THEY ARE IN EARNEST

EDWARD YARNOLD, S.J.

THEY ARE IN EARNEST

Christian unity in the statements of
Paul VI, John Paul I, John Paul II

Foreword by the Archbishop of Canterbury

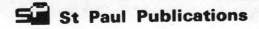 St Paul Publications

Acknowledgements are made to the undermentioned publishers for permission to quote from the following works:

Information Service of the Secretariat for Promoting Christian Unity, Vatican City State.

Austin Flannery O.P. (editor), *Vatican Council II: Conciliar and Post Conciliar Documents,* 1981 edition, Dublin, Dominican Publications/ Northport, Long Island, Costello Publishing Co.

Karol Wojtyla, *Sources of Renewal.* English translation © 1980 William Collins Sons & Co. Ltd., London, and Harper and Row Publishers Inc., New York.

St Paul Publications
Middlegreen, Slough SL3 6BT, England

Copyright © 1982 St Paul Publications
First published in Great Britain April 1982
Typeset by Grove Graphics, Tring, and
printed by Billing & Sons, Guildford,
Worcester, Oxford and London
ISBN 085439 212 2

St Paul Publications is an activity of the priests and brothers of the Society of St Paul who promote the Christian message through the mass media.

CONTENTS

FOREWORD
BY THE ARCHBISHOP OF CANTERBURY

I AM glad to have the opportunity of writing a Foreword to this collection of Papal statements on ecumenism. There can be no doubt that the Papacy in recent years has frequently reiterated its commitment to unity, and it is good that this record is being made widely available through the editorial work of Fr. Edward Yarnold, who has devoted much of his time and energies to ecumenism in recent years and who has served on the Anglican/Roman Catholic International Commission since its beginning.

But some will say words are not enough. Indeed there does come a time when intentions have to be turned into decisions.

In May this year, after fifteen years of official dialogue and widespread pastoral collaboration, Pope John Paul II and I will meet in Canterbury Cathedral. It will be a historically unique opportunity. I hope and pray that both Churches will grasp it in the light of the Final Report of the Anglican/Roman Catholic International Commission.

Karl Rahner has written of ecumenical progress:
"It seems to me, the initiative in this question must pass from the theologians to the office-holders."

Fr. Yarnold's collection of statements points to the greatest office-holder in the Christian tradition taking such an initiative in Canterbury. I, as one who also holds office, will encourage him to do so.

Robert Cantuar

INTRODUCTION

MOST Orthodox Churches did not accept Pope John XXIII's invitation to send observers to the first session of the Second Vatican Council. Centuries of separation and suspicion made it inevitable that they would fear that the Pope's invitation was a scheme to lure them into a union which would make them subjects of the Roman See. In the spring of 1963 the Anglican Bishop of Ripon, John Moorman, went to Constantinople to persuade the Ecumenical Patriarch Athenagoras that Pope John simply wanted to restore friendly relations between the Catholics and Orthodox, and to initiate talks on a basis of equality. When he met the Patriarch, Bishop Moorman's simple message was: 'They are in earnest'. Orthodox observers from Constantinople attended the remaining sessions of the Council, and official dialogue was soon begun.

I hope that this book will convince readers that Pope John's three successors, in their frequent references to reunion, are in earnest too.

There seemed to be three ways in which I could have collected these papal statements. The first way would have been an anthology of sayings in chronological order; the second a similar anthology arranged according to subjects. I preferred a third method. I have connected the statements by a narrative of events, and in the last chapter drawn the various themes together.

Although this is a book about papal statements, I have also included some other material. It seemed useful to give an account of the Council documents which bore on ecumenism, as they provide the context for assessing what the popes have said. I have also included one or two other documents, such as some statements by the President of the Secretariat for Christian Unity, who evidently cannot make major statements of policy without the approval of the Pope. I have also allowed myself the latitude of giving some of the statements of the other Church leaders with whom the Pope entered into dialogue. Among them the Ecumenical Patriarch Athenagoras I – he whom Bishop Moorman visited so fruitfully – stands out for his vision, his generosity in breaking free from traditional rivalries, and his courageous leadership of fellow churchmen, many of whom were indifferent or hostile to his ecumenical ideals. However, despite this additional material, this book is intended as a study of papal statements on ecumenism, and not as a general study of the three papacies, still less of all developments in the Church.

I have given the popes' statements generally in the official Vatican translation, allowing myself the occasional correction when it seemed necessary.

In compiling this material I owe a great debt to the excellent reporting of *The Tablet*, and to the Information Service of the Secretariat for Promoting Christian Unity. Xavier Rynne's four books on the Council proved helpful. I have quoted the conciliar documents in the translation contained in the edition of Austin Flannery, O.P. I am grateful to Peter Hebblethwaite for drawing some facts to my attention, and for the help I derived from his book *The Year of Three Popes*. Finally I owe the warmest thanks to Fr Robert F. Healey, S.J., for generously undertaking to read the whole work in typescript, and for saving me from many slips.

Oxford
Feast of St Edmund Campion
1 December 1981

To my colleagues at ARCIC
'veterans, seasoned workers in
a great cause'

POPE PAUL VI

1. GIOVANNI BATTISTA MONTINI

WHEN Cardinal Montini was elected Pope on 21 June 1963, he had already proved himself to be capable of taking new initiatives on behalf of Church unity. In 1956 he had invited six Anglican priests to be his guests in Milan. He had encouraged the American Jesuit John Courtney Murray in his preliminary work on what came to be the revolutionary Decree on Religious Liberty of the Second Vatican Council. During the first session of the Council, while still Archbishop of Milan, he had spoken of the inadequacy of the current understanding of the Church as a visible society founded by Christ; it was rather Christ himself using human beings as instruments to bring salvation to all mankind. By thus conceiving the Church in theological rather than juridical terms, Montini was embracing a view which made it possible to include non-Catholics within the Church. Consequently it was not surprising that two newspapers saw his choice of the name Paul as 'a symbol of ecumenical unity, embracing the Catholics, the Protestants and the Orthodox'.

On 18 August 1963 he made his first major statement on ecumenism as Pope. He drove the few miles from Castel Gandolfo to the Uniate Byzantine monastery at Grottaferrata, where he took this theme as the subject for his address. He recalled that he had sent a Swiss bishop to Moscow to take part in the celebration of the eightieth birthday of the Patriarch of that city. He explained his intention 'of paying homage, of showing that there were no motives of rivalry, of prestige, of pride, of ambition, nor any desire to perpetuate discords, disagreements which in the past perhaps had reason to exist but which now seem to be completely anachronistic.' Orthodox Churches, he declared – and he was often to repeat this statement during his pontificate – shared with the Catholic Church the same baptism, the same fundamental faith, a valid hierarchy and sacraments.

> I long to make mine the wish which spontaneously and generously welled up in the hearts of my predecessors, especially John XXIII . . . , that we can truly make our voice like an angel's trumpet which says, 'Come, let the barriers which separate us fall!' Let us explain the points of doctrine which are not common to us but are still subjects of controversy; let us seek to render our creed a joint one and a solid one; let us seek to draw together in an articulate hierarchical union.

3

In words that recalled Cardinal Mercier's watchword concerning the Anglican communion, 'united not absorbed', the Pope expressed his wish 'neither to absorb nor to modify the great flowering of Eastern Churches, but we wish it to be regrafted again on to the one tree of the unity of Christ.' It is significant that he does not speak of regrafting on to the Roman Catholic Church, as if that were the only surviving Church endowed with the life of the Spirit.

The Gospel of the Sunday was the episode of the healing of the deaf mute. 'We are all a little deaf, we are all a little dumb,' the Pope commented. 'May the Lord open us up, open us up to understand the voices of history, the voice of the Holy Spirit. His voice, the Gospel, which should still be our law, our force.'

Twice in the following week he referred at general audiences to the return of 'separated brethren'. To non-Catholics he addressed a remark which again implied their membership of the Church: 'Your coming to the house of the Vicar of Christ is evidence not only of our universal fatherhood but also of your membership in the great and mysterious family of Christ.' With them he felt not among strangers but among people with whom he enjoyed a spiritual relationship. 'We should like you to make yourselves promoters of Christian unity; to work and pray that the sons of the Church be always faithful to their mother, that the separated brethren may enjoy one day our happiness . . .'. This affirmation that Catholics enjoyed a privileged position in comparison with other Christians is notably absent from many of his later addresses.

Paul VI's address to the Roman Curia on 21 September 1963 contained no direct reference to ecumenism, but it had an indirect bearing on the subject. Although the Pope is sometimes remembered for a 'Hamlet-like' indecisiveness, which could lead him to weaken some of his most original insights by balancing against them other more traditional remarks, he could, as in this instance, act with rapidity and decision. Only three months after becoming Pope, he announced plainly to the Curia that it needed to be reformed. He was able to say this with tact, for, as he reminded his hearers, he had himself served in the Curia for thirty years, and appreciated their 'faithful, competent, devoted service'. Nevertheless it is understandable how, in the passage of time, the Curia has 'grown ponderous with its own venerable age, how it feels the disparity of its organs and of its practices with respect to the needs and customs of new times, how at the same time it feels the need of being simplified and decentralized and the need of being broadened and made fit for new functions.'

In the years since Vatican II, many ecumenists from other

Churches have come to recognize the value of a papacy conceived in terms of a universal primacy, serving the universal Church by being the focus and the servant of its worldwide unity. But most of these theologians are understandably reluctant to accept such a primacy if it involves putting all Christians under the authority not so much of a primate as of a central bureaucracy, whose original sin is to wish to impose a uniform, traditional, italianate pattern on every aspect of Church life. Consequently such words as the following have considerable ecumenical significance.

> Let the Roman Curia be a true community of faith and charity, of prayer and action, of the Pope's brothers and sons who do everything, each with respect for the competence of the other and with a sense of collaboration in serving him in his work for the brothers and sons of the Universal Church and of the entire world.

Eight days later, on 29 September, the Pope inaugurated the second session of the Council, which had been conceived and opened by his predecessor John XXIII. He took advantage of the occasion to deliver a speech of more than an hour setting out his expectations for the Council. Nearly ten minutes of it he devoted to the theme of Christian unity.

John XXIII had already put before the Council the question of those 'whom we have not the happiness of numbering among ourselves in the perfect unity of Christ, which only the Catholic Church can offer them'. The terms in which Pope Paul speaks of these other Christians are significant. The thing which they necessarily lack is membership of 'the perfect unity of Christ', which 'objectively speaking, should be theirs by baptism'. It is also 'something which, virtually at least, they already desire'. Paul VI is taking the concept of an implicit desire, already commonly employed in Catholic theology to explain how unbaptized people can be saved through 'baptism of desire', and using it to explain how baptized non-Catholics have an implicit desire of membership of the Catholic Church. The implication (which the Council's Decree on Ecumenism would attempt to spell out) is that the Roman Catholic Church is the one true Church of Christ; non-Catholics, while not belonging to its visible unity, to some extent participate in its life.

> Recent movements . . . show clearly two things. The first is that the Church of Christ is one alone and therefore must be unique. The second is that this mystic and visible union cannot be attained except in identity of faith and by participation in the

same sacraments and in the organic harmony of a single ecclesiastical control, even though this allows for a great variety of verbal expressions, movements, lawful institutions, and preference with regard to modes of acting.

This last half-sentence is of great importance, for in it, right at the beginning of his pontificate, the Pope stated his conviction, contained already in germ in his remark of 18 August about absorption, that a united Church need not be one in which every part was a carbon copy of every other, but that it could contain 'a great variety' of forms. This variety can embrace 'movements, lawful institutions, and preference with regard to modes of acting'. Such acceptance of practical differences between sections of a united Church contains nothing new; they already exist among the Uniate Churches in communion with the Roman See. Of much greater significance is Paul's widening of the scope of permissible variety to include 'verbal expressions'. This implies that faith in the fullness of the Christian revelation can be expressed in other formulas besides those employed in Roman Catholic dogma. It is true that the Pope had not yet reached the point of saying that such variety was not only tolerable but a positive necessity, since any single dogmatic statement will succeed in expressing only one aspect of the many-sided truth. In this new vision of a diversified but united faith, one detects the influence of John XXIII's simple but compendious maxim contained in the speech he delivered when opening the Council on 11 October 1962: 'The substance of the ancient doctrine of the deposit of faith is one thing, and the way in which it is presented is another.'

In official documents the Council was described as an 'ecumenical' council, that is to say, a council of the whole Church throughout the world. Catholic tradition has come to regard Vatican II as the twenty-first ecumenical council. But the Orthodox resent this terminology, maintaining that a council cannot represent the whole Church if they themselves are not present: they recognise as ecumenical only the first seven, which were held before the Photian Schism in the ninth century formalised a breach between the East and the West that had been widening over many centuries. The difference in terminology reflects different understandings of the nature of the Church. For Catholics, the Church remains essentially one; this unity has endured within the Roman Catholic Church, from which other Churches have detached themselves; therefore a General Council of the Roman Church is by definition an ecumenical council representing the one Church of Christ. For Orthodox, and for

Anglicans, they as well as Rome are part of the Church, whose unity has been broken by schism; therefore a council of the Roman Catholic Church alone has no claim to ecumenicity. Paul VI, while not abandoning Vatican II's claim to ecumenical status, goes so far as to admit that, in the absence of the other Churches, its ecumenicity is not *fully* realised. In saying this he is implying once more that the traditional view equating the one Church of Christ with the Roman Catholic Church does not take into account the fact that non-Catholic Christians have some degree of membership of the Church:

> The Council aims at complete and universal ecumenicity – that is at least what it desires, what it prays and prepares for. Today it does so in hope that tomorrow it may see the reality. This council while calling and counting its own those sheep who belong to the fold of Christ in the fullest and truest sense, opens the door and calls out, too, in anxious expectation to the many sheep of Christ who are not present within the unique fold.
>
> It is a council, therefore, of invitation, of expectation, of confidence, looking forward towards a more widespread, more fraternal participation in its authentic ecumenicity.

Although these words clearly indicate a defect in the Church membership of non-Catholics, they are remarkable for their admission that separation from them constitutes a defect in the Roman Catholic Church too.

The Pope proceeded to welcome the observers from other Churches, introducing a theme to which his statements on Church unity often returned: Roman Catholics share the blame for divisions among Christians:

> If we are in any way to blame for that separation, we humbly beg God's forgiveness and ask pardon too of our brethren who feel themselves to have been injured by us. For our part, we willingly forgive the injuries which the Catholic Church has suffered, and forget the grief endured during the long series of dissensions and separations. May the heavenly Father deign to hear our prayers and grant us true brotherly peace.

The Holy Father held out no hopes of a rapid removal of the causes of Christian divisions:

> We are aware that serious and complicated questions remain to be studied, treated and resolved. We would wish that this could be done immediately on account of the love of Christ that 'urges

7

us on' (cf. 2 Cor 5:14). But we also realise that these problems require many conditions before satisfactory solutions can be reached – conditions which are as yet premature. Hence we are not afraid to wait patiently for the blessed hour of perfect reconciliation.

He then communicated to the observers 'some points in our attitude towards reunion . . . We believe that these points are well known, but it is useful to repeat them here.'

The first point was an assurance that the observers need have no fear that they had been invited to the Council with any ulterior motives, political, proselytizing or polemical. 'We lay no snares.'

> We owe our faith – which we believe to be divine – the most candid and firm attachment.
> But at the same time we are convinced that this does not constitute an obstacle to the desired understanding with our separated brethren, precisely because it is the truth of the Lord and therefore the principle of union, not of distinction or separation.

In other words, if Catholics state their faith clearly, other Christians, being obedient to the Word of Christ, will recognise its truth.

But, secondly, this does not mean that Catholics believe they have a monopoly of the truth. 'We look with reverence upon the true religious patrimony we share in common, which has been preserved and in part even well developed among our separated brethren. We are pleased to note the study made by those who seek sincerely to make known and to honour the treasures of truth and of genuine spirituality, in order to improve our relations with them.' Paul VI expressed the hope that, reciprocally, other Christians 'would also wish to make a closer study of our doctrine and its logical derivation from the deposit of Divine Revelation.'

On 17 October 1963 the Pope received the observers in audience and reaffirmed this message,

> here in our library where we receive private audiences we can say it in a manner which is completely intimate and friendly . . . The sincerity of our words and of our feelings allows us, in fact urges us, to express this new opening of our heart in the simplest language, one which is able to express far better than the solemnity of Latin something which we feel towards you in the depths of our soul.

So the same points recur. 'Our attitude conceals no hidden

snares nor tries to hide the difficulties which lie in the way of a complete and final understanding . . . Good faith and charity are the bases which we offer you.' He endorsed a remark of John XXIII's: 'One's mind is tempted to look backwards to the past. But this would mean getting lost in the labyrinth of history and would certainly reopen wounds which have not yet completely healed.'

> We took the liberty . . . of talking above all of Christian forgiveness: a reciprocal one if possible. . . .
> We are looking towards something new to create, a dream which must become reality. Let us quote the words of St Paul: 'Forgetting those things which are behind, and reaching forward unto those things which are before, I press towards the mark for the prize of the high calling of God in Christ Jesus' (Phil 3:13-14). Hope is our guide, prayer our power, and charity our method, in the service of the divine truth which is our faith and our salvation.

Professor Kristen Skydsgaard, President of the World Lutheran Federation, speaking on behalf of the observers, had quoted St Augustine: 'Search to find, and find to search still more.' The Holy Father stated his agreement, and added: 'a real Christian can never be static.' His emphasis on creating something new, on reaching forward, on deepening one's understanding of the truth, on not being static, shows clearly that he saw ecumenism as a Spirit-led mutual convergence, not an invitation to non-Catholics to enter an unchanging Catholic Church.

There would be neither 'miraculous nor immediate solutions. The fruits that we are hoping for will have to ripen very slowly, through study and prayer.' But the Pope spoke movingly of his longing for progress.

> As for us, like the watchman, of whom Isaiah spoke – 'Watchman, what of the night?' (Is 21:11) – we are on the alert, craning to see, and happy each time we do, those signs in the heart of the night heralding the dawn. By this we mean signs that some progress has been made in the dialogue that has been started on, some step forward towards a rapprochement with those who are sustained by the same gospels and who hear resounding in the depths of their souls the same glorious appeal of St Paul to the Ephesians: 'One Lord, one faith, one baptism, one God and Father of all; who is above all and through all, and in all' (Eph 4:4-6).

The Pope's address which closed the second session of the

Council on 4 December 1963 made no mention of ecumenism, until at the end of his speech he announced his intention of making a pilgrimage to Palestine in the following January to visit the places where Christ lived, died, rose and ascended, 'whence Peter set forth and where not one of his successors has returned'. But his motives were not only those of personal piety. '. . . We shall return there as an expression of prayer, penance and renovation to offer to Christ his Church, to summon to this one holy Church our separated brethren, to implore divine mercy on behalf of peace among men . . .'. Although he saw that reunion would require a growing together by all the Churches, his conviction that the Roman See was the divinely ordained focus of the Church's unity led him sometimes, as on this occasion, to speak as if all that was required was a return of the separated brethren.

Church leaders generally welcomed the Pope's proposal. Most enthusiastic was the Ecumenical Patriarch Athenagoras of Constantinople, the first-ranking patriarch of the Orthodox Churches. As he will feature several times in this narrative, it is worth while dwelling on his statement, the words of which reveal a man of sanctity, humility and courage, who, in obedience to Christ, would pursue all paths to unity that were open to him, without fear of what the shape of the united Church would be. His communiqué states that he regarded the Pope's decision to be 'inspired by God', and that he observed

> that it would be truly a work of providence if, during this godly pilgrimage all the heads of the Eastern and Western Churches were able to meet each other in the holy town of Zion, in order to ask, in fervent prayer together, and with pious contemplation having as its source the Christian soul, on their knees, with tears in their eyes and in a spirit of unity, on Golgotha which was watered by the most holy blood of Christ and before the holy sepulchre from which reconciliation and repentance have sprung – to ask that a way may be opened for a total re-establishment of Christian unity in accordance with the holy will of the Lord, for the glory of the holy name of Christ and for the profit of the whole of humanity.

The Patriarch had expressed his intention of being in Jerusalem for the feast of the Epiphany. It seems likely that Pope Paul took the idea of a pilgrimage to the Holy Places from him. It seems even more likely that it was the Patriarch who first conceived the idea of a meeting with the Pope. What is certain is that, when the two Church leaders met in Jerusalem, there was a meeting of kindred spirits which recalls the famous meeting of

10

St Francis and St Dominic. Under the spotlight of the media, before the eyes of the world, in their three meetings in four years they showed how ecumenism should be pursued, in obedience to God's will, in charity, humility, in the spirit of self-sacrifice and service, with hope and courage to face an uncharted future, and above all with prayer.

Not all reactions. even within Athenagoras' own patriarchate, were so favourable. The London *Times* reported that the Pope's proposal 'has been received by the Church of Greece with the reserve and mistrust with which Greek prelates habitually greet the Ecumenical Patriarch's initiatives on Christian unity'. The Archbishop of Athens told his Synod on 17 December: 'Behind the friendship of the Catholic lies trickery.' The Patriarch of Moscow, however, expressed approval. The Greek Church eventually gave its consent.

How much was the ready rapport that sprang up between Paul and Athenagoras due to another man of warmth and vision, John XXIII, who, as Angelo Roncalli, had been Apostolic Delegate in Turkey and Greece from 1934 to 1944, when he had done so much to improve relations between Rome and Constantinople?

In the days that followed, the text of a letter was published which Pope Paul had written to the Patriarch of Constantinople in September, long before the Jerusalem pilgrimage was announced, in which he thanked Athenagoras for his message of congratulation on his election as pope. 'The responsibility which the Lord has entrusted to us,' Paul wrote, '. . . fills us with a lively desire with regard to the union of Christians and all that can contribute towards re-establishing perfect concord among them.' The Pope anticipated some of the points he made to the observers on 17 October: we must think of the future rather than the past, 'reaching forward unto those things which are before' (Phil 3: 13). He then turned to what the two Churches have in common:

He has made us his own through the gift of the same baptism, the same priesthood, celebrating the same Eucharist, the unique sacrifice of the unique Lord of the Church. And this celebration always strengthens in us the feelings which were those of Christ Jesus and which enable us to penetrate deeply into the sense and the demands of his prayer to his Father: 'That they may all be one . . .' (Jn 17:21ff). May the Lord open our hearts to the inspiration of his Spirit and lead us towards the full realisation of his will.

11

The Patriarch's reply of 22 November was published on 18 December. After expressing the 'joy and love' with which he received Paul's letter, he continued:

> . . . We are particularly delighted now, being informed by your letters also of the deep response which the prayer of the Alpha and the Omega of the faith, Christ our God, is having at the moment for the unity of those who believe in him, and the exhortation of the Apostle to forget all that was behind, and being informed also at the same time of the fervent desire of Your Holiness for the full realisation of the Lord's desire for unity.
>
> And we also, instructed by the Lord to have friendly relations with one another, as befits the members of his most holy Body, which is the Church, and having, by virtue of the relation of the members between themselves, only one Lord and Saviour, thanks to whom we have communion in the sacraments, we think that we could not bring each other anything more precious than the offering of communion in love, which, according to the Apostle, 'bears all things, believes all things, hopes all things, endures all things' (1 Cor 13 : 7) – a communion which was formerly firm in the link of the peace of our holy Churches, and which is renewing itself now 'by the grace of the Lord . . . to the praise of his glory' (Eph 1 : 12 and 14).
>
> . . . Let us observe the will of the Lord from the height of charity, with a contrite heart and pure eye. Let us put ourselves and one another, as well as our life, at his disposition to find grace and so that the kingdom of God will reign on the face of the earth.

In his first Christmas Message, broadcast on 23 December 1963, after speaking of the problems connected with hunger and peace, Pope Paul turned to the unity of the Church.

> The true sociology of human peace takes its rise from Christian religious unity. It is this unity, introduced by Christ into human thought and history, that we earnestly desire for the peace, concord, mutual understanding and happiness of all men of good will.

He then turned to the ecumenical dimension of his forthcoming pilgrimage to Jerusalem. 'Our journey will be that of Peter's witness: we wish to include in our own faith that of the whole Church, and, with Peter at Caesarea Philippi, say to Jesus: "Yes, Lord, you are the Christ, the Son of the living God." ' The journey would also be a 'journey of offering'; like the Magi he would bring 'the offering of his Church'.

It will also be a journey of search and hope: search for all those who are for us sons and brothers in Christ. In the atmosphere of the Gospels, evoked by the land of benediction, how can we not ask ourselves: Where is the full flock of Christ? Where are the lambs and the sheep of his fold? Are they all here? Which ones are missing? And so we cannot but implore Jesus the Good Shepherd, using his own words: 'May there be one fold and one Shepherd.'

And our heart will reach out also to those outside the fold of Christ, and our good intentions will embrace all the peoples of the earth. . . .

These words are worth studying, for they cast light on his understanding of the relationship between non-Catholics and Christ's Church. They are the 'full flock of Christ'; they are 'of his fold'. But they are not 'here' – not, that is to say, included in the visible unity of the Church, which is represented by the Bishop of Rome. However, the context and the capital letter suggest that the 'one Shepherd' is not – as in a common Roman Catholic prayer for unity – the Pope, but Christ himself.

On 28 December the Ecumenical Patriarch's envoy, Metropolitan Athenagoras of Thyatira and Great Britain, visited the Pope. As a Vatican official pointed out, this was the first time in several centuries that an official representative of the Patriarchate had come to Rome. The Metropolitan spoke of the historical significance of the forthcoming meeting between the Pope and the Patriarch in Jerusalem.

After centuries of silence, the Latin West and the Greek East, moved by mutual love, by the respect stirred in them by the Gospel, and by their Christian hearts, are moving towards a meeting, for an exchange of views and of brotherly greetings, and in order to start, if possible, a dialogue of understanding for the peace of the world and the progress of the Church of God.

The two leaders were to 'climb the same mountain, the mountain of the Lord, from different sides'. The Metropolitan called for prayers that 'they may meet on the top, on the ground sanctified by their common Redeemer, near his cross and his empty tomb, and that they may from then on walk together trying to rebuild in Christian solidarity the broken bridges, so that all may be one as Christ is one with his Heavenly Father.'

The Holy Father arrived at Amman airport in the early afternoon of Saturday, 4 January 1964. This is not the place to give an account of all the prayers, actions and speeches that filled his crowded forty-nine hours in the Holy Land. There is

13

room only for the events of directly ecumenical importance, among them a meeting in Nazareth with a Rabbi representing the Chief Rabbi of Israel.

Protocol required that the Pope's first meeting should be with the Orthodox Patriarch Benedictos of Jerusalem. Patriarch Athenagoras had tactfully announced beforehand: 'Of course Patriarch Benedictos of Jerusalem will have precedence in receiving the Pope in Jerusalem. The Pope and ourselves will simply meet and then pray together for world peace and the union of all Christian Churches.'

The first meeting with the Ecumenical Patriarch took place on the Sunday evening at the Apostolic Delegation on the Mount of Olives, where the Pope spent the two nights of his brief pilgrimage. There, in an historic gesture, Pope and Patriarch exchanged the kiss of peace. The Patriarch expressed his 'immense joy' at the meeting, which he attributed to God's call, help, grace and goodwill. He regarded it as 'an event of extraordinary significance and importance for the history and life of the Church'.

> With our whole heart we wish that the good intentions which of recent times come to light so frequently on both sides and which are now confirmed, we wish that this blessed meeting of persons and this brotherly and sincere embrace may be the prelude to mutual understanding as well as complete submission to the holy will of God.

On the Monday morning, the feast of the Epiphany, after saying an early Mass at Bethlehem, at the traditional site of our Lord's birth, Paul VI delivered the major address of his pilgrimage. A substantial part of it he devoted to the theme of Church unity.

> We are living at the historic hour when the Church of Christ must live its deep and visible unity. It is the hour for us to answer the wish of Jesus Christ: 'That they may become perfectly one, so that the world may know that thou hast sent me.' To the internal unity of the Church corresponds externally its apologetic and missionary strength.

Accordingly he asked for a 'unanimous effort' in co-operation with the Council: 'This is our message to the Catholics who already belong to Christ's sheepfold'. It is surprising that, after clearly implying in his Christmas message that non-Catholics were part of Christ's fold, he now unambiguously implies the contrary. But perhaps his following words concerning 'our

14

Christian brothers who are not in complete communion with us' might be taken as implying that they belong to Christ's fold in an incomplete way.

From now on it is clear to all that one cannot avoid the problem of unity. Today this desire of Christ thrusts itself on our minds and forces us to undertake, with wisdom and charity, everything that is possible in order to allow all Christians to enjoy the great blessing and supreme honour of the unity of the Church.

However, 'such an outcome cannot be obtained at the expense of the truths of the faith. We cannot be unfaithful to this patrimony of Christ: it is not ours but his, and we are only its depositaries and interpreters.' The Pope apparently supported the Ecumenical Patriarch's recommendation of a meeting of the leaders of all Christian Churches:

. . . we are ready to take into consideration every reasonable means capable of smoothing the roads of dialogue, in respect and in charity, with the aim of a future meeting – please God it may be near – with our Christian brothers who are still separated from us. The gate of the sheepfold is open.

The Holy Father was evidently sensitive to the resentment that might be aroused by his insistence that Christ's fold is the Roman Catholic Church. So he continued:

The step to be taken is awaited with all our affection: it can be made with honour and in honour and in mutual joy. We will refrain from asking for steps that would not be made freely and with full conviction, that is to say moved by the Spirit of the Lord, who bloweth when and where he listeth. We will wait for this blessed time. For the moment all we ask of our very dear separated brethren is what we ask of ourselves: that the love of Christ and of the Church may inspire every eventual step towards rapprochement and meeting. . . . We will put our trust in prayer. Even if it is not yet in common, it can at least be said simultaneously and rise, parallel from our hearts, as from the hearts of the separated Christians, to join together at the feet of the Most High, the God of unity.

Thanking the assembled Church leaders for sharing in his pilgrimage, Paul paid 'homage to the share they possess of the authentic treasure of the Christian tradition, and to them we express our desire for an agreement in the faith, in the love and in the discipline of the one Church of Christ.' This last phrase must mean, not that all Christians must accept Roman Catholic

15

discipline, but that it is to be hoped that all Christians will come to agree about the essential practical demands of membership of Christ's Church.

The Holy Father expressed his 'deference' to 'whoever professes monotheism and with us pays religious worship to the one and true God, the living and supreme God, the God of Abraham, the Most High, he whom on this soil . . . Melchisedech celebrated as the "God Most High, maker of heaven and earth" ' (Gen 14: 19). This address was so phrased as to embrace both Jews and Arabs.

Back in Jerusalem, the Pope paid his return visit to the Ecumenical Patriarch that same morning at the patriarchate on the Mount of Olives. He expressed his joy and his gratitude to God because 'after centuries of silence and expectation, the Catholic Church and the Patriarchate of Constantinople meet once again in the persons of their highest representatives.' (The Pope was aware that Athenagoras was meeting him solely as Patriarch of Constantinople, not as representative of all the Orthodox Churches.)

Paul acknowledged that the initiative had been taken by Athenagoras. 'You have desired this meeting ever since the time of our unforgettable predecessor John XXIII, your esteem and affection for whom you did not conceal, and to whom, with striking intuition, you applied the words of the evangelist: "There was a man sent from God, whose name was John" (Jn 1: 6). He too yearned for this meeting, as you well know, but his early death prevented him from realising this desire of his heart. The words of Christ: "That they may be one", *ut unum sint,* repeated frequently by the dying Pope, leave no doubt as to one of his most cherished intentions, those for which he offered God his long agony and valuable life.' (Typically, Athenagoras, on his way to the meeting, had already attributed the initiative to Pope Paul.)

The Holy Father acknowledged that, for both Churches, 'the roads which lead to union may be long and sown with difficulties. But these two paths converge towards one another and eventually reach the sources of the Gospel.' But their meeting manifested

the great goodwill which, thanks be to God, animates ever more all Christians truly worthy of that name: the will, that is, to work to surmount disunity, to break down barriers, the will to engage resolutely upon the path which leads to reconciliation.

Divergencies of a doctrinal, liturgical and disciplinary nature will have to be examined, at the proper time and place, in a spirit of fidelity to truth and of understanding in charity. What

16

UNITAPES— WHAT ARE THEY?

Unitapes began as cassette recordings of the series of Evening Talks given at UNI in 1976. Since then the Evening Talks at UNI have been recorded and each is available on a separate cassette. In addition to the Evening Talks an increasing number of other talks is now available.

DISCUSSION PACKS

UNI now produces Study Packs designed especially for group work. These Packs contain a cassette tape on which are four complete discussions of about fifteen minutes duration, plus an accompanying sheet outlining the tape's contents and suggesting questions for group discussion.

The views expressed by individuals on Unitapes try to reflect current theological thinking and are offered for thought and discussion. They do not necessarily bear the authority of the Bishops or of the Institute.

The UPHOLLAND NORTHERN INSTITUTE, or UNI, is a conference centre with a residential teaching staff which was established by the Northern Bishops in 1976 as a sign of the Church's commitment to adult Christian education. By providing its own courses and promoting other meetings and conferences UNI seeks to encourage adults to study, reflect on and discuss the implications of being an adult Christian today.

As a residential centre UNI offers full accommodation facilities in beautiful and extensive grounds.

The UNI teaching staff is available for courses and conferences at the centre and in parishes and deaneries. Full details of these facilities as well as an up to date programme of courses can be obtained by writing to:-

The Institute Secretary
Upholland Northern Institute
Skelmersdale
Lancashire WN8 0PZ
Tel: Upholland (0695) 625255

THE PAPAL VISIT:
ECUMENICAL HOPES AND FEARS?

The historic visit of Pope John Paul II to Britian has opened up fresh discussions about the nature of the Papacy itself and about his own possible contribution to furthering the cause of Christian Unity in these islands. Frs. Wilkinson and Crowley discuss the personality of the present Pope, his conflicting characteristics, his doctrinal stances, and his possible message to the Christian churches of Britain. They look first at the Papal witness to ecumenism given by John XXIII, Paul VI and John Paul II, and then at some sensitive ecumenical questions like Anglican Orders, Papal Authority and Primacy, Papal Infallibility and Intercommunion. This tape should be of considerable help to ecumenical groups or parish groups who wish to explore more fully the meaning of the Papacy and the attitudes of the present Pope.

UNITAPE 243

The Papal Visit:
Ecumenical Hopes & Fears

Rev. Patrick Crowley &
Peter Wilkinson

UPHOLLAND
NORTHERN
INSTITUTE

243 **THE PAPAL VISIT: ECUMENICAL HOPES
AND FEARS?** Rev. Patrick Crowley & Peter Wilkinson

can and must now commence to develop is that fraternal charity, which is ingenious in finding out new ways of showing itself, which, taking its lessons from the past, is ready to pardon, more ready to believe well than evil, carefully above all to conform itself to the divine Master and to allow itself to be drawn and transformed by him. Of such charity the symbol and example should be the kiss of peace which Our Lord has permitted us to exchange in this Holy Land, and the prayer which Jesus Christ taught us and which we shall shortly recite together.

We cannot express how touched we are by this your gesture nor are we alone in this: the Church of Rome and the Ecumenical Council will learn with deep joy of this historic event. As for us, we raise towards God a grateful prayer, and we beg him to help us follow along this path, and to bestow upon you and upon us, who have undertaken it with faith and confidence, that blessing which will ensure happy results. With these feelings, it is not a 'goodbye' that we say to you, but, if you allow us, an *au revoir,* based upon the hope of other fruitful meetings in the name of the Lord, *in nomine Domini.*

After his speech, the Pope said in French 'We are going to read together chapter 17 of St John's Gospel.' Paul and Athenagoras then recited Christ's great prayer for unity antiphonally, a verse in Greek read by the Bishop of New Rome being answered by one in Latin read by the Bishop of Old Rome. They then embraced and recited the Lord's Prayer in the same two languages on the Mount of Olives, where Jesus is said to have taught it to his disciples. They both gave a blessing. *The Tablet* reports that the Patriarch was heard to say, 'This means we are in agreement.'

After their meeting the two leaders issued a joint communiqué. In it they are careful to prevent the occasion from being misinterpreted as already constituting an act of union between the two Churches. It must be seen, they said, simply as a 'fraternal gesture', but one which they prayed might be 'the sign and prelude of things to come'.

That evening at Rome airport, giving his impressions of his visit, the Pope spoke of his 'benevolent remembrance' of 'all our brothers in Christ, particularly beloved and dear, whose presence in the Holy Places sharpens for us the desire of the hoped-for reunion'.

The Ecumenical Patriarch commented on the meeting in the course of his journey home. At Amman airport, when asked if the meeting would lead to a 'merger' between Rome and Orthodoxy, he replied, 'A merger is impossible, for the Churches have never been unified at any time in the past. But we aim at creating a unified Christian front to face our common problems.' In rejecting the idea of a merger, the Patriarch was presumably rejecting the acceptability of 'absorption' of the Orthodox Churches by Rome, as indeed Paul had ruled out the idea not long before.

Back at Istanbul airport he spoke of the possibility of another meeting. 'It was the meeting of two brothers. It was the first time in the history of the two Churches that a meeting took place in such an atmosphere of brotherhood and mutual understanding.'

Pope Paul later compared his journey to the Holy Land to 'the movement of a plough through old, hard-beaten earth', and suggested that its significance could be discerned by 'those who know how to read the signs of the times'. The year 1964 was to provide may more signs for the instruction of the pope-watcher.

Any light that the Pope shed on his own understanding of the papacy was obviously of great ecumenical importance. Speaking to the Roman nobility on 14 January 1964 he referred to the changes in the structure of the papacy which time had brought.

> As you well know, we are no longer the temporal sovereign around whom in past centuries there gathered the social classes to which you belong. For we are no longer what we were yesterday. . . . Although he finds in his sovereignty over the State of Vatican City the shield and sign of his independence of every authority of this world, the Pope cannot and must not any longer do anything more than exercise the power of his spiritual keys. . . . The duty that is incumbent on the Holy See of attending to the government of the universal Church and of entering upon an apostolic dialogue with the modern world . . . obliges it to look realistically at the resources at its disposal, . . . to discriminate and to prefer, within its heritage of institutions and customs, what is essential and vital . . .

It would soon become apparent that the changes in the papacy he envisaged were not limited to the renunciation of the trappings of temporal power.

In the same month, in an Apostolic Exhortation addressed to the bishops of the whole world, he turned to his recent meeting with Patriarch Athenagoras.

> All this we would like to regard as the first fruits of complete unity in the one Church of Christ, however far distant that goal may be.

In his Maundy Thursday address, delivered at St John Lateran on 26 March, the Pope gave his reasons for choosing to celebrate the liturgy in person; among them was the connection between the celebration and the unity of the Church, which is closely linked with the Eucharist:

> The second motive concerns . . . every priest, every bishop; but it concerns us principally, our mission and our person, whom Christ has placed at the heart of the unity of the whole Catholic Church, which at the dawn of her existence was said by one of the Fathers to be the 'president of charity'. . . . It is for us to prepare a table in this place to which all the bishops, priests and faithful of the earth are mystically invited. That which is being celebrated here is the fraternity of all the children of the Catholic Church. Here, indeed, is the very fount of Christian society; . . . this is the source of its buoyant energy that is fed not by earthly interests. . . . It is nourished, rather, by a superior and divine current, by the current of charity that urges us on, that charity which Christ obtained for us from God, which he infuses in us to help us to 'be one' as he himself is one with his Father.
>
> . . . here we find the school of the higher love of individuals for others, the profession of mutual esteem, of engagement in fraternal co-operation and gratuitous service, the motivation for a wise tolerance; here we discover the precept of mutual forgiveness. . . .
>
> . . . It is our desire . . . to build up, with the help of Christ, a community of souls, one with the widest possible dimensions.

He addressed this message of love first of all to the faithful of the Roman Catholic Church; then to his brother Christians, 'still sadly separated from us, but busy looking for the unity which Christ wished his Church to have'. He referred first to the Ecumenical Patriarch and the other patriarchs he had met in the Holy Land, then to the Anglican Church, 'which we hope we will be able to see one day resuming her honourable place (*ricomposta onoratamente*) in the one and only fold of Christ.' (It is not said explicitly that Anglicans are outside the fold.) He continued:

> Greeting and peace to all the other Christian communities born of the Reformation in the sixteenth century which has separated them from us. May the virtue of Christ's Easter show us the right, and perhaps long, road for us to walk along towards perfect communion. Meanwhile let us now, with mutual respect and with reciprocal esteem, search for ways of shortening the distances between us and of practising the charity which we hope to see one day victorious.

He also greeted the non-Christian believers in God, and the whole of humanity.

Perhaps it was because he had thus given ample expression to the ecumenical dimension of the feast that the Pope made little allusion to other Christians in his Easter Sunday message. But in an Apostolic Letter *Spiritus Paracliti* of 30 April, which called for prayers for the Council at Whitsun, he returned to the subject. In it he spoke of Rome as 'the summit and, as it were, centre of Catholic unity'. He continued,

> let us not cease from quiet and reverent meetings with our separated brethren, who will not refuse calm and friendly discussions; and, being more solicitous for their convenience than our honour, let us seek together by what ways and what means brotherly union may be restored, rooted in unity of faith and the necessity of mutual love, as Christ prescribed for his Church.

At the end of April too the text was published of a letter that the Pope had sent to his 'beloved brother in Christ', Patriarch Athenagoras, on the occasion of the Greek Easter. He wished, he said, 'to renew the kiss of peace exchanged on the Mount of Olives and to tell you again how you yourself, your clergy, and all your faithful are present in our prayer.' He hoped the message, conveyed by three members of the Secretariat for Unity, would be an occasion 'for strengthening the ties that already exist and for seeing how they can be drawn closer . . . May the risen Christ, by whose death we are reconciled to the Father, be our inspiration in our efforts to restore the unity of all those who are redeemed by him and who believe in his name.'

On Whit Sunday, announcing the creating of a Secretariat for Non-Christian religions, the Pope reflected on the implication of the name 'Catholic':

> The habitual use of words often weakens their force and the marvel of their meaning. We use with extreme facility the word Catholic, almost without noticing the fullness it embraces, the dynamic it generates, the beauty it opens up, the engagement it imposes. It often becomes in common use a defining term, and thus something which circumscribes and limits the true Church, to distinguish it from other fractions, worthy of respect and endowed with immense Christian treasures, yet separate from the Catholic fullness. . . .
>
> But if the meaning of 'Catholic' penetrates us truly, all egoism is conquered, all class-consciousness yields to social solidarity, all nationalism gives way to the good of the world community, all racism is condemned, all totalitarianism revealed in its inhumanity: the little heart cracks, or, better, it achieves an unheard-of capacity to dilate.

20

Once more we observe in Paul's words that other Christian bodies, though 'endowed with immense Christian treasures', lack the 'fullness' which exists in the Roman Church. The Pope's conviction that to be a Christian is to be committed to seeking full communion with all other Christians is here seen to be part of a wider movement reaching out to the whole human race.

On 26 May 1964 the Pope returned to the subject of the function of the papacy in a letter to the Bishop of Middlesbrough commemorating the thirteenth centenary of the Synod of Whitby.

> Union with Rome, loyalty to the Vicar of Christ, is not a servitude, but a brotherhood; it derives from the true traditions of the Apostles, for Peter, though their Prince [unfortunately this word carries associations of royal splendour not intended by the Pope], referred to by himself as *consenior* [*co-presbyter* or *fellow elder*] and emphasised that government in the Church should not be by constraint but willingly, not by lording it over one's charges but by becoming from the heart a pattern to them (cf 1 Pet 5:1-3). The faithfulness asserted and strengthened at Whitby has made religious life in Britain most fruitful, producing saints and scholars, noble institutions and admirable organisations.

The Holy Father did not make it clear whether he included the Anglican and other Churches among the 'noble institutions'; his frequent expressions of respect and esteem for other Churches in many other speeches suggests that he did. But more important is his statement that the papacy should be a moral leadership, based on example and evoking a free response, rather than an authoritarian dictatorship.

Next month Pope Paul performed one of the imaginative gestures which marked his pontificate when he announced his intention of returning to Patras the skull of St Andrew, which had been removed from there to Rome in 1462 to preserve it from capture by the Turks. Pius II had written that he received the relic 'under particular circumstances . . . with the intention that one day, please God, it should be returned'. Paul's fulfilment of his predecessor's promise cannot have failed to speed the improvement in the relations between Rome and Constantinople. It may have influenced Athens's decision to take part in a Pan-Orthodox Conference to be held at Rhodes later in the year to consider, among other things, initiating a formal dialogue with Rome. Athens had sent no representative to the second Pan-Orthodox Conference in the autumn of 1963. While announcing this decision to return the relic the Pope considered the events of the first year of his pontificate. Speaking of his 'pilgrimage' to the Holy Land, 'which we can, in all simplicity, call historic,' he referred to his meetings with Orthodox leaders, and hoped they would prepare the way for greater contacts with the leaders of other Churches, and be the prelude to the restoration of unity which he hoped for.

Another ecumenical gesture was the removal of the vacant Latin Patriarchates of Constantinople, Alexandria and Antioch from the list of Sees in the 1964 *Annuario Pontificio*. The Greek Orthodox had long regarded the existence of these patriarchates as a sign of Roman aggressive intentions. The Pope also sent a contribution towards the rebuilding of an Orthodox Cathedral in Yugoslavia.

So ended the first year of Paul VI's papacy. He had shown he believed passionately that ecumenism was a duty imposed on all Christians by their love of Christ. He longed to extend the service he performed for Roman Catholics to all Christians, and receive them all into full communion with the 'centre of unity'. He was aware that ecumenism was a voyage over an uncharted sea, leading to an unexplored land. Nevertheless there remained in his thinking traces of a one-sided ecclesiology according to which the Church was an organised society coextensive with the Church of Rome, which therefore excluded the other Christian bodies. How Paul's vision broadened and clarified, the passing of the years of his pontificate will show.

2. FIRST ENCYCLICAL, THE COUNCIL

IT was not until the fourteenth month of his pontificate that Pope Paul published on 6 August 1964, the Feast of the Transfiguration, the customary encyclical setting out the principles according to which he hoped to fulfil the first years of his office. He had presented a brief sketch of his views in the address with which he opened the second session of the Council on 29 September 1963. Some people may attribute the delay to the 'Hamlet-like' indecisiveness which the media chose to regard as a leading trait in his character. Others might see it rather as evidence of the deep personal thinking which underlay the encyclical; with none of the customary reliance on speech-drafters, he wrote every word himself, after first compiling a careful dossier of notes, and in the final version he speaks of the difficulty of his subject.

As the title of the letter, *Ecclesiam Suam*, shows, his thoughts took the form of reflections on the Church. His aim, he says, was not to provide a doctrinal treatise on its nature, for that was the task of the Council. Setting out a clear programme of the contents, he explains that he had three ideas in mind. The first is that at the present time the Church needs 'to deepen its consciousness of itself . . . to meditate on that mystery which is peculiar to it'. This leads him to his second point: consideration of God's ideal for the Church leads it to seek its renewal by 'correcting the defects of its own members and . . . leading them to greater perfection'. The third thought, which follows from the first two, is that the Church must make contact with the whole human community. 'Thus we meet what has been termed the problem of the dialogue between the Church and the modern world.' In his Latin original the Pope used the Italian word *dialogo* for the sake of its contemporary associations; the Latin translators, being stylistic purists, preferred the classical word *colloquium*.

Discussing the nature of the Church, the Pope rejected the view that its aim was to keep itself isolated from the contaminating influence of the world; on the contrary, 'the Church has her roots deep in mankind, . . . she is part of it, . . . she draws her members from it, . . . she receives from it precious treasures of culture, . . . she suffers from its historical vicissitudes, . . . she favours its progress.' But the Church must not go to the extreme and 'disavow herself and take up the very latest and untried ways of life'. This danger will be avoided if the members of the Church become

23

more vitally and consciously united to Christ. For it is not only theologians who understand the mystery of the Church: every true Christian is deeply marked with the 'sense of the Church', which is a matter of living experience, not abstract knowledge. (This understanding of the *sensus Ecclesiae* is essential if the Catholic understanding of teaching authority is to be presented to other Churches in a properly balanced form.) In concluding this section with a brief discussion of baptism, the Pope showed that all the baptized are 'by virtue of this sacrament inserted into the Mystical Body of Christ, that is, into the Church'.

It is the third section, on dialogue, which is of most relevance to ecumenism. The Pope proposes three stages in dialogue: the first that we should 'reverently, persistently and lovingly approach' others so as to understand how their minds work; secondly, 'we should put before them the gifts of truth and grace' of which God has appointed the Pope to be the guardian; thirdly, we should share with them the redemption and hope which we have received. (It has been rightly pointed out that this concept of dialogue is one-sided in that the Church learns *about* its partners in dialogue in order to change them, not in order to learn *from* them.) The 'origin' of this dialogue is God's dialogue with man, namely the revelation contained in the incarnate life itself of Christ, as well as his Gospel. (This analogy again shows that Paul envisages the Church as the possessor of truth which is communicated to the partners in dialogue.)

The Church should take the initiative, and not wait to be called to dialogue by others. 'But no one is compelled by force to come to the dialogue of salvation, far from it; rather they are invited by the attractive power of love.' The papacy should function in the same way:

> although it announces the certain truth and necessary salvation, it will not choose any method of external coercion; on the contrary it will proceed along the legitimate paths of courtesy and politeness, of interior conviction, of shared dialogue; it will offer the gift of salvation without violating the freedom of any private individual or citizen.

In initiating such dialogue 'it is good to consider the slow progress of human history, and wait for the time when God will make the dialogue fruitful'.

> This type of relationship indicates a proposal of courteous esteem, of understanding and of goodness on the part of the one who inaugurates the dialogue: it excludes the *a priori* condemnation, the offensive and time-worn polemic, the ostentatious

pursuit of a fruitless discussion. If this approach does not aim at effecting the immediate conversion of the partner, inasmuch as it respects both his dignity and his freedom, nevertheless it does aim at helping him, and tries to dispose him for a fuller sharing of sentiments and convictions.

(Once more the lack of reciprocity in the Pope's conception of dialogue is evident.) This dialogue requires the character of one 'who realises the seriousness of the duty to be an apostle; who is convinced that he cannot separate his own salvation from that of others.'

Eventually the Holy Father considers what the Catholic can gain from dialogue:

> One readily perceives that the light of faith can be reached in various ways, which can converge on a single destination. Although the ways are different, they can sometimes complement one another and lead our reasoning a little way away from the traditional path, so that sometimes we are compelled to consider our own position more deeply or to improve the terms in which we express it.

This procedure 'will help to find some elements of truth even in the ideas of the other side'. (The concession that Catholics have something to learn from others is made in grudging terms, but it is a vital concession for all that.) However, 'the desire to come together as brothers must not lead to a watering down of the truth or to any subtraction from it'. *Irenismus* (false irenicism) and *syncretismus* (eclecticism) must be avoided, for they are forms of scepticism.

In terms that should please Protestants, the Pope spoke of 'the supreme importance which attaches to the preaching of God's word . . . Apostolate and preaching are almost synonymous. Our ministry [does he mean the papal ministry?] is above all the ministry of the word.'

The Church can be envisaged as the centre of a set of concentric circles. The outer comprises the whole of humanity. In words that echo the Latin poet Terence, Paul declared: 'All things human are our concern.' The next circle includes those 'who adore the one, supreme God whom we too adore', above all the Jews and the Moslems. The third circle contains all Christians, while finally at the centre is the Roman Catholic Church.

It is what the Pope says about the third circle that most concerns us here. What has been said above about the proper procedure for dialogue applies to the dialogue between Catholics and other Christians. 'In some areas it has begun to make satisfactory progress.' Our method should be 'first to discover what all have in common before indicating the issues that divide.'

> But we wish to say more than that. With regard to many points of difference concerning tradition, spirituality, canon law and worship, we are ready to study means of satisfying the legitimate desires of our Christian brothers still separated from us. For nothing is closer to our heart than to be able to embrace them in perfect unity of faith and charity.

Nevertheless this recognition that differences are acceptable (though the Pope does not explicitly include differences of doctrine or even theology) must not lead us to make any compromise with 'the integrity of the faith and the duties of charity'.

> Since the Catholic Church has chosen to undertake the restoration of the one fold of Christ, it will not cease to apply the greatest prudence and care; it will not cease to affirm that the prerogatives which set it apart from brothers outside its threshold do not spring from ambition based on the memory of the past or from crazy theological speculations, but from the will of Christ. It will not cease to affirm that, if the purpose of these prerogatives is properly understood, they benefit everyone, for they promote common unity, common freedom, and the common fullness of Christian life.

Among these 'prerogatives' the Pope turned his attention to the papacy itself:

> it fills our heart with sorrow that many brothers separated from communion with the Apostolic See think that we ourselves, while supporting the idea of reconciliation, are actually an obstacle to it because of the primacy of honour and jurisdiction which Christ conferred upon the Apostle Peter and which we have received in succession to him. Do not some people say that, if the primacy of the Bishop of Rome were abolished, it would be easier for the separated Churches to be united with the Catholic Church in a single body? Accordingly we beg our brothers who are separated from communion with us to ask themselves whether their opinion can be sustained in the light of two facts: first, that without the Pope the Catholic religion would cease to be Catholic; and secondly, that if Christ's Church lacked a supreme Petrine pastoral office endowed with the power to act and make decrees, its unity would fall apart . . . This office, which is like the main hinge of the Church, is not a supreme authority puffed up with spiritual pride or eager for human domination, but a primacy of service, ministration and love. It is not empty rhetoric which confers upon the Vicar of Christ the title of 'servant of the servants of God'.

26

The Pope spoke of the joy and confidence he experienced when he saw how the faithful all over the world were longing for unity. He spoke of his pleasure at his meetings with Patriarch Athenagoras, and thanked the observers at the Council. He promised his 'watchful and devoted attention to every spiritual matter connected with the question of unity'.

His final remarks, addressed to Catholics, throw light on his conception of the Church. Catholics are 'our sons who are in the house of God, that is the one, holy, catholic and apostolic Church, of which the Roman Church is the mother and head'. By 'Roman Church' he must mean the diocese of Rome. The statement that Catholics are in the one Church headed by the Roman See, while implying that non-Catholics are not in it, refrains from stating whether they have any affiliation to it at all. This was an issue much debated at the Council in the course of the formulation of the Decree on the Church.

The encyclical is probably most notable for its repeated insistence that the Church should be inserted into the world. It met with a generally lukewarm reception from ecumenists of other Churches, because of its one-sided conception of dialogue and its strong insistence on papal primacy. A more sympathetic reading would have noticed its originality: its insistence that dialogue must involve listening, searching for common ground, and even changing one's mind; its conviction that the papacy must prove itself to be in practice a service and not a threat to other Christians.

There is a revealing passage in the encyclical where Pope Paul, discussing his relationship with the Council, shows how at this stage he understands papal teaching authority. Most properly and considerately he states that he will avoid writing on those aspects of the doctrine of the Church still being considered by the Council, so as to leave that body its 'freedom of investigation and debate'. The words that follow, however, intended apparently to recall that a Council's decrees are not valid until given papal ratification, give the impression that he conceives the papacy as a source of doctrine which is not only superior to the Council but is also separate from it:

> . . . as our apostolic office of teacher and pastor requires, the office which we enjoy as head of the Church, at the proper moment and in the appropriate manner we shall express our mind, and then we shall be most happy if we can present it in perfect accord with that of the Council Fathers.

Paul was here touching on the question of collegiality, the relationship between the Pope and the bishops, which the Council had already been discussing as it worked on the Decree on the Church.

It is not without precedent in history that a pope should refuse to ratify the decision of a council. But the overtones of the Pope's words jarred, suggesting as they seemed to do that the Council was a body which must indeed be allowed its freedom of debate, but whose voice was in the last resort only advisory.

The title 'head of the Church' recurs in conjunction with others in Paul's speech at the opening of the third session of the Council on 14 September 1964, where he describes himself as 'your brother, the Bishop of historic Rome, and as the humble but authentic successor of the apostle, Peter, . . . and therefore as the unworthy but true head (*Moderator*) of the Catholic Church and Vicar of Christ, servant of the servants of God'. The following words cast more light on his understanding of the link between the papacy and the unity of the Church: 'recapitulating (*complectimur*) in our persons and in our functions the universal Church, we proclaim this Council ecumenical'; and the Council is 'the exercise of unity, . . . the exercise of universality'.

The claim to 'recapitulate' the Church at first reading sounds like an extreme form of papalism which implies that the Church derives its existence and its power from the pope. But this is not what Paul is saying. To say that the pope recapitulates the Church could be no more than to say that he is the universal primate; for a primate has the duty to represent the whole Church, liturgically, symbolically and in his teaching. The term 'recapitulate' may, however, have been intended to add an extra dimension to the notion of primacy, namely that the pope is, as it were, an ikon or sacramental sign of the presence of the Holy Spirit working through the Church. (That very original Anglican theologian Austin Farrer described priests as 'walking sacraments'.)

The Pope spoke of the task of the Second Vatican Council as completing the work of the First in explaining the nature of the Church. Vatican I defined the papal powers, an action which 'has appeared to some as having limited the authority of the bishops, the successors of the apostles, and as having rendered superfluous and prevented the convocation of a subsequent Ecumenical Council'. Vatican II is required therefore to produce a 'clarification consonant with the doctrine of the papacy which will place in its splendid light the role and mandate of the episcopate.'

The Pope went on to expound his understanding of the relationship between the papacy and the episcopate. His words go some way towards removing the misgivings that *Ecclesiam Suam* could arouse. The Council is not just an advisory body, but has its 'sacred authority'; the pope is not apart from this body, but belongs to it as its head; interventions which the pope may make are for the sake of the unity of the Church.

As successors of Peter and, therefore, as possessors of full power over the entire Church, we have the duty of heading the body of the episcopate, although we are surely unworthy of this dignity. It is not our intention to deprive you of the authority which belongs to you. On the contrary, we are among the first to respect that sacred authority. If our apostolic duty requires us to impose restrictions, to define terminology, to prescribe modes of action, to regulate the methods which concern the exercise of episcopal authority, you realise that this is done for the good of the entire Church, for the unity of that Church which has proportionately greater need of centralised leadership as its worldwide extension becomes more complete, as more serious dangers and more pressing needs threaten the Christian people in the varying circumstances of history, and we may add as more rapid means of communication become operative in modern times.

No one should regard as a device formulated by pride such centralisation, which will surely be always tempered and balanced by an alert and timely delegation both of authority and facilities for local pastors.

We assure you, our brothers in the episcopate, that this centralisation is rather a service and a manifestation of the unifying and hierarchical spirit of the Church . . .

Such centralisation strengthens rather than weakens the authority of bishops, whether that authority be considered in the individual bishop or in the collegiality of the bishops . . .

For your part, dispersed as you are all over the world, if you are to give shape and substance to the true catholicity of the Church, you have the need of a centre, a principle of unity in faith and communion, a unifying power, such as, in fact, you find in this chair of Peter.

Then, after addressing the Roman Catholic auditors at the Council, he turned to the observers from other Churches:

We welcome and thank you, we wish to assure you once more of our purpose and hope to be able one day to remove every obstacle, every misunderstanding, every hesitancy that still prevents us from feeling fully of one heart and one soul in Christ, in his Church (Acts 4: 32).

For our part, we shall do all that the possibilities allow to this end . . .

It is something new, in contrast with the long, sad history which led up to the various separations, and we shall wait patiently for the conditions to ripen that will make possible a positive and friendly solution.

It is something, too, of deepest significance, having its roots in the mysterious counsels of God, and we shall strive, in humility and faith, to dispose ourselves to deserve so great a grace. We recall the words of the Apostle Paul, who brought the gift of the Gospel to all nations, seeking to become all things to all men (1 Cor 9: 22). Such an adaptability as we might today be tempted to call pluralism in practice; at the same time we recall how the same apostle has exhorted us to preserve the unity of the Spirit in the bond of peace because there is only one Lord, one faith, one baptism, one God and father of all (Eph 4: 2, 5-6).

We shall therefore strive, in loyalty to the unity of Christ's Church, to understand better and to welcome all that is genuine and admissible in the different Christian denominations that are distinct from us, and at the same time we beg of them to try to understand the Catholic faith and life better and, when we invite them to enter into the fullness of truth and charity which, as an unmerited blessing but a formidable responsibility, Christ has charged us to preserve, we beg them not to take it in bad part, but as being prompted by brotherly love.

This address brings out clearly what seem to be the two leading ideas in Paul's conception of ecumenism. The first is the conviction that the papal office is of the nature of the Church, for which it provides an indispensable service as the minister and focus of unity. The second is the passionate desire that all Christ's followers should be fully one, the appreciation of the diversity of the gifts of the Spirit among non-Catholics as well as Catholics, and the desire for this diversity to be cherished and not extinguished in a united Church. In one passage these two convictions are expressed together very eloquently :

O Churches that are so far and yet so close to us; Churches for whom our heart is filled with longing; Churches, the nostalgia of our sleepless nights; Churches of our tears and of our desire to do you honour by our embrace in the sincere love of Christ – O may you hear, sounding from this keystone of unity, the tomb of Peter, apostle and martyr, and from this Ecumenical Council of brotherhood and peace, the loving cry we send you.

There is one sentence in the address which contains an ecumenical principle of the first importance. Pope Paul's words on many occasions show that he sees an identity between the one, holy, catholic and apostolic Church founded by Christ and the Catholic Church in communion with the Roman See. But this does not mean that other Christians have simply detached themselves from this true Church leaving it whole and unharmed. Here Paul shows that he understands the separation of the other Christians as something which stunts the full growth of Christ's

Church not merely in a numerical way: 'that fullness of truth and charity will be made the more manifest when all those who profess the name of Christ are reassembled into one'. That is to say, the Church's conception of the truth is incomplete because of the divisions among the Christian Churches.

Paul VI's address to the observers delivered in the Sistine Chapel on 29 September 1964 showed again his characteristic desire to admit the fullest possible diversity for the sake of Christian unity, while insisting upon 'certain doctrinary requirements' from which the Catholic Church 'cannot deflect'.

> And so here we are again, seeking, on both sides, a definition of our respective positions. As for our position, you already know it. You will have noticed that the Council has only had words of respect and gladness for your presence and for the Christian communities which you represent. Indeed, words of honour, charity and hope in your regard. This is no small thing if we think of the disputes of the past; and if we think that this changed attitude is sincere and heartfelt as well as profound. Moreover, you may observe how the Catholic Church is prepared for an honourable and serene dialogue. It is in no hurry, but wishes to begin this, leaving it up to divine goodness to end it, when and how he decides. We still remember the proposal you made to us last year, in similar circumstances to the present ones – that of founding a research centre for study of the history of salvation, to be carried out in collaboration; and we hope to achieve this initiative, in memory of our journey to the Holy Land last January. We are considering whether this is possible.
>
> This proves to you, gentlemen and brothers, that the Catholic Church, although it cannot deflect from certain doctrinary requirements to which it must, in duty to Christ, remain true, is ready to study how difficulties can be removed, misunderstandings cleared away, the genuine treasures of truth and spirituality respected (which you possess). The Church is prepared to broaden and adapt certain canon laws to help the recomposition of unity between the great Christian communities now separated from us.

Once again there is discernible in the Holy Father's words a tension between the insistence on an unchangeable doctrinal position on the one hand, and on the other the admission that the other Churches are endowed with 'genuine treasures' not only of custom and spirituality, but also of truth. In other words, he is coming close to allowing the possibility of a pluriformity in doctrine as well as in faith.

On 18 October 1964 the Pope canonised the twenty-two Ugandan martyrs who were killed between 1885 and 1887. In his

31

homily the Holy Father referred to the Anglicans who also gave their lives for the faith in the same persecution.

The Pan-Orthodox Conference which Patriarch Athenagoras had worked so hard to convene met at Rhodes on 31 October with the intention of discussing ways of entering into dialogue with Rome. Since so far even the Ecumenical Patriarch, when meeting the Pope, had represented only his own Church of Constantinople and not the whole of Orthodoxy, that this conference came together at all was a significant step forward. Pope Paul sent a message to the Council, in which he evidently took great care to say nothing which could cause offence. Promising to follow the work of the conference with prayer and attention, he wrote:

> while your brothers of the Roman Catholic Church, gathered in Council, are asking themselves about the ways to follow to be ever more faithful to the design of God for his Church in this epoch so rich in possibilities but also so full of trials and temptations, you also, responding to this will of the Lord, are preparing yourselves to turn to the same problems.

The Conference did not invite other Christian Churches to send observers, but welcomed representatives of the Catholic and Protestant press. Greeting them Bishop Spyridon of Rhodes quoted with approval the words of Pope Paul in *Ecclesiam Suam*: 'Before we observe or study what divides us, let us bring to mind many common points of unity.' The members of the Conference sent the Pope a telegram expressing unanimous thanks for his 'very friendly' message, and appreciation for his 'words of love and peace'.

Unfortunately the outcome of the Pan-Orthodox Conference was not so happy. The Conference of the previous year had agreed in principle to dialogue with Rome 'on equal terms', and the 1964 Conference was convoked with the express intention of implementing that decision. In the event the decision was to reopen theological discussion with the Anglicans and Old Catholics, but that conditions were not yet suitable for equivalent discussions with Roman Catholics. However the text of the decision tried to avoid giving offence:

> This, however, does *not* mean that any of the local Orthodox Churches is *not* free to continue to cultivate sisterly relations with the Roman Catholic Church, providing she does this on her own behalf and not in the name of all Orthodoxy, in the conviction that in this way the difficulties at present existing may be neutralised.

On 21 November 1964, the final day of the third session of the Council, three more documents were passed to add to the Decrees on Liturgy and the means of Social Communication already passed the previous year. As the subject of this book is papal statements there will not be space to attempt a detailed analysis of these new documents. But as two of them contained passages which touched on ecumenical issues and the third dealt explicitly with ecumenism, they form the context within which later papal utterances need to be assessed. It will therefore be necessary to devote a little space to them.

The *Dogmatic Constitution on the Church* presented an official Catholic ecclesiology with which other Christians could feel they had much in common. While reiterating the traditional picture of the Church as a visible, hierarchical society headed on earth by the Pope, its first two chapters depicted the Church in quite distinct (though of course not incompatible) terms. The first chapter, speaking of the Church as a 'mystery', at once raises the subject from the organisational to the spiritual level: so too does Chapter Five, on the call of the whole Church to holiness. The second chapter employs the biblical language of the 'People of God', and examines the links in the Holy Spirit between the Roman Catholic Church and 'the baptized who are honoured by the name of Christian, but who do not however profess the Catholic faith in its entirety or have not preserved unity or communion under the successors of Peter' (n. 15). Chapter Three, which puts forward the idea of the episcopate as a college, of which the Bishop of Rome is both a member and the president, points the way to a conception of papacy which might be acceptable to other Christians. Chapters Two and Four expound the biblical doctrine of the priesthood of all the faithful. Chapter Eight, on the Blessed Virgin Mary, places Roman Catholic teaching on the Mother of God within the doctrines of the Communion of Saints and the Church.

Of most explicit ecumenical importance is paragraph eight, which treats of the relationship of the visible societies of the Roman Catholic Church and other Christian bodies to the Church. A draft of the text affirmed a simple identity between Christ's Church and the Roman Catholic Church which would leave other Christians outside. In the final version of the document a form of words was chosen which would assert a unique relationship between the visible Church of Rome and Christ's Church, without totally excluding non-Catholics. The 'unique Church of Christ',

> constituted and organised in the world as a society, in the present world subsists in the Catholic Church, which is governed by the successor of Peter and by the bishops in common with

33

him. Nevertheless many elements of sanctification and of truth are found outside its visible confines. Since these are gifts belonging to the Church of Christ, they are forces impelling towards Catholic unity (n. 8).

Much paper has been used up in the discussion of that key-word 'subsists'. The most plausible suggestion seems to be that, since the Church willed by God needs to have a sociological, institutional realisation or embodiment on earth, the Roman Catholic Church *is* that embodiment; God's will for the salvation of mankind through the Church is fulfilled in many ways among other Christian bodies (perhaps sometimes more effectively than in the Roman Catholic Church), but these bodies, being separated from the Bishop of Rome, who is the divinely appointed centre of unity, *are* not Christ's Church. This theology of the Church is conceived in terms of a visible society. Recent Roman Catholic studies have pointed out that these are not the only terms in which the Church can be conceived (the Constitution itself, as we have seen, speaks of the Church also in other terms). Accordingly, if the Church is conceived, for example, as a fellowship or communion of all who believe in Christ or all who are baptized, or as the body of all who share the life of the Holy Spirit in Christ, non-Catholic Christians form part of the Church. This is evidently an area in which much work remains to be done.

The second document ratified by the Council that day was the *Decree on the Eastern Catholic Churches*. This decree dealt with the Uniate Churches, which, though in communion with the Roman See, did not follow Latin canon law or Latin liturgical norms, but enjoyed their own 'liturgical rites, ecclesiastical traditions and their ordering of Christian life' (n. 1). The subject was of great ecumenical importance, for, if the Anglican and Orthodox Churches were to be reunited with Rome, this uniate pattern seemed to provide the most promising basis for an arrangement. The statement that the uniate rites were 'of equal rank' with the Roman rite was welcomed by non-Catholic critics. On the other hand, the Orthodox theologian Alexander Schmemann found fault with the text for its 'uniatism', i.e. its apparent assumption that the differences between East and West could be reduced to differences of practice.

> But it is precisely this reduction which forms the basis of 'uniatism' that the Orthodox reject, for they affirm that the liturgical and canonical tradition of the East cannot be isolated from doctrinal principles which it implies and which constitute the real issue between Roman Catholicism and Eastern Orthodoxy (A. Schmemann in *The Documents of Vatican II*, ed. W. M. Abbott and J. Gallagher, London, Dublin, etc., 1966, p. 387).

The same criticism was made from the Catholic side by Dom Emmanuel Lanne ('Pluralism and Unity: the Possibility of a Variety of "Typologies" within the same Ecclesial Allegiance', *One in Christ* 6 [1970] p. 445).

The third document was the *Decree on Ecumenism*, which, according to a Protestant commentator 'marks the beginning of a new era in the relation of the Churches to one another' (S. M. Cavert in W. M. Abbott and J. Gallagher, op. cit., p. 367). The Decree confesses that Catholics share the blame for the existence of divisions among Christians.

The Catholic Church accepts other Christians as brothers. 'Men who believe in Christ and have been properly baptized are put in some, though imperfect, communion with the Catholic Church. Some, even very many, of the most significant elements and endowments which go together to build up and give life to the Church itself, can exist outside the visible boundaries of the Catholic Church. . . . All of these, which come from Christ and lead back to him, belong by right to the one Church of Christ.' It is not that non-Catholics *as individuals* possess these endowments: their communities 'as such' are of 'significance and importance in the mystery of salvation. For the Spirit of Christ has not refrained from using them as means of salvation which derive their efficacy from the very fullness of grace and truth entrusted to the Catholic Church' (n. 3).

Nevertheless these non-Catholic bodies necessarily suffer from a radical defect:

> . . . our separated brethren, whether considered as individuals or as communities and Churches, are not blessed with that unity which Jesus Christ wished to bestow on all those to whom he has given new birth into one body, and whom he has quickened to newness of life. . . . For it is through Christ's Catholic Church alone, which is the universal help towards salvation, that the fullness of the means of salvation can be obtained (n. 3).

However, it does not follow from the Council's words that separated Christians necessarily suffer from any defect apart from the lack of the unity which comes from being in communion with the Bishop of Rome. Making use of the term already used in the Constitution on the Church, the Decree on Ecumenism affirms that the unity 'which Christ bestowed on his Church from the beginning . . . *subsists in* (my italics) the Catholic Church as something she can never lose' (n. 4).

The Decree established an order of importance in ecumenical activity.

Catholics must assuredly be concerned for their separated brethren, praying for them, keeping them informed about the Church, making the first approaches towards them. But their primary duty is to make a careful and honest appraisal of whatever needs to be renewed and done in the Catholic household itself, in order that its life may bear witness more clearly and faithfully to the teachings and institutions which have been handed down from Christ through the apostles (n. 4).

In a very important passage, the Decree transcends the 'uniatism' that had been detected in the Constitution on the Church, expressing not only a tolerance but even a welcome for pluralism in the Church, and extending the scope of this pluralism so that it includes not only practice but also doctrine:

while preserving unity in essentials, let everyone in the Church, according to the office entrusted to him, preserve a proper freedom in the various forms of spiritual life and discipline, in the variety of liturgical rites, and even in the theological elaborations of revealed truth (n. 4. Cf. E. Lanne, op. cit., p. 447).

The same paragraph spoke of the 'truly Christian endowments . . . which are to be found among our separated brethren', and recognises 'the riches of Christ and virtuous works in the lives of others who are bearing witness to Christ, sometimes to the shedding of their blood'. Indeed, divisions in the Church constitute a wound in the Church (i.e. presumably the Roman Catholic Church), for it is prevented

from realising the fullness of catholicity proper to her in those of her sons who, though joined to her by baptism, are yet separated from full communion with her. Furthermore, the Church herself finds it more difficult to express in actual life her full catholicity in all its aspects.

The second chapter of the Decree is entitled 'The Practice of Ecumenism', and begins with the statement that 'the concern for restoring unity involves the whole Church, faithful and clergy alike.' Essential to ecumenism is 'interior conversion' (n. 7).

This change of heart and holiness of life, along with public and private prayer for the unity of Christians, should be regarded as the soul of the whole ecumenical movement, and merits the name, 'spiritual ecumenism' (n. 8).

The importance of prayer in common is affirmed, but the need for limiting principles is maintained.

Catholics 'must become familiar with the outlook of our separated brethren' (n. 9), and theology and Church history should be taught 'with due regard for the ecumenical point of view' (n. 10).

Guidelines are laid down for ecumenical dialogue.

> The manner and order in which Catholic belief is expressed should in no way become an obstacle to dialogue with our brethren. It is, of course, essential that the doctrine be clearly presented in its entirety. Nothing is so foreign to the spirit of ecumenism as a false irenicism which harms the purity of Catholic doctrine and obscures its genuine and certain meaning . . .
>
> When comparing doctrines with one another, they should remember that in Catholic doctrine there exists an order or 'hierarchy' of truths, since they vary in relation to the foundation of the Christian faith (n. 11).

Unfortunately the Council did not explain how this principle concerning the hierarchy of truths was to be applied in practice.

The third chapter of the Decree concerned 'the two principal types of division which affect the seamless robe of Christ'. The Churches of the East (e.g. the Orthodox and the Copts) have much in common with the Roman Church, especially the honour they pay to our Lady, 'true sacraments, above all – by apostolic succession – the priesthood and the Eucharist, whereby they are still joined to us in closest intimacy' (n. 15). The Council reaffirmed its appreciation of Eastern traditions : 'such diversity of customs and observances only adds to her beauty and contributes greatly to carrying out her mission.'

> To remove all shadow of doubt, then, this holy Synod solemnly declares that the Churches of the East, while keeping in mind the necessary unity of the whole Church, have the power to govern themselves according to their own disciplines, since these are better suited to the character of their faithful and better adapted to foster the good of souls. The perfect obedience of this traditional principle – which indeed has not always been observed – is a prerequisite for any restoration of union (n. 16).

The same principle applied to 'legitimate variety . . . in legitimate expressions of doctrine.'

> In the study of revealed truth East and West have used different methods and approaches in understanding and confessing divine things. It is hardly surprising, then, if sometimes one tradition has come nearer to a full appreciation of some aspects of a mystery of revelation than the other, or has expressed them

37

better. In such cases, these various theological formulations are often to be considered complementary rather than conflicting (n. 17).

In seeking to restore communion with the East, one must 'impose no burden beyond what is indispensable' (Acts 15 : 28) (n. 18).

When it comes to the second type of division, that which arose in the West as a result of the Reformation, in one way the links Rome has with the Reformation Churches are closer than those with the East, because of the 'specially close relationship' which results from 'the long span of earlier centuries when the Christian people had lived in ecclesial communion'. But there are 'very weighty differences not only of a historical, sociological, psychological and cultural character, but especially in the interpretation of revealed thruth' (n. 19). Among these Churches, 'the Anglican communion occupies a special place' (n. 13). The Decree picks out baptism as 'the sacramental bond of unity existing among all who through it are reborn',.but adds the reservation that

> baptism, of itself, is only a beginning, a point of departure, for it is wholly directed towards the acquiring of fullness of life in Christ. Baptism is thus ordained towards a complete profession of faith, a complete incorporation into the system of salvation such as Christ himself willed it to be, and, finally, towards a complete integration into eucharistic communion (n. 22).

However, the separated Western ecclesial communities 'lack the fullness of unity with us which flows from baptism, and . . . we believe they have not preserved the proper reality of the eucharistic mystery in its fullness, especially because of the absence of the sacrament of Orders' (n. 22).

Because of this difference between the separated Churches of the East and the West, whereas with the East 'some worship in common (*communicatio in sacris*), given suitable circumstances and the approval of Church authority, is not merely possible but is encouraged' (n. 15), nothing similar is said about the West, where the faithful are urged 'to abstain from any frivolous or imprudent zeal', which can 'cause harm to true progress towards unity' (n. 24).

The Decree contains a reference to a principle of great ecumenical significance which is preserved in Orthodox tradition, without however endorsing it on behalf of the Catholic Church. This is the Eastern understanding of the importance of the local Church:

> of primary concern and care among the Orientals has been, and still is, the preservation in a communion of faith and

charity of those family ties which ought to exist between local Churches, as between sisters (n. 14).

In the last session of the Council, however, the Decree on the Pastoral Office of Bishops was to adopt this principle into official Catholic teaching:

> A diocese is a section of the People of God entrusted to a bishop to be guided by him with the assistance of his clergy so that, loyal to its pastor and formed by him into one community in the Holy Spirit through the Gospel and the Eucharist, it constitutes one particular church in which the one, holy, catholic and apostolic Church of Christ is truly present and active (n. 11).

In summarising the main points of ecumenical interest contained in the three decrees of the third session of the Council, we have had no room to give an account of the dramatic debates that preceded their promulgation. Something must, however, be said about Pope Paul's intervention in the final formulation of the section of the Constitution on the Church which dealt with the doctrine of collegiality. A week before the date fixed for the promulgation of the three decrees, the Pope (his name was not mentioned but his authorship is not in doubt) issued a 'Preparatory Explanatory Note', which was to form part of the acts of the Council, defining the sense of Chapter Three of the Constitution; the Fathers were asked to vote for or against the chapter in the light of this authoritative interpretation. The Pope may have taken this unprecedented step, not because he was dissatisfied with the text, but because he wanted to convince those bishops who disapproved of the chapter that, if it was properly understood, they had nothing to fear. This was only one of several such interventions: the Pope was soon to require last-minute changes in the text of the Decree on Ecumenism. The incidents are important in so far as they show Pope Paul's conception of collegiality in practice.

In the closing address which he delivered on 21 November 1964, the Pope gave further evidence of his awareness of the possibility of diversity and change in the Church, when he spoke of the Council's efforts 'to discover the innermost significance and substantial truth of the constitutional law of the Church herself, to determine what is immobile and certain therein and what is a derivation by a process of natural and authoritative evolution from basic principles.' He commented too on the way in which the Constitution had shown the 'successor of Peter' to be 'not different and extraneous' to the college of bishops, but rather its 'centre and head'.

He then turned his attention to other Christian Churches:

> We also hope that the same doctrine of the Church will be benevolently and favourably considered by the Christian brothers who are still separated from us. We wish that this doctrine, completed by the declarations contained in the schema on Ecumenism, likewise approved by this Council, might have in their souls the power of a loving leaven for the revision of thoughts and attitudes which may draw them closer to our communion, and finally, God willing, may merge them in it.

The last part of his address he devoted to one of the most sensitive of ecumenical subjects, the Blessed Virgin Mary.

> Truly, the reality of the Church is not exhausted in its hierarchical structure, in its liturgy, in its sacraments, in its juridical ordinances. The intimate, the primary source of its sanctifying effectiveness is to be sought in its mystic union with Christ; a union which we cannot conceive as separate from her who is the Mother of the Word Incarnate and whom Jesus Christ himself wanted closely united to himself for our salvation. Thus the loving contemplation of the marvels worked by God in his Holy Mother must find its proper perspective in the vision of the Church. And knowledge of the true Catholic doctrine on Mary will always be a key to the exact understanding of Christ and of the Church.

Accordingly he went on to 'proclaim' Mary to be 'Mother of the Church'. 'It is precisely by this title, in preference to all others, that the faithful and the Church address Mary'. The Pope's action was clearly not intended as an *ex cathedra* dogmatic definition, but as the official commendation of a widespread devotion.

The Pope had already announced his intention of making this proclamation, a proposal which 'very many Council Fathers made their own, pressing for an explicit declaration at this Council of the motherly role of the Virgin among the Christian people.' Nevertheless, the Council's Theological Commission had rejected the proposal that the title should be included in the Marian section of the Constitution on the Church, explaining:

> From the ecumenical point of view, the title can certainly not be recommended, although it can be admitted theologically. The Commission therefore deemed it sufficient to express the idea in equivalent terms.

The Holy Father's utterances during the third session had offered fresh evidence of his longing for unity. But some of his words and actions showed a readiness to override the voice of the bishops which could not fail to be an obstacle, and perhaps an unnecessary obstacle, to non-Catholic understanding of the value of the papacy.

3. INDIA, ANATHEMAS,
THE END OF THE COUNCIL

POPE PAUL had little time for rest after the tensions of the third session of the Council. Early in December he resumed his role of pilgrim pope to attend the Eucharist Congress in Bombay.

On 3 December 1964 he gave an address to the non-Catholic Christians at the Congress. He spoke of his joy at the 'atmosphere of fraternal charity and mutual understanding', which was

> a sign that the Holy Spirit has been working in a special way in the minds and hearts of all those who bear the glorious name of Jesus Christ. It is with joy that we express our graditude to God for his pouring out of gifts of his Spirit especially in these days. For if the divisions which exist among Christians are causes of pain to all who desire to serve their Lord faithfully, the fact that so many initiatives have already been taken to repair these divisions is a source of joy and consolation.

The Pope spoke of the initiative which the Catholic Church had taken towards the reconciliation of all Christians, and on his own repeated emphasis on this movement in his addresses and letters. He reminded his hearers of the recently promulgated Decree on Ecumenism.

> However, the initiatives which we are taking are not to be made in isolation. Rather it is our hope that our efforts can accompany yours, can mingle with yours so that together in humility and charity and mutual understanding we can seek out ways by which Christ's will that 'all may be one' can one day be fully realised.

He reiterated that he 'must remain faithful to that which we have received from the Apostles and the Fathers of the Church'. But his following words suggest that he acknowledges that other Christians have a similar duty of fidelity to their traditions, and that such fidelity on both sides will lead to a growing together, not a divergence:

> But we are also confident that fidelity to Christ and to his Gospel, which is the touchstone of all sincere ecumenical activity, will bring it about that God, who will never be wanting to those

who serve him in love, will crown the efforts of all of us with blessings of true peace and reconciliation among Christians themselves, even as he has reconciled us to himself in the Blood of his Son.

Within four days of his return to Rome, he spoke again of ecumenism at a General Audience, reiterating the need for diversity in the Church.

Christianity is not linked to any one civilisation, but is designed to express itself according to the character of each, so long as the civilisation is truly human and open. The duty immediately arises of knowing better those people with whom we come in contact by reason of the Gospel, recognising all the good they possess, not only in their history and civilisation, but also in the heritage of moral and religious values which they possess and preserve. This attitude of Catholics towards non-Catholics is now sharpening and developing. . . .

We are easily led to believe that the extension of unity to mankind in the practical order of reality is not only universality but uniformity. . . . We [must] progress to the reflection that all that multiplicity must be recognised, respected and indeed promoted and verified.

The theme of the Pope's Christmas message was brotherhood. After speaking of various obstacles to brotherhood, he again rejected the view of an intolerant, monolithic Church:

Listening to our message, some may ask: is not religion a motive for the division among men, and especially the Catholic religion, so dogmatic, so demanding, so discriminating? Does it not impede an easy conversation and a spontaneous understanding among people? Oh yes, religion, Catholic no less than any other, is an element of distinction among men, even as is language, culture, art and the professions, but it is not of its very nature a divisive element. It is true that Christianity, by the newness of the life which it brings into the world, can be a motive of division and of contrast because of that which brings good to humanity: it is a light shining in darkness, differentiating the various areas. But it is not of the nature of religion to oppose itself to people. It is on behalf of people, it stands in defence of all that is sacred and unsuppressible in them, of their fundamental aspiration to God, and their right to manifest this externally in a worthy form of worship.

Meanwhile the Ecumenical Patriarch, undeterred by the setback at Rhodes to his hopes of establishing formal dialogue between Rome and Orthodoxy, in his Christmas message reaffirmed his optimism:

> Our Orthodox communion, not neglecting or ignoring its responsibility, from the depth of its heart will work for the mutual cultivation of sisterly relations with the Roman Catholic Church, according to the common desire expressed at Rhodes by all the Orthodox Churches.

Early in January 1965 the Pope wrote to the Patriarchs of the Arab countries on the occasion of the anniversary of his visit to the Holy Land. The letter urges co-operation between the Christian and Muslim communities. 'We could complete one another in the cultural sphere and be enriched by our very differences.' But the importance of the letter for our purposes lies not in its reiteration of the value of diversity, but in the fact that it was addressed to both Catholic and Orthodox Patriarchs.

The same month Pope Paul spoke of ecumenism in three addresses in connection with the Church Unity Octave. In all of them he concentrated on the difficulties that arose once progress towards unity began to be made. On 17 January he said:

> Little by little, as the Christian conscience is aroused to this great ideal of union and charity, so also do the difficulties grow and the obstacles come into evidence: obstacles which are understandable but which are so painful, yet all the same, in our opinion, not insurmountable.

Three days later he returned to the difficulties:

> To those who know only superficially the question of the reunion of all Christians, the solution seems extremely easy and capable of swift realisation. But those who know the historical, psychological and doctrinal aspects of the question itself are aware of the great and numerous difficulties of every kind and from every quarter, so much so that some despair whether they can be resolved, while others still hope but see that perhaps a long time will be needed and certainly a special, almost miraculous intervention of God's grace.

There was a temptation to water down the Catholic faith for the sake of unity. But Christianity 'is a divine truth which was given to us not to change but only to ascertain and to accept for our salvation. . . . The intention is good; the method is not.'

> It is good from the Catholic point of view to want to recognise how much good is still found in the heritage of the Christian

44

Churches and confessions separated from us. It is good to want to present Catholic teaching in its authentic and essential aspects, prescinding from its debatable and non-essential aspects. It is again good to seek to present controversial points in terms that can make them more exact and better understood even with regard to those who do not share them. This is brotherly patience, this is good *apologia,* this is charity in the service of truth. But it is not a good service to pretend to resolve doctrinal difficulties by seeking to discredit or disregard or conceal affirmations which the teaching authority of the Church declares binding and definitive. It is not a good service for the cause of union because it creates among the separated brethren mistrust, the suspicion of being tricked, or else it generates the notion of misleading possibilities; and because it creates in the Church fear that union is being sought at the price of truths that are not open to discussion, and gives rise to suspicion that the dialogue is being concluded at the expense of sincerity, loyalty, and truth.

The tone of these remarks sounds disappointingly negative and anxious. But Paul was a man with a developed political sense. One wonders whether his aim was to induce the conservatives in his own Church to accept the ecumenical methods the value of which he was taking for granted ('it is good . . .'), by showing that he agreed with them that over-enthusiastic ecumenical utterances were not only inconsistent with Catholic faith but also hampered rather than promoted true union among Christians.

After creating twenty-seven new cardinals, the Pope explained at a General Audience on 27 January 1965 that one of his motives had been 'to spread the idea of ecumenism, to which the Council in the course of its existence has given so much splendour and so much hope. . . . It is our intention to give the Sacred College an expression of a fuller communion and more effective representation of authority, of collegiality, of experience, of traditions, of culture, and of worth.' Among the cardinals were three uniate Catholic patriarchs.

Meanwhile various ecumenical contacts were being pursued. Patriarch Athenagoras sent two metropolitans to Rome to inform the Pope of the decisions of the previous year's Pan-Orthodox Conference. They brought with them a letter dated 25 January 1965 in which the Patriarch was clearly at pains to counteract the check which the Conference had administered to Catholic/ Orthodox dialogue. The Orthodox Church, Athenagoras stated, had 'decided and proclaimed its aspirations and desire to cultivate fraternal relations with your venerable Church of the elder Rome in order to promote the spirit of unity in Christ'. The Pope in an equally discreet reply to the two metropolitans said:

> It is necessary by means of ever more frequent brotherly contacts to build up again what has been destroyed by the time of mutual isolation: an atmosphere must be created in all fields of the life of both Churches that will make it possible to begin a fruitful theological dialogue when the time comes.

The following month the Pope performed another of his gestures which did so much to encourage an atmosphere of trust and reconciliation between Rome and the Orthodox, when he authorised the return to the East of two relics which had fallen into the possession of the Venetians in their days of power. The relics of St Sabas were to be given back to the Greek Orthodox Patriarch of Jerusalem, and the head of St Titus to the Greek Orthodox Metropolitan of Herakleion.

In an audience given on 31 March 1965, the Pope reminded his listeners of the need for unity within the Roman Catholic Church.

> A lot is being said now about re-establishing unity with the separated brethren, and this is a good thing: this is a most deserving undertaking, and we should all collaborate in its progress with humanity, with perseverance, and with faith. But we must not neglect the duty of working all the more for the internal unity of the Church, which is so necessary for its spiritual and apostolic vitality.

It was impossible for the Catholic Church not to be *intrinsically* united; this was a gift of the Holy Spirit, who brought together dissimilar people without destroying the differences; this was the gift of catholicity or universality. However,

> unity is not merely a prerogative of the Catholic Church. It is a duty, a law, an obligation. That is, the Church's unity must be accepted and recognised by each and every member of the Church and be fostered, loved, and defended by them. It is not enough for people to call themselves Catholics: they must be effectively united.

Characteristically, the Pope pointed out, claiming the support of St Thomas Aquinas, that this unity of the Church required not only the unity of communion of the members with one another, but also unity of convergence, linking the members with Christ, the head of the Church, whose representative on earth is the Bishop of Rome.

The same day the Pope wrote to Patriarch Athenagoras thanking him for the letter he had written earlier in the year communicating the decisions of the Pan-Orthodox Conference. In it he wrote:

> The programme drawn up in these [decisions] seems to us to correspond to the needs of the concrete situations bequeathed to us by history and thus to those of the common journey towards the unity desired by the Lord, the desire for which has been so wonderfully kindled by his Spirit of love in the heart of Christians of our time. Your Holiness will recall that solicitude to contribute towards the restoration of unity among all Christians was one of the principal motives that inspired our predecessor of venerated memory to summon the Second Vatican Council. We can assure you that this preoccupation continues to concern us and that it is shared by all the Fathers of this Council, just as they demonstrated this by solemnly approving the decree on ecumenism. This important document, which in fact begins with the words *Unitatis redintegratio* (the restoration of unity), is entirely animated by the desire for dialogue and the conviction of the necessity of creating auspicious conditions and a favourable atmosphere for its fruitful development. Is not the fortunate harmony which it is easy to observe between the decisions of the Rhodes Conference and those of the Vatican Council a new sign of the action of the Holy Spirit?
>
> The object of our efforts will be the realisation of this joint programme of brotherhood and collaboration, which are being progressively rediscovered at all the levels of the life of our Churches and their activity. Neither the length of the road to be traversed nor the difficulties to be met with on it, both foreseen and unforeseen, can stop us, for our determination is based on that hope that cannot deceive.

A further sign of the growing trust between Catholics and Orthodox was a pair of articles written by Professor Alivizatos, State Procurator of the Greek Orthodox Synod, speaking of four official acts by which Pope John XXIII and his successor had 'opened wide the gates of understanding with those outside the Roman Catholic Church.' They were the decision to invite observers from other Churches to the Vatican Council, Pope Paul's decision to meet the Ecumenical Patriarch in Jerusalem as equal with equal, his visit to India in order to emphasise the importance of Christianity among the modern Gentiles, and the same Pope's decision to write a letter addressed directly to the Pan-Orthodox Conference in November 1964.

Another indication of the increasing cordiality was given at Easter 1965, when the Pope and the heads of the Eastern Churches separated from Rome exchanged greetings. But the thaw was not universal among the Orthodox Churches. In June the Archbishop of Athens told his Synod: 'As long as I live there will be no rapprochement with the Roman Catholic Church'.

On 1 May the Pope issued his second encyclical, *Mense Maio,* in which he made an urgent plea for 'united prayer' for peace 'from the whole Christian people'.

That same day *Civiltá Cattolica* published the text of a letter that the Pope had written to all bishops of the world the previous December. The subject was collegiality. The 'discordant and confused' modern world 'needs an example of true and complete spiritual harmony'.

> And here is the holy Church, raised up like an ensign for the nations (cf. Is. 11:12) and showing itself flowering with that miraculous unity that has again been proclaimed, strong with that internal bond of faith, love and discipline which binds together the episcopal order and the holy people of God.

The summer of 1965 saw several incidents of ecumenical importance. In June the Pope received the new British minister to the Holy See, and asked him to convey to the English people 'something of the care, both discreet and respectful, with which the Holy See favours, in God's good time, the perfect reconciliation between the Catholic Church and the Church of England'. On 14 July, addressing a general audience on the subject of authority in the Church, the Pope spoke of authority as a pastoral service, and denied that it tended to stifle legitimate variety.

> Again you will ask us, must, then, an authority so qualified and destined to make of mankind one single flock, level everyone and make everything uniform according to one single type of religious faithfulness? We will answer you with a phrase of St Gregory the Great: *In una fide nihil officit sanctae Ecclesiae consuetudo diversa* – 'When faith is one, diversity of customs does not harm the Church.' The unity of the Church is not uniformity, unless it be of faith and love.

Through most of the year 1965 it seems that ecumenism was no longer in the forefront of the Pope's thoughts, and that other issues had a prior claim on his attention, especially the question of world peace. His address on 14 September at the opening of the last session of the Council contained nothing that bore on reunion, apart from one brief sentence welcoming the observers. That this fact implied no decline in his interest in ecumenism, would be amply proved before the year was ended. The speech concluded with an announcement of the utmost importance: the Holy Father declared his intention of establishing a synod of bishops, as an organ of collegiality, after which he repeated the news that he would attend the twentieth anniversary of the United Nations Organisation and bring to that assembly an appeal for peace from the Council.

A significant exchange of telegrams took place at the opening of the last session of the Council. The Ecumenical Patriarch sent the Holy Father 'our brotherly congratulations and our wishes for a conclusion to its blessed and great work to the profit of the entire Church of Our Lord Jesus Christ'. The Pope told the Patriarch that the message would be read at the opening of the fourth session, saying that it 'touched us profoundly. We share your desire that the labours of the Council shall be blessed by God and bring fruitful results to the benefit of the whole Church of Jesus Christ.' A commentator pointed out that both prelates had used the phrase 'entire/whole Church of Christ' in such a way as to suggest that the Roman Catholic and Orthodox Churches were part of the same Church. This ecclesiology advances far beyond the 'subsists in the Catholic Church' of the Constitution on the Church.

That the Council's endeavours for Christian unity had suffered something of a check was acknowledged by Cardinal Bea, the President of the Secretariat for Christian Unity, when he addressed the observers on 18 September. He referred to

> the difficulties at the last minute with the text on ecumenism, the disappointment it caused to many, together with apprehensions for the future of the ecumenical dialogue. I do not mean to minimise the difficulties. I know that there were great efforts made by many for the return of calm and serenity little by little, and I am not saying that it has returned everywhere. But the simple fact remains that, in spite of all this, important steps forward have been made in the ecumenical field.

On 4 October 1965 the Pope absented himself from Rome in order to make his lightning visit to New York and address there the United Nations. He spoke, he said, 'not only in our own personal name and in the name of the great Catholic family: but also in that of those Christian brethren who share the same sentiments which we express here, particularly of those who so kindly charged us explicitly to be their spokesman here'. Commenting on the role of the Organisation to be 'a bridge between peoples, ... a network of relations between states,' he suggested that

> your chief characteristic is a reflection, as it were, in the temporal field, of what our Catholic Church aspires to be in the spiritual field: unique and universal. In the ideological construc-

tion of mankind, there is on the natural level nothing superior to this, your vocation is to make brothers not only of some, but of all peoples, a difficult undertaking, indeed: but this is your most noble undertaking. Is there anyone who does not see the necessity of coming thus progressively to the establishment of a world authority, able to act efficaciously on the juridical and political levels?

These words illuminate Paul's conceptions of the papacy as a bridge, the centre of a network of relations, uniting all Christians and for this purpose endowed with juridical authority. That day in New York one had a vision of the future, when the universal primate of all Christians could speak in their name to the world, affirming the value of Christian principles for the promotion of justice and peace.

On 24 October the Pope again saw himself in relation to all Christians in his Mission Sunday appeal for a great development in evangelisation.

Our ever more agonising, more urgent, more conclusive appeal is directed to the entire Christian people, so that all children of God who are already within the house of their Father may remember their brothers who yet stand outside, and that they may unite themselves with us in prayer and in works of united and brotherly love.

It is noteworthy that Pope Paul includes non-Catholic Christians 'within the house of their Father'.

The five documents promulgated half-way through the last session of the Council on 28 October 1965 all had some ecumenical relevance. As was pointed out in the preceding chapter, the *Decree on the Pastoral Office of Bishops* put forward a theology of the local church which could point to a model of a reunited Church as a community of local churches. The *Decree on the Renewal of Religious Life* commended the life of the religious vows to non-Catholics by showing its connection with the call of all Christians to holiness which sprang from their baptism, and by viewing it as a call to serve the Church. The *Decree on the Training of Priests* stressed the need for training for the ministry of the word (n. 4); candidates should 'receive a most careful training in holy Scripture, which should be the soul, as it were, of all theology' (n. 16). They should also 'be introduced to a fuller knowledge of the Churches and ecclesial communities separated from the Holy See, so that they may be able to take part in promoting the restoration of unity between all Christians according to the decisions of the Council' (n. 16).

The *Decree on Christian Education*, while recommending the existence of Catholic schools, 'attaches particular importance to those schools, especially in the territories of newly founded Churches, which include non-Catholics among their pupils' (n. 9). Theological education should be encouraged, among other reasons, in order that 'dialogue with our separated brethren and with non-Christians be promoted' (n. 11). Finally, the 'wider ecumenism' with non-Christians was recommended in the *Declaration on the Relation of the Church to non-Christian Religions*. Preaching on the day of the promulgation, the Pope expressed the wish that 'our Christian brethren, still separated from the full communion of the Catholic Church' might 'wish to contemplate this new manifestation of its [the Church's] renovated face'.

The Pope's thoughts were now turning to the future: to the spirit in which the Council's decrees would need to be implemented, and the organisation that would have to be set up to formulate norms for the practical realisation of the principles the decrees contained. Thus preoccupied, in his addresses to the Council of 4 and 18 November he did not pay even customary courteous acknowledgement to the non-Catholic observers.

However, of the two decrees promulgated on 18 November 1965, one was of enormous ecumenical importance. This was the *Dogmatic Constitution on Divine Revelation*. Many Catholic theologians had taught a 'two-source' theory of revelation which made tradition a source which was independent of scripture. The Constitution clarified the Church's teaching in a way which could not fail to be more acceptable to Protestants. Scripture and tradition are not two independent sources: they are closely united, springing as they do from the *one* source of revelation, which is God. However there was not sufficient unanimity among the Council Fathers to allow the connection between scripture and tradition to be given more precision. The second document, the *Decree on the Apostolate of Lay People*, had only indirect relevance to ecumenical questions: for example, it chooses terms which suggest a concern with all Christians and not only with Roman Catholics, in speaking of the 'apostolic activity of the People of God' (n. 1).

The Pope did, however, redirect his attention to the subject of reunion when, preaching to the observers at a service held at St Paul's Outside-the-Walls on 4 December 1965, he attempted to sum up the contribution the Council had made to the ecumenical cause.

... we can first of all register the fact of an increased awareness of the problem itself, a problem which concerns and obligates us all. We can add another fruit, still more precious: the hope that the problem – not today, certainly – but tomorrow – can be resolved slowly, gradually, honestly and generously. That is a great thing!

And this shows that other fruits have ripened too. We have come to know you a little better, and not only as the representatives of your respective confessions. Through you we have come into contact with Christian communities which live, pray and act in the name of Christ, with systems of doctrines and religious mentalities, and – let us say it without fear – with Christian treasures of great value.

Far from arousing our jealousy, this rather increases our fraternity and desire to re-establish the perfect communion between us desired by Christ. And this leads us to discover still other positive results on the road to our peace.

We have recognised certain failings and common sentiments that were not good. For these we have asked pardon of God and of you. We have discovered their un-Christian roots and have proposed to ourselves to change them, on our part, into sentiments worthy of the school of Christ; to abstain from preconceived and offensive controversy and not to bring into play questions of vain prestige; to try, rather, to keep in mind the often-repeated exhortations of the Apostle at whose tomb we are this evening: 'lest perhaps there be found among you contentions, envyings, animosities, dissensions, detractions, gossiping, arrogance, disorders' (2 Cor 12:20). We want to resume human, serene, benevolent and confident relations.

The Pope then spoke of his meetings with Church leaders and their representatives, making special mention of his meeting with the Ecumenical Patriarch. He then spoke of the way the Council 'has gone forward to meet you in many ways':

from the consideration which the Council Fathers have not ceased to show for your presence, so dear to them, to the unanimous effort to avoid any expression lacking in consideration for you; from the spiritual joy of seeking your élite group (*groupe d'élite*) associated with the religious ceremonies of the Council to the formulation of doctrinal and disciplinary expressions able to remove obstacles and to open paths as wide and smoothed as possible for a better evaluation of the Christian religious inheritance which you preserve and develop.

There is a notable tendency throughout the sermon to express appreciation, not only of the traditional practices of the other Churches, but also of their 'systems of doctrines'.

The Pope went on to speak of the Catholic Church's

good will to understand you and to make itself understood. It has not pronounced anathemas but invitations. It has not put any limits to its waiting, any more than to its fraternal offer to continue a dialogue in which it is engaged.

In words that presumably refer to eucharistic sharing, Pope Paul states that the Council

would have liked, with Pope John XXIII, to whom goes the merit of this conversation which has again become trusting and fraternal, to celebrate with you, with some of those among you, the decisive and final meeting. But it realises that in this is a too human haste and that in order to reach full and authentic communion there is still a long way to go, many prayers to be made to the Father of Lights (James 1:17), many vigils to keep. May we at least at the end of the Council record a victory: we have begun to love each other once more. And may the Lord will that, at least in this, the world may recognise that we are truly his disciples, because we have re-established between us a reciprocal spiritual love (cf. Jn 13:35).

You are about to leave. Do not forget the charity with which the Roman Catholic Church will continue to think of you and to follow you. Do not think it insensible and proud if it feels it is its duty to preserve jealously the 'trust' (cf. 1 Tim 6.20) which it has carried with it since its beginnings. And do not accuse it of having betrayed or deformed this trust if, during the course of its age-old, scrupulous and loving meditations, it has uncovered treasures of truth and life which it would be a breach of faith to renounce.... And think that truth dominates us and frees us, and also that truth is close to love.

He told a story of Soloviev, who once spent a whole night walking up and down past a door which he could not recognise in the dark, but which became obvious with the first light of dawn.

The truth is near. Beloved brothers, may this ray of divine light allow us all to recognise the blessed door.

That is our hope. And now let us pray together at the tomb of St Paul.

The significance of the event is shown by the fact that several Catholic bishops sent a message to the Pope protesting at this act of *communicatio in sacris* with heretics.

On 7 December 1965 a most significant ecumenical gesture was made. The Pope and the Orthodox Patriarch of Constantinople mutually lifted the excommunications of 1054, which had formalised the breach between the two Churches. The joint declaration of Pope Paul and the Ecumenical Patriarch, recalling their meeting in the Holy Land, affirmed that they had

> not lost sight of the determination each then felt to omit nothing thereafter which charity might inspire and which could facilitate the development of the fraternal relations thus initiated between the Roman Catholic Church and the Orthodox Church of Constantinople. They are persuaded that in acting this way, they are responding to the call of that divine grace which today is leading the Roman Catholic Church and the Orthodox Church, as well as all Christians, to overcome their differences in order to be again 'one' as the Lord Jesus asked of his Father for them.

Speaking of the excommunications of 1054, they continued:

> One cannot pretend that these events were not what they were during this very troubled period of history. Today, however, they have been judged more fairly and serenely. Thus it is important to recognise the excesses which accompanied them and later led to consequences which, in so far as we can judge, went much further than their authors had intended and foreseen. They had directed their censures against the persons concerned and not the Churches; these censures were not intended to break ecclesiastical communion between the sees of Rome and Constantinople.
>
> Since they are certain that they express the common desire for justice and the unanimous sentiment of charity which moves the faithful, and since they recall the command of the Lord: 'If you are offering your gift at the altar, and there remember that your brother has something against you, leave your gift before the altar and go, first be reconciled to your brother' (Mt 5: 23-24), Pope Paul VI and Patriarch Athenagoras I with his synod, in common agreement, declare that:
>
> a) They regret the offensive words, the reproaches without foundation, and the reprehensible gestures which, on both sides, have marked or accompanied the sad events of this period.
>
> b) They likewise regret and remove both from memory and from the midst of the Church the sentences of excommunication which followed these events, the memory of which has influenced actions up to our day and has hindered closer relations in charity; and they commit these excommunications to oblivion.
>
> c) Finally, they deplore the troublesome precedents and later events which, under the influence of various factors – among them, lack of understanding and mutual trust – eventually led to the effective rupture of ecclesiastical communion.
>
> Pope Paul VI and Patriarch Athenagoras I with his synod realise that this gesture of justice and mutual pardon is not sufficient to end both old and more recent differences between the Roman Catholic Church and the Orthodox Church. Through

the action of the Holy Spirit, those differences will be overcome through cleansing of hearts, through regret for historical wrongs, and through an efficacious determination to arrive at a common understanding and expression of the faith of the Apostles and its demands.

They hope, nevertheless, that this act will be pleasing to God, who is prompt to pardon us when we pardon each other. They hope that the whole Christian world, especially the entire Roman Catholic Church and the Orthodox Church, will appreciate this gestures as an expression of a sincere desire, shared in common, for reconciliation, and as an invitation to follow out, in a spirit of trust, esteem and mutual charity, the dialogue which, with God's help, will lead to living together again, for the greater good of souls and the coming of the kingdom of God, in that full communion of faith, fraternal accord and sacramental life which existed among them during the first thousand years of the life of the Church.

The Metropolitan of Heliopolis was present as the Ecumenical Patriarch's representative when the document was read out in St Peter's; when he knelt to kiss the Pope's ring, Paul raised him up, and they exchanged a kiss of peace to a 'thunderous burst of applause' from the Council Fathers. Simultaneously a similar ceremony took place at Constantinople between the Ecumenical Patriarch and Cardinal Shehan of Baltimore. Predictably the reaction of the Orthodox Archbishop of Athens was hostile:

> The Church of Greece [he wrote] has learned with great disappointment of the initiative of the Ecumenical Patriarch. No individual has the right to undertake acts of such importance on his own. This right belongs to the whole of Orthodoxy.... We seek peace and Christian love. We do not want to be subjected to the Vatican. I am convinced that the Patriarch's gesture will not be recognised by any of the other Orthodox Churches.

The same day, 7 December 1965, saw the promulgation of the Council's last four decrees. The *Declaration on Religious Liberty* was one of cardinal importance to the ecumenical movement. It affirms that all human beings have a duty to 'seek the truth ... and to embrace it and hold on to it *as they come to know it*' (n. 1, my italics). They are bound to follow their conscience, and must not be forced to act against it, or prevented from acting in accordance with it (n. 3). 'Nobody is to be forced to embrace the faith against his will', for 'the act of faith is of its very nature a free act' (n. 10). The *Decree on the Church's Missionary Activity* urges a search for 'ways and means for attaining and organising fraternal co-operation and harmonious relations with the missionary undertakings of other Christian communities, so that as far as possible the scandal of division might be removed' (n. 29). What is said in Chapter Three about the need to respect 'the philosophy and wisdom of the people' (n. 22), and for the local Church and the universal Church to 'increase the life of the Mystical Body' by a 'mutual outpouring of energy' (n. 19) applies to the old Churches separated from Rome as much as to the young Churches in developing countries. The *Decree on the Ministry and Life of Priests* shows that Catholics and Protestants share many insights into the nature of ministry, particularly the belief that 'it is the first task of priests as co-workers of the bishops to preach the Gospel of God to all men' (n. 4); the same can be said of the reaffirmation of the priesthood of all the faithful (n. 2). The *Pastoral Constitution on the Church in the Modern World* develops the thoughts Pope Paul had put forward the previous year, in his encyclical *Ecclesiam Suam*, on the Church's obligation to make all human concerns its own. The Pastoral Constitution is addressed not only to Roman Catholics but to 'all who call upon the name of Christ', and 'the whole of humanity' (n. 2). 'The Catholic Church,' it states,

> values what other Christian Churches and ecclesial communities have contributed and are contributing co-operatively to the realisation of this aim [of humanising the family of man] (n. 40).

The unity of Christians is seen to be a 'harbinger of unity and peace throughout the whole world'.

> Let us, then, join our forces and modify our methods in a way suitable and effective today for achieving this lofty goal . . . (n. 92).

The Council closed on 8 December with an address by the Pope. It was a sign of the deepening relationship between the Pope and the observers that he no longer felt it necessary to devote a courteous paragraph to them at the end of his speech. Instead, the whole speech was addressed to them as much as to the Catholic listeners. In the greeting in the opening paragraph, the 'observers belonging to so many different Christian denominations' are mentioned after the cardinals, bishops, representatives of governments and civic dignitaries, and before 'faithful and sons' of the Catholic Church.

So ended the Council, at which much had been said about reunion, and where Council Fathers, *periti* and observers had learnt to understand and trust one another, and had formed deep friendships. The time had now come to turn the words into deeds, and to make the spirit of trust spread from the participants at the Council throughout the whole of their Churches.

4. ROME, CANTERBURY, CONSTANTINOPLE

EARLY in 1966 it was announced in London that the Archbishop of Canterbury, Archbishop Michael Ramsey, was to pay a visit to Pope Paul in March. The visit to Rome, it was stated, would be 'one of courtesy, made in the spirit of the renewed fellowship between all the Christian Churches'. The Vatican Secretariat for Unity pointed out that the Archbishop would be calling on the Pope not only as Primate of the Province of Canterbury, but 'as president of the Lambeth Conference of the bishops of the Anglican Communion'. Although this was not yet the beginning of official dialogue, still less of negotiations leading up to reunion, the Primate was able to represent all Anglicanism, unlike the Patriarch of Constantinople, who could meet the Pope only as the representative of his own patriarchate. The visit which Archbishop Ramsey's predecessor, Geoffrey Fisher, had paid in 1960 to Pope John XXIII in Rome was made by private initiative, and the Archbishop had felt it necessary to make it clear that he did not claim to be representing anyone at all. Nevertheless it had been of great importance as a symbol of the improved relations between the two Churches and of the growing recognition that ecumenism was an imperative, not an option.

Dr Ramsey was reported as having said in a press interview that the greatest difficulties in Anglican/Catholic dialogue were the Marian dogmas of the Immaculate Conception and the Assumption. Speaking of the facts which had made fruitful conversations between the two communions possible, the Archbishop pointed to the Council's emphasis on the collegiality of the bishops 'to balance the authority of the Pope', on the 'unity of all who have been baptized in the Mystical Body of Christ,' and on the importance attached to 'the study of Scripture and the place of Scripture in doctrinal and spiritual life'. Asked about the doctrine of papal infallibility, he replied:

> I have observed that there have been different interpretations among Roman Catholic theologians of the doctrine of papal infallibility. It is possible to interpret infallibility in terms of the authority of the whole Church with the Pope as the spokesman of this collective authority. If infallibility is interpreted in this manner, then it will be possible for Anglicans and Roman Catholics to discuss it more profitably.

Archbishop Ramsey's meeting with the Pope on 23 March 1966 took place in the shadow of an Instruction on Mixed Marriages issued five days earlier by the Congregation for the Doctrine of the Faith (as the remodelled Holy Office was now named). This document could be regarded as the first test of how the ecumenical good intentions of the Council were going to be put into effect. The text itself states that

> one must not in the least forget the way in which Catholics must now behave towards their brethren separated from the Catholic Church as solemnly decreed by the Second Vatican Council in its Decree on Ecumenism.

However, the document scarcely lives up to its own exhortation, for while much is said about the duty of the Catholic partner to ensure the baptism and education of the children 'in the Catholic religion', there is not the slightest acknowledgement of any corresponding rights and duties on the side of the non-Catholic partner.

On 23 March the Archbishop and the Pope met in the Sistine Chapel. After some private conversation they exchanged addresses. In his address Dr Ramsey greeted the Pope 'in my office as Archbishop of Canterbury and as President of the Lambeth Conference of Bishops from every part of the Anglican Communion throughout the world'. He continued:

> I have come with the longing in my heart, which I know to be in your heart also, that we may by our meeting together help in the fulfilment of the prayer of our Divine Lord that all his disciples may come to unity in the truth.

The Archbishop praised the work of John XXIII and Paul VI for unity, and prayed: 'May the grace of God enable us to serve his divine purpose by our meeting, and enable Christians everywhere to feel the pain of their divisions, and to seek unity in truth and holiness'. He went on to speak of 'formidable differences of doctrine', and of his hope for increasing dialogue between theologians of the Roman Catholic, Anglican and other traditions. He spoke too of 'difficult practical matters about which the consciences and feelings of Christian people can be hurt'.

> All the more therefore must such matters be discussed together in patience and charity. If the final goal of unity is yet some way ahead, Christians can rejoice already in the fact of their common baptism into the name of the Triune God, Father, Son and Holy Spirit, and they can already pray together, bear witness to God together and together serve humanity in Christ's name.

Finally the Archbishop pointed out that the Christian appeal to the world for peace would carry no conviction if they remained divided. 'It is only as the world sees us Christians growing visibly in unity that it will accept through us the divine message of peace.'

Pope Paul, returning Dr Ramsey's greeting, spoke of the 'singular importance of this encounter'. He recalled the meeting between Dr Fisher and John XXIII.

> . . . you rebuild a bridge which for centuries has lain fallen between the Church of Rome and the Church of Canterbury: a bridge of respect, of esteem and of charity. You cross over this yet unstable viaduct, still under construction, with spontaneous initiative and sage confidence – may God bless this courage and this piety of yours!
>
> We would wish that your first impression, upon crossing over the threshhold of our residence, should be this: your steps do not resound in a strange house; they come to a home which you, for ever valid reasons, can call your own. We are happy to open its doors to you and, together with its doors, our heart; for, applying to this event the words of St Paul, we are both happy and honoured to welcome you not as 'strangers and sojourners, but . . . fellow citizens with the saints and members of the household of God' (cf. Eph 2: 19-20). Surely, from heaven, St Gregory the Great and St Augustine look down and bless.

The Pope spoke of the historical importance of the meeting:

> It appears to us great, almost dramatic, and fortunate, if we think of the long and sorrowful story which it intends to bring to an end, and of the new developments which this hour can inaugurate in the relations between Rome and Canterbury – from now on, friendship must inspire and guide them.

The meeting also had a civil importance, as an example for peace among the nations; an ecumenical importance; and 'the truly spiritual and religious value of our common quest for a common profession of fidelity to Christ, and of a prayer, old and new, which may harmonise minds and voices in celebrating the greatness of God, and his plan of salvation in Christ for all mankind'. However,

> in the field of doctrine and ecclesiastical law, we are still respectively distinct and distant; and for now, it must be so, for the reverence due to truth and to freedom; until such time as we may merit the supreme grace of true and perfect unity in faith and communion. But charity can, and must, from now on be exercised between us, and show forth its mysterious and prodigious strength: 'Where there is charity and love, there is God.'

59

Two points here deserve comment. The first is that the Pope is careful not to appear as one claiming authority over the Archbishop: they are both 'fellow citizens'. Secondly, perfect unity is a grace but it can be 'merited', which means presumably prepared for, now.

The following day, 24 March, the two Church leaders took part in a joint service at St Paul's Outside-the-Walls. In the course of it the following Common Declaration was read.

In this city of Rome, from which St Augustine was sent by St Gregory to England and there founded the cathedral see of Canterbury, towards which the eyes of all Anglicans now turn as the centre of their Christian Communion, His Holiness Pope Paul VI and His Grace Michael Ramsey, Archbishop of Canterbury, representing the Anglican Communion, have met to exchange fraternal greetings.

At the conclusion of their meeting they give thanks to Almighty God who by the action of the Holy Spirit has in these latter years created a new atmosphere of Christian fellowship between the Roman Catholic Church and the Churches of the Anglican Communion.

This encounter of the 23 March 1966 marks a new stage in the development of fraternal relations, based upon Christian charity, and of sincere efforts to remove the causes of conflict and to re-establish unity.

In willing obedience to the command of Christ who bade his disciples love one another, they declare that, with his help, they wish to leave in the hands of the God of mercy all that in the past has been opposed to this precept of charity, and that they make their own the mind of the Apostle which he expressed in these words: 'Forgetting those things which are behind, and reaching forth unto those things which are before, I press towards the mark for the prize of the high calling of God in Christ Jesus' (cf. Phil 3 : 13-14).

They affirm their desire that all those Christians who belong to these two Communions may be animated by these same sentiments of respect, esteem and fraternal love, and in order to help these develop to the full, they intend to inaugurate between the Roman Catholic Church and the Anglican Communion a serious dialogue which, founded on the Gospels and on the ancient common traditions, may lead to that unity in truth, for which Christ prayed.

The dialogue should include not only theological matters such as Scripture, Tradition and Liturgy, but also matters of practical difficulty felt on either side. His Holiness the Pope and His Grace the Archbishop of Canterbury are, indeed, aware that serious obstacles stand in the way of a restoration of complete communion of faith and sacramental life; nevertheless, they are of one mind in their determination to promote responsible contacts between their Communions in all those spheres of Church life where collaboration is likely to lead to a greater understanding and a deeper charity, and to strive in common to find solutions for all the great problems that face those who believe in Christ in the world of today.

Through such collaboration, by the Grace of God the Father and in the light of the Holy Spirit, may the prayer of Our Lord Jesus Christ for unity among his disciples be brought nearer to fulfilment, and with progress towards unity may there be a strengthening of peace in the world, the peace that only he can grant who gives 'the peace that passeth all understanding', together with the blessing of Almighty God, Father, Son and Holy Spirit, that it may abide with all men for ever.

The dialogue which the Pope and the Archbishop called for was soon to be initiated with the establishment of the Anglican/ Roman Catholic Preparatory Commission. The spirit of forgetting the past and reaching forward towards the future marked its discussions and those of its successor, the Anglican/Roman Catholic International Commission.

In his Easter message the following month, the Pope quoted several lines from the Decree on Ecumenism recalling the Father's will that Christ 'might by the process of redemption give the human race new life and unity'. He added these comments of his own:

The resurrection of Christ is the beacon of the spiritual and moral union of mankind, a union of men with God, to whom they have been reconciled by means of that miracle of mercy and of love which consists of the redemption suffered for us and offered to us by Christ.

His resurrection floods with light the unity of men whose faith is rooted deep in a counsciousness which is overflowing with the grace, the peace, the joy of Christ himself. His resurrection highlights the unity of men among themselves. Having been united to the one and only Master and made capable of a higher love, they can now find happiness in loving one another and in doing good to each other.

We speak confidently of the possibility of the triumph of this unity in love and justice, in liberty and progress, because of the great strength and encouragement we receive from the paschal mystery, history's eternal springtime which this year, too, is in flower on the earth that has been given by the blessed resurrection of the Lord.

The Pope then spoke with sadness of the divisions in the world, and of its need for Christ.

On 6 July 1966 the Pope spoke with approval at a general audience of a new liturgical office of St Peter adopted by the

Greek Orthodox Church. The office commemorates 'the glorious and most illustrious apostle and first leader (*coryphaeus*) Peter' on 28 August. 'This office,' the Pope said, 'draws from ancient texts which had disappeared from editions of the Greek liturgical books, the most beautiful expressions in honour of the apostle Peter and of the mission entrusted to him.' Paul VI quoted several of these expressions, e.g. 'Peter, unbreakable rock of the Church', saying they were the echo of ancient traditions which had been suppressed from the liturgy after the fourteenth century as a result of anti-Latin polemics. 'They now renew the noble and authentic voice of the piety of the Eastern Church, and, just as they are a happy and faithful reminder of ancient times, so they seem to us a welcome sign of new times.' As the text seems to have been composed by a hymnwriter attached to the Constantinople patriarchate, the ecumenical sensitivity of Athenagoras is again apparent.

A few weeks later the Ecumenical Patriarch in a press interview gave further evidence of his strong desire for full union with Rome.

> We are already in union with the Church of Rome and, in the name of Christ, we are seeking to set up that inter-communion which will cancel for ever all traces of our centuries-old and therefore even more absurd separation. The theologians are already at work for this noble purpose.
>
> What a stupidity our separation was, and it took place only because of a quarrel between a patriarch and a cardinal. In fact, the schism was never decreed, nor sanctioned. Now we are in unity, above all thanks to the greatness and wisdom of the Christian spirit of Paul VI. The name of this Pope will be remembered in the history of mankind.
>
> My dream is to go to Rome, the great city of Christendom, to embrace its bishop, Paul VI, as soon as possible . . .
>
> I should not say it, but theologians are difficult men. But we shall succeed, I feel it. We have the same cross, the same Christ, and we must defend his sacrifice. Therefore, we must consolidate our unity, which, not by chance, was revived in Jerusalem and not far from Calvary. This unity seemed impossible to achieve, as if it were at the peak of a forbidding mountain. But in Jerusalem, it was on the slope of a gentle hill.

On 28-29 October 1966 a plaque was unveiled in Malines Cathedral commemorating the Malines Conversations. The Holy Father sent Cardinal Suenens the following telegram :

> On the occasion of the fortieth anniversary of the Malines Conversations, which took place under the presidency of your most eminent predecessor Cardinal Désiré-Joseph Mercier and

of Lord Halifax, we are glad that there should be a ceremony to commemorate the efforts of those pioneers in searching out the ways of the Lord to bring together the Roman Catholic Church and the Church of England. The Malines Conversations marked an epoch in the striving, the preparation for perfect unity among all those who believe in Christ. Though of a private nature, they were marked by a spirit of frankness and Christian fraternity which allowed them to broach delicate and sometimes difficult questions dividing the two communions: to broach them in a common effort towards re-establishing unity in truth and charity.

We associate ourselves with the ceremony celebrated today at Malines and in the Holy Spirit we pray with you and with all those assembled with you to the Lord of the Church, that he may be pleased to bless the efforts and aspirations of all who believe and hope in him, that 'there may be but one fold and one Shepherd'.

That month an Anglican centre was opened in Rome, one of the most important features of which was to be a library of up to 10,000 books. Pope Paul gave a private audience to the committee of the centre. The Pope spoke of 'that spiritual affinity which binds us to it [the Anglican Church] and the hope we must cherish in our hearts of a perfect communion with it. . . You come to Rome to set up a centre which may serve to make the Anglican Church better known, and, reciprocally, promote better knowledge of the Roman Catholic Church. This is the first step in practical ecumenism – to know. To know each other.' He suggested a motto: 'Knowledge prepares the way for love: love leads to unity.' (The affirmation of the 'spiritual affinity' between Anglicans and Roman Catholics is significant; up till now such language had been used only of the Orthodox Church.)

On 28 April 1967 the Pope made an important speech to the Secretariat for Christian Unity, in which he spoke of 'the perspicacity and the charity of our unforgettable and venerated predecessor John XXIII' in setting up the Secretariat, and of its achievements. He went on to discuss 'some of the points which seem to us the most significant among those which are raised today in the Catholic world by the question of ecumenism.'

First of all, the ecumenical question has been raised by Rome in all its gravity, its breadth, and its innumerable doctrinal and practical implications. It has not been considered with an occasional and passing glance, but has become the object of permanent interest, of systematic study and of unceasing charity.

It remains such, in accordance with a line which has by now become part of our apostolic ministry. The Council makes this an obligation for us and traces the way for us.

The conciliar documents which deal expressly or incidentally with the question of the recomposition of the unity of the one Church by all who bear the name of Christian are so authoritative and so explicit, they have such a force of orientation and obligation, that they offer Catholic ecumenism a doctrinal and pastoral basis that it never had before.

We must admit that we have here a fact in which the Holy Spirit, who guides and animates the Church, plays the principal and decisive part. We will be docile and faithful to him . . .

Secondly: an ecumenical spirit has been created and is developing. This is a merit of the Council, and also the merit of the undertaking, which had already spread and become known everywhere, of celebrating a 'week of prayer' for the recomposition of the unity of the Christians in the one Church of Christ . . .

The conviction that unity is willed by Christ, that it is an important and urgent question not only for Christianity but also for the spiritual destinies of the world, the conviction that it is no longer a matter of dwelling on discussion of the historical causes from which present divisions originate but that it is necessary to form friendly and loyal relations between the Catholic Church and all other Christian communities which sincerely pursue ecumenical aims, that a fundamental unity betwen all baptized Christians already exists in the faith in Christ and in the invocation of the Most Blessed Trinity, this conviction – we were saying – already full of so many factors favourable to ecumenism, is by now present and active in every vigilant Christian heart and this seems to us a great achievement.

Charity inspires the entire Christian process and aims at expressing itself in external forms. Respect, loyalty, esteem, trust mark with a Christian seal the friendly and practical relations which are being established in determined fields between Catholics and Christians of other confessions. They prepare, God willing, for agreements which may still at this stage seem delicate and difficult but promise already to be full of truth and of joy in the spirit of the Lord.

Thirdly: the series of meetings to which we have referred must be attributed to the mysterious inspiration of the Holy Spirit.

The Holy Father made special mention of his meeting with Patriarch Athenagoras, 'which inaugurated a friendship marked, on our part, by veneration, admiration and cordiality'.

Is it perhaps an illusion, or is it on the contrary a hope founded on revealing truths, if we believe that there already exists between the venerable Orthodox Church and the Catholic Church a kind of dawning communion, the prelude of the one we will attain on the blessed and bright day of our total and profound reconciliation?

A similar joy and hope we must express regarding the visit, marked by so much courtesy and piety, of the Anglican Archbishop of Canterbury, the very venerable Dr Michael Ramsey. It semed to us at that moment that history was marking a new and wonderful hour, truly an hour of Christ.

He spoke also of other 'visits, conversations and promises', naming Orthodox and Protestant visitors, which 'are carved in our memory as so many dazzling signs, as the mysterious prelude of the forthcoming apparition of the Christ among us, announcing his ineffable peace and manifesting his unfailing presence there where it is truly in his name that we have gathered.'

These are not signs of the ageing of Christianity, as some have insinuated, but are further proofs, instead, of its ever renewed youth.

These rapprochements are not based on an equivocal irenicism aiming at the elimination of doctrinal and canonical difficulties. No, they are the fruit, rather, of a mutual and spontaneous effort of reciprocal understanding, aiming at the discovery of the truths of the faith and of the concrete demands of ecclesial charity – the sole bases of an authentic and perfect unity . . .

The Pope's fourth point concerned the difficulties. 'Incomprehension and opposition which has lasted for centuries cannot be dispelled in a few years. Patience is an ecumenical virtue. Psychological maturing is no less difficult than theological discussion.'

The possibility alone of having to abandon old positions, stiffened by bitter memories and mixed up with questions of prestige and subtle controversies, reawakens reactions of principle on which it would seem impossible to compromise.

The habit of being resigned to a Christianity torn within itself might lead one to fear the prospect of a reconciliation which would restore to it its primitive hierarchical and community features, presenting it to the world without those aspects to which we have become accustomed – incomprehensible sectarian exclusiveness, and pluralism which extends to essentials and is therefore intolerable. In the face of such a fear, each turns in afresh on himself, resists and rebels. Ecumenism comes to a standstill.

Pope Paul spoke of two problems: those of 'proselytism' and 'the canonical discipline of mixed marriages'. He alluded, on the other hand, to 'a certain ecumenism which would be too precipitate', which went 'beyond the confines marked by theological reality and established rules – as sometimes in the "*communio in sacris*" [shared worship]'.

Finally he spoke, as he had in *Ecclesiam Suam*, 'of the difficulty to which our separated brothers are always so sensitive . . . which comes from the function that God has assigned to us in the Church of God and which our tradition has sanctioned with such authority'.

> The Pope, as we well know, is undoubtedly the gravest obstacle in the path of ecumenism. What shall we say? Should we refer once more to titles which justify our mission? Should we once more attempt to present it in its exact terms such as it is really intended to be – the indispensable principle of truth, charity, and unity? A pastoral mission of guidance, of service and of brotherhood which does not challenge the liberty and honour of anyone who has a legitimate position in the Church of God, but instead protects the rights of all and demands no other obedience than that which is demanded from the sons of a family?
>
> It is not easy for us to make our apologia. It is you who with words of sincerity and mildness will know how to make it when the occasion and the possibility arises. As far as we are concerned, in all serenity we prefer to remain silent and pray.

The Holy Father asked for prayers for this end especially during the 'year of commemoration of the martyrdom of the Apostles St Peter and St Paul, the year of faith as we have called it'. In conclusion he said:

> If there is a cause in which our human efforts prove unable to attain any good results and show themselves to be essentially dependent on the mysterious and powerful action of the Holy Spirit, it is precisely this one of ecumenism. This awareness of our weakness, of the disproportion between our forces and the results to be obtained make us humble to the point where we are tempted to believe that our plans are naïve, that our undertakings are in vain, that it is all a matter of the dreams of people who do not know the laws of history and of human psychology.
>
> But trust, or rather, the certainty that divine aid will not fail us, that Christ is with us, that the Father is for us a father, that the Holy Spirit is still fruitful with prodigies, strengthens us, sets us free and gives us the inner stimulation to continue on the road we have begun.

It may be necessary to emphasise some of the more important, but less obvious, points that Pope Paul made in this address.

First, he does not equate the Church with the Roman Catholic Church, as if the object of ecumenism were to bring non-Catholics into the already existing unity of the Church; on the contrary, the unity of the Church requires 'recomposition', as does 'the unity of the Christians in the one Church of Christ'. Secondly, there exists already a 'fundamental unity' among all the baptized; in addition, there is already a 'dawning communion' of Roman Catholics with the Orthodox Church and also, apparently, with the Anglican Communion. Thirdly, ecumenism requires the 'discovery of the truths of the faith' in the other side's position. Fourthly, ecumenism will require both sides to 'abandon old positions'. Fifthly, the obstacles to reunion are psychological just as much as theological. Sixthly, the passage about the papacy, when compared with the corresponding passage in *Ecclesiam Suam*, on the one hand takes a more serious view of the difficulty it constitutes in the ecumenical movement, which is now said to be 'the gravest obstacle'; but on the other hand, the service which the papacy is meant to provide to the Church is more clearly stated.

As we have seen, within a few months of becoming Pope, Paul VI had met the Ecumenical Patriarch Athenagoras of Constantinople in Jerusalem and exchanged with him the kiss of peace on the Mount of Olives. In December 1965 these two passionate seekers after the reconciliation of the Churches of the East and West had issued a joint statement lifting the mutual excommunication of 1054 which was the symbol and culmination of a breach the first cracks of which had already appeared in the second century. In 1967 the Pope and the Patriarch continued their work of healing.

It is hard to imagine any ecumenical gesture more significant than a visit by the Pope to the Patriarch in his own See of Constantinople. To the beleaguered Greek Patriarch, in his tiny enclave within an unfriendly and non-Christian Turkish population, subject to an obstructive Turkish government, and having to contend with Moscow for the leadership of Orthodoxy, this papal visit could not fail to provide comfort and support. In announcing in Rome less than a fortnight in advance his intention to pay the visit, the Pope spoke of his desire to discuss with the Patriarch 'the best way to promote theological and canonical studies to smooth the path towards the re-establishment of a perfect communion between the Catholic and Orthodox Churches', as well as co-operation between the two Churches over the administration of the Holy Places in Jerusalem. He also planned to visit Ephesus, wishing 'to honour in the dawn of this Year of Faith, among the various illustrious historical cities of that eastern land, the memory of the important Ecumenical Councils held there and also at

67

Ephesus'. (Constantinople had in 381 been the venue of the Council which extended the Creed of Nicaea into a form closely resembling that used in the liturgy today. Three other Councils had been held there subsequently in the sixth, seventh and ninth centuries, the first two being recognised as Ecumenical by both Catholics and Orthodox. Ephesus was the scene of the Council which in 431 had clarified the unity of the man Jesus with the Divine Word by giving official approval to the title of Theotokos (God-bearer) which popular piety had already accorded to Mary. The Pope also expressed his desire to pay his respects to the civic authorities of Turkey, and to meet the leaders of the other Churches and the representatives of the non-Christian religions.

The terms of the Pope's announcement revealed the respect and the warm affection which existed between Paul and Athenagoras: 'We should like thus to make an act of honour towards the illustrious and venerable Ecumenical Patriarch, to exchange the gestures of courtesy he has often made towards us and the Roman Catholic Church by sending his representatives both as observers to the Ecumenical Council and as visitors and personal delegates in various circumstances.'

When Pope Paul arrived at Istanbul airport on 25 July, Athenagoras was there to greet him, together with the Armenian Patriarch and other religious leaders. That evening the Pope visited the Patriarch at his residence known as the Phanar. The two leaders exchanged a warm embrace, then walked hand in hand to the Orthodox Cathedral of St George, where they took part together in a liturgical service modelled on the Great Doxology of the Byzantine Church. There they prayed together for ecumenical understanding and world peace. After the service the Pope and the Patriarch exchanged formal addresses.

'Can we not see,' the Pope asked, 'the working of Divine Providence in the fact that this pilgrimage affords us the opportunity of fulfilling the hope of meeting again, which we both expressed in Jerusalem after Your Holiness had told us that, "having sought to meet with one another, together we had found the Lord"?' It is significant that the Holy Father referred to his visit as a 'pilgrimage'. That one word at once removed the visit from the sphere of ecclesiastical politics and placed it in a spiritual context; more importantly, it made it clear that he was not coming as the first patriarch of Christendom visiting the second, still less as the Supreme Pontiff inviting the submission of a separated subject, but as a follower of Christ paying his devotions at a place which had exercised a significant influence on the growth of the faith.

The Pope alluded once more to several of his favourite ecumenical themes. It is fidelity to Christ which is the source of ecumenical progress; and this progress is a process of rediscovery of the past. 'Is not the secret of our meeting, of the gradual rediscovery of our churches, that unceasing search for Christ and for fidelity to Christ, who unites us in himself?' This progress 'can only be the work of the Spirit of Love'.

With great emphasis he spoke of the deep unity between the two Churches. 'In the light of our love for Christ and of our brotherly love, we perceive even more clearly the profound identity of our faith, and the points on which we still differ must not prevent us from seeing this profound unity.' The Holy Father made no attempt to minimise these differences, but offered two considerations which helped to put them in perspective.

First, he recalled how in the fourth century the Latin Father St Hilary and the Greek Father St Athanasius had made identical contributions to the healing of a schism that had developed among those who, resisting the Arian heresy, had remained true to their faith in the divinity of Christ. (The Latin bishops had adhered to the statement of the Creed of Nicaea that the Son was of the same being as the Father [*homoousios*]; many Greeks, interpreting that term in a different sense, had thought it safe only to say that he was of similar being with the Father [*homoiousios*].) Hilary and Athanasius had the vision to perceive 'the sameness of faith underlying the differences of vocabulary'. What had enabled them to discern the truth in the other side's position was 'charity'. In the same way, later in the same century, when the divinity of the Holy Spirit was now in question, 'pastoral love' prompted St Basil 'to refrain from using certain terms which, accurate though they were, could have given rise to scandal in one part of the Christian people.' So too in the following century, when two Greek Churches, those of Alexandria and Antioch, were bitterly divided over the correct ways of expressing the unity between the humanity and the divinity in Christ, St Cyril of Alexandria consented 'to abandon his beautiful formulation of theology in the interests of making peace with John of Antioch, once he had satisfied himself that in spite of divergent modes of expression, their faith was identical.' So too today, when East and West were suffering from their long-standing division, 'charity must come to our aid'. (The Holy Father is not simply expressing a pious platitude, but is formulating an ecumenical principle of great importance. Love of our separated brethren should impel us to look for truth in statements of faith which seem to be contrary to our own. And the same love should impel us to refrain from insisting upon cherished traditions even in matters of faith, and even to be prepared to abandon them ourselves, provided the formulations of the other side are true to the Gospel. In other words, we should never grumble, as some lukewarm ecumenists do, that 'our Church seems to be the one that is making all the concessions'. Love implies a willingness to be the one to make the greater sacrifices.)

Secondly, 'while unity of faith is required for full communion, diversity of usages is not an obstacle to it – on the contrary'. The Pope cites St Irenaeus in the second century, who said that diversity of usages 'confirms the accord of faith', and St Augustine in the fifth, who saw it contributed to the 'beauty of the Church of Christ'.

But love, besides begetting mutual understanding, also 'makes us suffer more painfully the present impossibility of seeing this unity expand into concelebration'. If Church leaders recognise and respect one another 'as pastors of that part of the flock of Christ which is entrusted to them', they will be able to 'lead the Churches along the path which leads to the rediscovery of full communion'. (Again the suggestion that unity is something lost which is there to be rediscovered.) At the same time the Pope is prudent in giving the warning that leaders must avoid 'all that could disperse' the people of God 'and throw confusion into its ranks'.

The Holy Father's reason for ruling out eucharistic concelebration is significant. Eucharistic sharing is the 'full manifestation of . . . charity', and that charity cannot be fully manifested if there is not 'communion in faith'. His implication seems to be that, if Catholics and Orthodox are not one in faith, this is because they do not love each other enough.

The Patriarch's reply was no less inspired by ecumenical boldness and wisdom. He was speaking, not as the leader of the whole of Orthodoxy, but on behalf only of his own Church, and of the other Christians, Orthodox and others, of Constantinople. Rising above the traditional disputes about the position of Rome, he referred to the Pope as 'you who have come here to bring the kiss of ancient Rome to its younger sister'. Even more significant was his reference to Paul – as 'very holy successor of Peter' – an explicit enough admission of a Roman primacy – 'who have Paul's name and his conduct, as a messenger of charity, union and peace'.

The Patriarch echoed several of the themes of the Pope's address in the more typological language of the East: 'Descending in peace from the Mount of Olives as from a first degree of conciliation, and taking the road towards Emmaus, walking along with the risen Lord and longing for the breaking of the bread, we have pursued our road until today, carrying on a dialogue in charity. Our hearts were burning and the Lord has not left us.'

Then he returned even more explicitly to the theme of Roman primacy. 'We have among us the Bishop of Rome, the first in honour among us, "he who presides in charity".' (The Orthodox had not been committed to the rejection of such Roman primacy, which had been affirmed at the first Council of Constantinople in 381. What the Orthodox traditionally denied was any primacy of jurisdiction which would entitle the Bishop of Rome to demand obedience from the bishops of the Churches of the East. Athenagoras transcended the terms of the dispute by speaking of the Pope, instead, in the words of St Ignatius of Antioch at the beginning of the second century as 'he who presides in charity'. In other words, the pre-eminent position of the Bishop of Rome is a pre-eminent responsibility for serving the whole Church. The Patriarch's imaginative and generous acknowledgement of papal primacy in these terms leaves the way open for Catholic theologians to show that to preside in charity requires jurisdiction. Service of the whole Church may require the power to command for the sake of the unity of the Church; and conversely such power must always be exercised in such a way that it is seen as a service of love and not as an autocratic imposition.)

Like Pope Paul, the Patriarch believed that the journey which the two Churches were making towards full communion was a reply 'to the exigences – unavoidable at the present hour – of a history of which God remains the master'. But he raised his eyes to wider horizons, and saw this converging path which the Catholics and Orthodox were following as part of their more general responsibility to the whole Church and the world.

> Called to be servants of the Lord of his Church and of the whole world, let us collaborate then in the design of God, who leaves the ninety-nine sheep to save the one of them who strayed (Mt 18:11) and towards whom we are held to a common care and a common witness.
>
> However, let us begin with ourselves. Let us make every possible sacrifice and suppress mutually, with a total abnegation, all that in the past seemed to contribute to the Church's integrity but which in reality ended by creating a division difficult to surmount.

Athenagoras called for 'reciprocal gestures' and 'the firm recognition of the common points of the faith and of canonical regulations'. Repeating and adding new emphasis to the Pope's appreciation of 'diversity of usage', the Patriarch spoke of the need for 'the liberty of a theological, spiritual and creative thought, inspired by the common Fathers, in the diversity of local usage admitted by the Church from its beginnings'. (He made it clear that diversity of usage included not only differing liturgical, devotional and canonical practices, but differing theological formula-

71

tions of a shared faith. But the difficult question of distinguishing differences of theology within such a shared faith from differences which spring from disagreement in faith, was raised by neither Pope nor Patriarch.)

In conclusion the Patriarch reiterated his wider vision.

> We will have in view not only the unity of our two holy Churches but also a higher service: to offer ourselves together to all dear Christian brothers as examples and artisans in the accomplishment of the whole will of the Lord, which is to reach the union of all so that the world may believe the Christ was sent by God.
>
> But there is more. We have in view all those who believe in a God, Creator of man and of the universe, and, in collaborating with them, we will serve all men without distinction of race, creed or opinion, to promote the good of peace in the world and to establish the kingdom of God on earth.

An exchange of gifts and private conversation followed.

Later that same evening, 25 July, the Patriarch went to the Nuncio's residence to return the Pope's visit. They went together to the Latin Cathedral of the Holy Spirit, where they took part in a specially prepared service. Towards the end of it, Bishop Jan Willebrands, the Secretary of the Secretariat for Promoting Christian Unity, read a message signed by the Pope. After returning to some of the themes contained in the two addresses which had been exchanged earlier in the day, the Pope spoke of the special affinity that existed between Catholics and Orthodox. In addition to baptism, by which 'we are one in Jesus Christ (Gal 3 : 28)', 'the priesthood and the Eucharist unite us even more intimately by virtue of the apostolic succession'. The text contains a reference to the Vatican II Decree on Ecumenism (n. 15), where possession of a hierarchy in the apostolic succession is held to be a link which binds Catholics with Orthodox in a unique way.

> Having become sons in the Son in all reality (cf. 1 Jn 3: 1-2), we have become also really and mysteriously brothers to each other. This mystery of divine love is realised in every local church, and is this not the reason for the traditional and so beautiful expression, according to which local churches like to call themselves sister churches?

Pope Paul here is not only reiterating the theology of the 'local church' which was expressed in the Council's Decree on the Pastoral Office of Bishops (n. 11; see above, p. 39). The published text of the speech gives a reference to the Decree on Ecumenism (n. 14), which attributed to Orthodox the view that local Churches are united by 'family ties', like sisters. Athenagoras had already adopted this terminology of 'sister churches' in speaking to the Pope. It is a matter of great significance that Pope Paul now made this terminology his own.

Catholics and Orthodox 'lived this life of a sister church for centuries, celebrating together the ecumenical councils which defended the deposit of faith against any alteration.' (In other words, the relation between the Catholics and the Orthodox Churches was of the same nature as that between, say, two local Catholic churches, sharing as they do the same sacraments and priesthood, and preserving the same faith.) During 'a long period of division and reciprocal incomprehension' this sisterhood was impaired or obscured; but now 'the Lord grants us that we rediscover ourselves as sister churches despite the obstacles which were then raised between us'. (The use once more of the verb 'rediscover' shows that Paul VI is not suggesting that the two Churches ever ceased to be sisters; rather, the sisters were estranged, and forgot that they were sisters.) It is therefore necessary to find ways in which the two Churches can actually live as sisters: 'we should work fraternally, seeking together those forms which are suitable and progressive towards development and actualisation in the life of our Churches of that communion which already exists, though imperfectly.'

In conclusion the Holy Father, echoing the Vatican II Decree on Ecumenism (n. 18), stated that 'care must be taken to "impose no burden beyond what is indispensable"' (Acts 15:28). Thus the address ended by reiterating that pluriformity was acceptable.

On the 25th and 26th the Pope exchanged visits and addresses with the Armenian Patriarch of Constantinople. He returned to the theme of the 'Year of Faith celebrating the anniversary of the martyrdom of the great Apostles Peter and Paul', in which he hoped that 'all Christians will strive to penetrate more deeply into the mystery of Christ'. In reply the Armenian Patriarch gave 'thanks to God that he has elected your Holiness, as well as our elder brother His Holiness Patriarch Athenagoras, to come together, and in holy embrace to dispel this fog of estrangement, which has been sitting for centuries over the two main centres of Christendom, and to feel again as brothers in faith and in Christ'.

In a busy two days, the Pope made several other speeches of ecumenical importance. Preaching to a Catholic congregation in the Cathedral of the Holy Spirit, he spoke of the progress towards unity which the people themselves had been able to observe, and reminded them that it was 'based first of all on the renovation of the Church and on the conversion of the heart. This means that you will contribute to this progress towards unity in the measure in which you enter into the spirit of the Council. An effort is demanded from each of us to revise our customary ways of thinking and acting to bring them more into conformity with the Gospel and the demands of Christian brotherhood.' Thus ecumenism is a duty shared by all Catholics, which they must fulfil first of all by conversion of heart and by entering into the Council's movement of *aggiornamento*.

From Ephesus he addressed a short message to the leaders of all Christian Churches throughout the world. To the patriarchs of the Orthodox Churches, though acknowledging 'real divergences' which remained, he spoke of the better understanding of the 'profound unity in the faith' which the two Churches shared. He spoke also of Rome's 'full respect for your customs and legitimate traditions'. Among the 'pastors of the other churches and ecclesial communities', Paul VI signaled out 'our dear brother, His Grace the Archbishop of Canterbury'.

In an address to the Grand Mufti, the head of the Moslem community in Istanbul, he said: 'We want to tell you of our esteem for the Moslems, who adore one God, living and existing, merciful and all-powerful, creator of the sky and the earth, who spoke to men.' He recalled the imperative declared by the Vatican Council 'to promote together, on that basis, social justice, moral values, peace and freedom'.

Three months later the Ecumenical Patriarch returned the visit. Arriving on 26 October, while the Synod was still in session, he drove to St Peter's, where the cardinals and bishops who constituted the synod had assembled to meet him. There he hung a lighted red lamp before the tomb of St Peter. In the moving words of the *Tablet* correspondent, 'the mind went back to the proud Humbert tossing the bull of excommunication on to another altar and striding out, and it was hard to hold back tears.' At a specially composed service, which included a common prayer of repentance and reconciliation, the two church leaders exchanged messages, which were not mere exchanges of courtesies or repetitions of the significant statements on Church unity which each had made when they met at Constantinople.

The Patriarch spoke first. In July he had addressed the Pope as 'first in honour' and 'he who presides in charity'. Now he placed the Roman primacy on a canonical basis by speaking of the Bishop of that city as 'first in honour *and order* in the living body of the Christian Churches scattered throughout the world' (my italics). (In Orthodox terminology, 'order' implies responsibility, though the associations are less legalistic than those of the Western term 'jurisdiction', which to some extent corresponds to it.)

74

He went on to speak of the Roman See's 'holiness, wisdom and struggles for the common faith in the undivided Church', referring to them as 'a permanent conquest and the treasure of the entire Christian world'. (Here we are light years removed from a traditional polemical stance in Orthodoxy according to which the Western Church is in heresy. Again we have expressed in the more mystical and unlegalistic language of the East the belief which underlies the Catholic doctrine of papal infallibility.)

Athenagoras called to mind again 'the journey towards a common Eucharist', and 'the holy work undertaken, that of the perfect recomposition of Christ's divided Church'. This work is a duty, not only because it is the Lord's will, but also because the world must be enabled to see 'the splendour of what is, according to our profession of faith, the Church's first property: unity'. Division in the Church is a 'weighty wrong'. The ecumenical movement has achieved already such success that 'it is not possible that there should be today a local Church, a responsible pastor or Christian teacher who does not realise the absolute urgency of healing the evil'.

Some familiar themes reappeared in the speech. The search for unity must be pursued 'in the sentiments of the Lord washing the Apostles' feet'. We have discovered that 'what unites us is more than what divides us'. We need charity in order to 'purify ourselves from all the negative elements we have inherited from the past', to 're-establish fully mutual brotherly trust', to create 'a new mentality – the mentality of kinship'.

The two Churches are engaged on a 'common journey, which will be a journey towards truth'. The 'dialogue of charity' must be intensified so as to prepare for the 'theological dialogue'. This formal theological discussion, when it begins, will have two ends: first, 'interpretation of what is already experienced in common in the Church'; secondly, 'research in a spirit of charity and edification, and . . . the expression of truth in a spirit of service'.

With great sensitivity the Patriarch chose a formula from a Latin theologian, Vincent of Lerins, to describe the goal of this common search for truth: 'what has been believed always, everywhere and by all.' He expanded his previous remarks about the scope for pluriformity:

> We hope to succeed in appreciating exactly and in distinguishing between those points of the faith which must necessarily be confessed in common and those other elements of the life of the Church which, since they do not touch on faith, can freely constitute, in accordance with the traditions of each of the Churches, the proper aspects of the life of each of them, aspects which are respected by the other.

But it is less clear here than in his Istanbul speech that these traditions include theological interpretations of essential Christian faith.

The Pope in his reply reiterated and gave new emphasis to many of his cherished ecumenical convictions. The meeting was timely, occurring as it did in the Year of the Faith, the centenary of the martyrdom of the founders of the Roman Church, Peter and Paul. 'The unity of Christ's disciples was given as the great sign that was to call forth the faith of the world.' Consequently 'this common witness, one yet varied, decided and persuasive, of a faith humbly self-confident, springing up in love and radiating hope, is without doubt the foremost demand that the Spirit makes of the Churches today.' (Never before had ecumenism been set so high in the scale of Christian duties.) Reunion is only possible through the action of the Holy Spirit, producing a 'change of heart' and the 'fruits of holiness and generosity' in every member of the Church, for only in this way can there come 'true lasting brotherhood'.

The Holy Father saw the Patriarch as 'the representative of the traditions of the Churches "of Pontus, Galatia, Cappadocia, Asia and Bithynia" to which "Peter, the apostle of Jesus Christ" (1 Pet 1 : 1), long ago wrote' his First Epistle.

> That letter with its instructions and exhortations also carried the greetings of the Church of Rome to those Churches (cf. 1 Pet 5: 13). It is thus a first testimony to the relations which developed so fruitfully in the following centuries, although we must admit that these have not been without clashes and misunderstanding.

The Pope then recalled the attempts in the thirteenth century at the Second Council of Lyons and in the fifteenth at the Council of Florence to repair the breach between the East and the West. Tacitly acknowledging that those efforts were partly inspired by ulterior motives, he asks whether there have ever been attempts at reunion more free than today's

> of every political element or of any other purpose than the sole desire of realising Christ's will for his Church. In fact, on both sides we are impelled by the single desire of purifying our souls in obedience to truth to love one another sincerely as brothers, loving one another sincerely from the heart (cf. 1 Pet 1 : 22), This rightness of our intentions and the sincerity of our decision are surely a sign of the Holy Spirit's action . . . that we are experiencing and marvelling at in the Church and in every member of the Christian faithful.

At the end of their meeting the Pope and the Patriarch issued a Common Declaration. Since it gave formal and common endorsement to many of the points made unilaterally and less formally, the Declaration is given in full here:

Pope Paul VI and the Ecumenical Patriarch Athenagoras I give thanks in the Holy Spirit to God, the author and finisher of all good works, for enabling them to meet once again in the holy city of Rome in order to pray together with the Bishops of the Synod of the Roman Catholic Church and with the faithful people of this city, to greet one another with a kiss of peace, and to converse together in a spirit of charity and brotherly frankness.

While recognising that there is still a long way to go on the road toward the unity of all Christians and that between the Roman Catholic Church and the Orthodox Church there still remain points to clarify and obstacles to surmount before attaining that unity in the profession of faith necessary for re-establishing full communion, they rejoice in the fact that their meeting was able to contribute to their Churches' rediscovering themselves still more as sister Churches.

In the prayers they offered, in their public statements and in their private conversation, the Pope and the Patriarch wished to emphasize their conviction that an essential element in the restoration of full communion between the Roman Catholic Church on the one side and the Orthodox Church on the other, is to be found within the framework of the renewal of the Church and of Christians in fidelity to the traditions of the Fathers and to the inspirations of the Holy Spirit who remains always with the Church.

They recognise that the true dialogue of charity, which should be at the basis of all relations between themselves and between their Churches, must be rooted in total fidelity to the one Lord Jesus and in mutual respect for each one's traditions. Every element which can strengthen the bonds of charity, of communion, and of common action is a cause for spiritual rejoicing and should be promoted; anything which can harm this charity, communion and common action is to be eliminated with the grace of God and the creative strength of the Holy Spirit.

Pope Paul VI and the Ecumenical Patriarch Athenagoras I are convinced that the dialogue of charity between their Churches must bear fruits of a co-operation which would not be self-seeking, in the field of common action at the pastoral, social and intellectual levels, with mutual respect for each one's fidelity to his own Church. They desire that regular and profound contacts may be maintained between Catholic and Orthodox pastors for the good of their faithful. The Roman Catholic Church and the Ecumenical Patriarchate are ready to study concrete ways of solving pastoral problems, especially those connected with marriages between Catholics and Orthodox. They hope for better co-operation in works of charity, in aid of refugees and those who are suffering and in the promotion of justice and peace in the world.

In order to prepare fruitful contacts between the Roman Catholic Church and the Orthodox Church, the Pope and the Patriarch give their blessing and pastoral support to all efforts for co-operation between Catholic and Orthodox scholars in the fields of historical studies, of studies in the traditions of the Churches, of patristics, of liturgy and of a presentation of the Gospel which corresponds at one and the same time with the authentic message of the Lord and with the needs and hopes of today's world. The spirit which should inspire these efforts is one of loyalty to truth and of mutual understanding, with an effective desire to avoid the bitterness of the past and every kind of spiritual or intellectual domination.

Paul VI and Athenagoras I remind government authorities and all the world's peoples of the thirst for peace and justice which lies in the hearts of all men. In the name of the Lord, they implore them to seek out every means to promote this peace and this justice in all countries of the world.

That same evening, 26 October 1967, a reception was given in the Apostolic Palace in honour of the Patriarch. In greeting Cardinal Bea and other guests, Athenagoras spoke of the apostolic succession, which forms a bond between Rome and Orthodoxy:

> You and we, bishops of the Holy Roman Catholic Church and in our Holy Orthodox Church, bear the Holy Spirit as in vessels of clay; we carry the priceless pearl of the apostolic succession, passed on without interruption to us through the imposition of hands.

The implication seems to be that that apostolic succession may be missing in other Churches. He spoke of the need to advance towards unity 'in a spirit of love and patience as each of us corrects the errors of the past and everything which has contributed to our division, and makes straight the ways of the Lord'.

In his farewell address to the Patriarch the Pope spoke of his joy that the visit had 'strengthened the bonds of fraternal charity between us'. He prayed to 'the almighty Father to guide your steps and ours in order that, faithful to the Spirit of truth and of charity, the Roman Catholic Church and the Orthodox Churches may move along together towards full communion.'

So ended a momentous chapter in ecumenical relations, significant not only for its symbolic value and for the affection and the trust which the two men showed for one another, but also for the important ecumenical principles which both enunciated: the need for a developing rediscovery of what the two Churches have in common, for a self-denying willingness to renounce anything except the truth which was an obstacle to reconciliation; the acceptability and even the desirability of pluriformity, though its extent was not yet defined. Especially remarkable was the Patriarch's acknowledgment of a Roman primacy of charity, honour and order. The spirit of the Washing of the Feet, recommended by the Patriarch, was evident throughout the meetings of the two great bishops, each of which was clearly bent on saying all he could to show a respect and a welcome for the tradition of the other Church.

Although during the years 1966 and 1967 the Roman ecumenical emphasis was on the Catholic Church's relations with the Orthodox and the Anglicans, the Churches of the Reformation were not forgotten. In October 1967, Cardinal Bea, as Secretary of the Secretariat for Unity, wrote to the President of the Lutheran World Federation on the occasion of the celebration of the 450th anniversary of the Reformation. Writing in consultation with the Pope, the Cardinal sent 'hearty greetings'. He continued:

> With all of you, we deeply regret that 450 years ago the unity of Western Christianity was broken. We do not wish to blame each other for this terrible schism; rather, together we wish to seek ways of restoring the lost unity.

In reply the President, Dr Fredrik Schiotz, spoke appreciatively of the work of the Vatican Council, and promised to participate in the Year of Faith.

Towards the end of the year the improvement in relations between Catholics and Orthodox spread to Russia. A group of Roman Catholic and Russian Orthodox theologians met at Leningrad Theological Academy on 9-13 December. The presence of Cardinal Willebrands at the head of the Catholic delegation showed that the talks were taken seriously.

5. JOURNEYS, MARTYRS, SISTER CHURCHES

IN MAY 1968, at the invitation of the Orthodox Patriarch of Moscow, the Pope sent a mission to take part in the fiftieth anniversary of the restoration of the Moscow Patriarchate. In it Pope Paul expressed the hope that 'this reaffirmation of your ancient tradition will serve to deepen the religious spirit of your people and that it will be a source of renewed strength for those Christians who seek to bear witness to Christ in a world that has so much need of him'. He continued:

> We are most happy also that God has granted that relations between our Churches should increasingly improve, particularly in recent years. If, in the past as in recent years, there have been difficulties and misunderstandings and especially some most regrettable happenings which have come between the Catholic and the Russian Orthodox Churches, we can see in the contacts which have been made in the recent past a token of a new development of brotherly love, of mutual understanding and of common effort to dispel the differences which still exist between the See of Rome and the Patriarchate of Moscow.

On 23 May 1968 the Pope received in audience a Bulgarian group of Catholic and Orthodox pilgrims. In his address the Pope spoke, apparently, of the Roman martyrs as 'those martyrs of the common faith of the undivided Church' – a phrase which once more showed that he refused to equate the Church with the Roman Catholic Church. 'We are delighted,' he continued,

> not only at the mutual respect with which you are motivated in the diversity of your opinions but also even more at the spirit of collaboration we know to exist between the Catholic and the Orthodox Churches in Bulgaria, to which your pilgrimage bears witness, just as reciprocal respect between Christians and those who do not share our faith presents one of the necessary conditions for the future happiness of your country, which will be worthy of its long and fruitful past.

The leader of the pilgrimage in reply spoke of the 'great impetus' Pope Paul had given 'not only within the Catholic Church but to all the Christian Churches and Communities in general. This has shortened the path to reconciliation between the Christian

Churches and between the separated brethren who profess the single faith of salvation.' He spoke appreciatively of the work of Pope John XXIII, who had served for nearly ten years as Vicar Apostolic in Bulgaria.

That same spring the Pope exchanged greetings with the Coptic Patriarch of Alexandria and the new Greek Orthodox Patriarch of the same city. At Easter he sent greetings to each of the patriarchs of the autocephalous Orthodox Churches, and to the catholicos and patriarch of each other ancient oriental Church. In the summer official Catholic observers were sent to the Fourth Assembly of the World Council of Churches at Uppsala and to the Anglican Lambeth Conference. Pope Paul in a message sent to the Lambeth Conference said that the 'diligent presence' of the seven Catholic observers and other guests 'will reflect the interest and be supported by the prayers of Roman Catholics everywhere. Our interest is sharpened by the fact that the Conference follows close on the profitable deliberations of the Joint Preparatory Commission between the Roman Catholic Church and the Anglican Communion. All that the Conference can do to advance further the cause of Christian unity will be blessed by God.' Proof of the Conference's concern with Roman Catholic relations was shown by the fact that two days were allotted to debate on the Encyclical *Humanae Vitae*, which had been promulgated in July. Although the members felt obliged to pass a motion stating that they were unable to agree with the Pope's teaching that all artificial methods of contraception were contrary to the 'order established by God', the motion went on to record their 'appreciation of the Pope's deep concern for the institution of marriage and the integrity of married life'. It is indicative of the new ecumenical climate that the motion regards the Pope as a brother with whom one is sorry to have to disagree, rather than an opponent off whom one is glad to be able to score a point.

On 30 June 1968 the Pope closed the Year of Faith by publishing his *Credo of the People of God*, which 'without being strictly speaking a dogmatic definition, repeats in substance, with some developments called for by the spiritual condition of our time, the creed of Nicaea'. In the article on the Church Pope Paul seemed to return to a form of words which equated the One Church with the Roman Catholic Church in a way which he had avoided in his recent statements. The passage paraphrases the 'subsists in' passage of Paragraph 9 of the Council's Constitution on the Church, though the implication that non-Catholics are 'outside' is stated now more sharply; whereas the Council had said they were 'outside the visible confines' of the 'sole Church of Christ', Pope Paul states that they are outside its 'organism'. The passage in the *Credo* runs as follows:

> Recognising also the existence, outside the organism of the Church of Christ, of numerous elements of truth and sanctification which belong to her as her own and tend to Catholic unity, and believing in the action of the Holy Spirit who stirs up in the heart of the disciples of Christ love of this unity, we entertain the hope that the Christians who are not yet in the full communion of the one only Church will one day be reunited in one Flock with one only Shepherd.

It would have been more typical of Pope Paul's usual sensitivity to non-Catholic feelings to reserve the phrase 'one Shepherd' to Christ, the Good Shepherd.

In August 1968 the Pope visited Columbia for the Eucharistic Congress. In the course of his visit, he spoke to representatives of the Jewish community at Bogota. He quoted the Council's Decree on the Relation of the Church to Non-Christian Religions: 'Since the spiritual patrimony common to Christians and Jews is thus so great, this sacred Synod wishes to foster and recommend that mutual understanding and respect which is the fruit above all of biblical and theological studies, and of brotherly dialogue.' The Pope continued:

> Among the riches of this great common inheritance we would like to recall to you today: faith in one God who transcends all human categories and yet is revealed as a Father. He has created man in his own image (Gen 1:26-28), and we share the belief that, in accordance with the great commandment of Love of God and of our neighbour (Deut 5; Lev 19), we are called to carry out the divine will and to put ourselves at one another's service. God grant that all of us may one day come to share in the fullness of his glory in a new heaven and a new earth (Is 65:17).
>
> We pray God that he will deign to bless our efforts at fruitful collaboration for the good of all humanity, until the day comes when all people call on the name of the Lord with a united voice and pledge him a united service.

On 28 March 1969 the Holy Father received a delegation of Protestant church leaders representing the National Council of Churches of Christ in the U.S.A. Responding to a statement by the delegation's spokesman, the Pope recalled some of his earlier remarks on the duty of ecumenism, and continued:

> What a consoling source of joy it is for us to know that the Roman Catholic bishops and faithful of the United States have

well understood and warmly accepted this serious engagement, so that already many fruitful accomplishments have been realised in close co-operation with your Council and those who belong to its member Churches.

Your distinguished spokesman has mentioned the common initiatives which you are making as Christians to help resolve the pressing problems of war and violence, of conflict between races and between the rich and the poor, of the gap between the generations. . . .

For we are convinced that doctrine and practice are inextricably intertwined in the common effort towards that unity through which Christ will truly be a sign to the world. Doctrine animates action; it guides it, gives it deeper inspiration and ensures that action is truly Christian. On the other hand, action gives a new and dynamic dimension to reflection upon the doctrine of Christ and its meaningful application to the concrete problems of today's world.

This dialectic between truth and love, doctrine and action, experience and reflection, is the fulfilment of those words of St Paul which form what could be called 'the great ecumenical commandment': *Veritatem facientes in caritate*: Speaking the truth in love, we are to grow up in every way into him who is the head, into Christ' (Eph 4 : 15).

Fidelity to that 'Pauline commandment' will help us to search out, understand and exploit those many bonds which already unite us as brothers in Christ, so that, both in our teaching and our common activity, the Good News of the Resurrected Lord may become more visible in the living practice of Christians. Such fidelity will indeed more clearly reveal the painful differences which still exist among brothers in Christ, but will help us discern better those ways of activity which can make an authentic contribution towards resolving those differences, and distinguish them from others which, though often inspired by sincere good will and love, in the final analysis impede rather than assist the search for that restoration of Christian unity which will make more vivid our common witness to the world.

On 31 May 1969 the Pope gave an audience to a delegation from the Lutheran World Federation. In his speech of welcome he spoke appreciatively of the contribution made by the Lutheran observers at the Vatican Council. He recalled Professor Skydsgaard's emphasis on 'the fundamental importance for the ecumenical movement of a theology of the history of salvation', a task which, the Pope said, would be undertaken by the new Ecumenical Institute of Jerusalem. He referred also to the study which the Roman Catholic/Lutheran World Fellowship working group had devoted to the problems of 'Gospel and Church'; 'we are convinced this question is one of the most central which still stands between us and without solution since the unhappy rupture of the time of the Reformation'.

The 'deep differences' between the two Churches must be taken seriously.

> We have, in addition, the hope that new ways and new possibilities of understanding and common vision will open under the inspiration of the Holy Spirit, on the condition that we face the difficulties with patience, seriousness, loyalty and an atmosphere of charity. . . .
>
> In this week of Pentecost, when we commemorate the outpouring of the Holy Spirit, we become particularly conscious of the fact of how much the event of the reconciliation between all Christians in the only and unique Church of Christ surpasses our strength and human capacities.
>
> That is why we put all our hope in the prayer of Christ for his Church, in the love of the Father for us, in the strength and the power of the Holy Spirit.

On 10 June 1969, in the course of a visit to Geneva at the invitation of the International Labour Organisation, the Pope took part in a meeting at the headquarters of the World Council of Churches. The General Secretary of the WCC, the Rev Eugene Carson Blake, in a speech of welcome, said that the Pope's visit

> signifies the growth of the ecumenical movement, through which Christ is gathering his Church in our century. This house itself is both a reminder of the divisions in the Christian community and a sign of growing fellowship among the churches. This fellowship is not primarily based on the efforts of men but seeks to be a response of the churches to the action of the Holy Spirit. It does not seek unity at the expense of truth but it attempts through the mutual enrichments of our living traditions to fulfil our common calling of witness to the Gospel in our days and service to all men.
>
> We are bold to describe our fellowship with a word used by that great and sainted teacher of the East, Basil the Great, 'Sympnoia', 'being together in one spirit'. This may sound almost presumptuous in the light of our failures to overcome our differences, to heal our divisions or even fully to understand the truth of the Gospel. Yet our experience of the presence of Christ in new and unexpected ways has brought us together in one spirit. Here, through mutual encouragement and mutual correction, we are finding new ways of living under his Lordship.

Pope Paul in his reply spoke of the World Council as 'a marvellous movement of Christians, of "children of God who are scattered abroad" (Jn 11: 52)'. He then took the opportunity of reformulating his conception of the papacy:

> We are here among you. Our name is Peter. Scripture tells us which meaning Christ has willed to attribute to this name, what duties he lays upon us: the responsibilities of the apostle and his successors. But permit us to recall other titles which the Lord wishes to give to Peter in order to signify other charisms. Peter is fisher of men, Peter is shepherd. In what concerns our person, we are convinced that without merit on our part, the Lord has given us a ministry of communion. This charism has been given to us not indeed to isolate us from you or to exclude among us, understanding, collaboration, fellowship and, ultimately, the recomposition of unit, but to allow us to carry out the command and the gift of love in truth and humility (cf. Eph 4:15; Jn 13:14). And the name Paul which we have assumed sufficiently points out the orientation which we have wanted to give to our apostolic ministry.

The General Secretary of the WCC in his report commented on this last sentence as a counterweight to the Petrine claims of the rest of the paragraph. On more than one occasion previously Pope Paul had discussed his understanding of his office, and of the essential service which it renders to the Church. Here he defines it in one short phrase as a 'ministry of communion', i.e. the responsibility for promoting the unity of all Christ's followers.

'Christian fellowship' already existed among the baptized, the Pope continued, but their communion was imperfect. God in the Spirit, however, was guiding all Christians in the search for the unity Christ wills for his one Church.

> This supreme desire of Christ, and the deep need of men who believe in him and have been redeemed by him, keep our spirit in a constant tension of humility, of regret for the present division among the followers of Christ; of a hope-filled desire for the restoration of unity among all Christians; of prayer and reflection on the mystery of the Church which is committed, for its sake and that of the world, to give witness to the revelation made by God the Father, through the Son and in the Holy Spirit. You may understand how at this moment this tension reaches a high degree of emotion in us, but far from troubling us, it rather makes our conscience clearer than ever.

The Pope referred to the activities of the joint working group set up by the Catholic Church and the WCC: 'theological reflection on the unity of the Church, the search for a better understanding of Christian worship, the deep formation of the laity,

85

the consciousness of our common responsibilities and the co-ordination of our efforts for social and economic development and for peace among the nations'. He spoke also of plans 'to find the possibilities of a common Christian approach to the pheno-menon of unbelief, to the tensions between the generations, and to relations with the non-Christian religions'.

Success in this work presupposes 'that at the local level the Christian people are prepared for dialogue and for ecumenical collaboration.... Our primary concern, of course, is more the quality of this manifold co-operation than the mere multiplication of activities.' He quoted a passage from the Decree on Ecumenism to the effect that growth in unity requires 'interior conversion, ... newness of attitudes, ... self-denial and unstinted love'.

> Fidelity to Christ and to his word, humility before the workings of his Spirit in us, service to one another and to all men – these virtues will give Christian quality to our reflection and work. Only then will collaboration among all Christians vividly express that union which already exists among them and set in clearer relief the features of Christ the Servant (cf. Decree on Ecumenism, n. 12).

The Pope then faced the question whether the Roman Catholic Church should join the WCC.

> In fraternal frankness, we do not consider that the question of the membership of the Catholic Church in the World Council is so mature that a positive answer could or should be given. The question still remains an hypothesis. It contains serious theo-logical and pastoral implications. It thus requires profound study and commits us to a way that honesty recognises could be long and difficult. But this does not prevent us from assuring you of our great respect and deep affection. The determination which guides us will always be the search, filled with hope and pastoral realism, for the unity willed by Christ.

He concluded with the prayer that 'we may move forward in our effort to fulfil together our common calling to the glory of the one God, Father, Son and Holy Spirit'.

On the same visit Pope Paul spoke to representatives of the non-Catholic Christian Churches of Geneva, 'who are united with us in faith in Christ the Saviour'. He recalled that 'Geneva is one of the cities of the world where one is most painfully conscious of division between Christians', but spoke of the 'climate of serenity and esteem' that marked the present meeting, and the good relations among the parishes of Geneva.

He went on to describe 'the spirit of healthy ecumenism':

This spirit lays down, as the first basis of every fruitful contact between different confessions, that each profess his own faith loyally. It calls for recognition, with no less loyalty, of the positive, Christian, evangelical values found in the other confessions. Finally, it is open to every possibility of collaboration in the fields where, already, common action seems possible and desirable: for instance in the field of charity and in the search for peace between peoples.

Animated by this spirit we come to you, animated by the sole care of the glory of God and the accomplishment of his will for men. May we be, as we so much desire, the pilgrim of reconciliation.

This description of the spirit of ecumenism must only be intended to apply to its initial stages, as the Pope makes no mention of shared prayer, or of growth towards full communion.

From 31 July to 2 August 1969 the Pope paid a 'religious and pastoral visit' to Uganda. On the last day of his visit the Pope consecrated an altar at Namugongo at the shrine dedicated to the Ugandan martyrs canonised in 1964. On the way he spent forty minutes at the shrine of the Anglican martyrs who had died in the same persecution. There, replying to a speech of welcome delivered by the Anglican Archbishop of Uganda, Rwanda and Burundi, the Pope spoke of his desire to meet 'the Anglican Church which flourishes in this country':

> We wished to pay homage to those sons of whom it is most proud: those who – together with our own Catholic martyrs – gave the generous witness of their lives to the Gospel of the Lord we have in common, Jesus Christ. . . .
> In the martyrs' spirit of ecumenism, we cannot resolve our differences by mere re-consideration of the past, or judgement upon it. Instead, we must press on in confidence that new light will be given us, to lead us to our goal; we must trust that new strength will be granted us, so that, in obedience to our common Lord, we may all be able to receive the grace of unity.

Speaking of the 'flourishing' Christian Council in Uganda, the Pope laid down the principle that 'there can be no growth towards unity without strong, deep local roots. . . . Thus, not only in Uganda, but in all the African continent, spiritual hunger will intensify to bring healing to that division of which the Second Vatican Council said that it "openly contradicts the will of Christ, scandalises the world, and damages the most holy cause, the preaching of the Gospel to every creature" (Decree on Ecumenism n. 1)'.

Pope Paul referred to the ecumenical co-operation in translating the bible, 'that rich source from which the minds and hearts of men receive the life-giving nourishment of divine revelation'. . . . This and all other forms of common work

> are gathered up in a single resolve. For this is the search we all pursue together, for that true, visible and organic unity which Christ so clearly willed, in order that the world may believe. . . .

Among the Anglicans present was Bishop Janani Luwum, who was soon to succeed to the Archbishopric of Uganda. A few years later, like the Martyrs, he was himself put to death by a tyrannous régime.

In 1969 further proof was given of the trust developing between the Roman Catholic Church and the Orthodox Churches. When the Synod of Bishops met in Rome in October, the Patriarch of Constantinople sent the Pope one of his typically considerate messages:

> Always in heart and spirit close to Your Holiness, we were particularly thinking of you and of your holy Roman Catholic Church during our divine liturgy yesterday in our own patriarchal shrine, on the occasion of the Holy Synod of Bishops assembled round you; we send to Your Holiness, whom we so love, and through you as intermediary to the venerable members of the Synod, our most cordial greetings and those of our Church. We pray to the Holy Spirit, the Paraclete, asking him to fortify Your Holiness in his heavy and holy responsibilities, and to guide well the work of the Synod under your inspired leadership, for the good of our well-loved sister, the Roman Catholic Church.

The same month the Metropolitan Nikodim of Leningrad visited Italy. His programme included an audience with the Pope in Rome. In November Cardinal Willebrands, who had succeeded Cardinal Bea as President of the Secretariat for Christian Unity, went to Constantinople to join in the celebration of the feast of St Andrew. The Ecumenical Patriarch spoke to the Cardinal of the visit as 'a fresh proof and further testimony of the fraternity of the two Churches and the notable progress which has been made, thanks be to God, towards re-establishing their communion and their firm resolve to go forward to the day when they will accomplish the mystery of the unity of the Church on earth . . .'. Concluding his speech, he said:

> None of us any longer summons one to the other, but, like Peter and Andrew, we direct each other towards Jesus, the one com-

mon Lord who unites us. We wish to remain with Jesus, to remain united, for the whole of the day, that endless day of the last times.

Cardinal Willebrands's reply contained a remarkable passage about the role of the papacy in a united Church:

> Desire for unity urges us to look for all possible ways and means of getting to the goal. The unity we are looking for is that which reigned in the college of the apostles. It is not a matter of all-absorbing uniformity, but of the unity of a body, the harmony which springs from all its members complementing each other. There is no question of silencing one or the other's voice, but of singing God's wonders in harmonious polyphony so that with one sole heart and 'one sole mouth we may glorify God, the Father of our Lord Jesus Christ' (Rom 15:6). We believe that Peter was the first choryphaeus [for the meaning of this term, which the Patriarch had used in his speech, in Orthodox tradition, see p. 62] of this college of the apostles, that he was not only at Jerusalem, but continued that ministry at Rome, and has transmitted it to his successors. This service of authority for the sake of unity needs to be studied once more in the light of the Gospel and of authentic apostolic tradition, in a dialogue of charity and truth between our Churches, as well as among all Churches and ecclesial structures of Christendom. . . .
>
> In order to hasten that day, we ought to work together with patience and perseverance to find ways of transmitting the rediscoveries made by their pastors to the entire structures of our Churches, even to the smallest parishes, and to draw the practical consequences for all aspects and all levels of their life and relationships.

A message from Pope Paul was read in which the Pope stated: 'This visit accords with our desire to see increasing contacts between our Churches and from time to time to examine together with Your Holiness everything that may favour our progress towards re-establishing full communion.'

The Synod of October 1969 had been devoted to the subject of collegiality. Speaking at an audience immediately after the Synod, on 29 October, the Pope linked collegiality with communion, in terms which implied that non-Catholics can share in the 'Church's life as a communion', even if they do not share in the 'external social fact':

> It [communion] means more than community, which is an external social fact; it means more than congregation, more than association, more than brotherhood, more than assembly, more than society, more than family, more than any form of human

solidarity and collectivity: it means Church, that is humanity inspired by one and the same interior principle, which is not only a sentimental and ideal, or cultural, principle, but also a mystical and real one – humanity inspired by Christ's spirit. . . .

If we wish to renew the Church's life, as a communion, we must take the greatest care to establish this personal and supernatural communion with Christ within ourselves.

At another audience a fortnight later Pope Paul returned to this theme. The Church, he said, is a communion;

in the formation of the new ecclesial mentality, which we can call post-conciliar, we must develop the sense of this. No matter how great may be our knowledge of our freedom and our personality, we must not forget that we are not alone, nor are we autonomous.

On 10 December 1969, speaking of the centenary of the First Vatican Council, which had defined the primacy of the Bishop of Rome, Pope Paul referred to the part the pope would have to play when Christians were reunited in a single Church: the papacy was the pinnacle and expression of Church unity.

On 18 January 1970 Cardinal Willebrands, the President of the Secretariat for Christian Unity, preaching in Cambridge, revealed some of the thinking of his secretariat on diversity within the unity of the Church. He made use of the term *typos* (character), and envisaged 'a plurality of *typoi* within the communion of the one and only Church of Christ'.

Where there is a long coherent tradition, commanding men's love and loyalty, creating and sustaining a harmonious and organic whole of complementary elements, each of which supports and strengthens the other, you have the reality of a *typos*.

Such complementary elements are many. A characteristic theological method and approach (historical perhaps in emphasis, concrete and mistrustful of abstraction) is one of them. . . . A characteristic liturgical expression is another. . . . A spiritual and devotional tradition draws much from many springs. . . . A characteristic canonical discipline, the fruit also of experience and psychology, can be present. Through the combination of all these, a *typos* can be specified.

. . . If a typology of Churches, a diversity in unity and unity in diversity, multiplies the possibilities of identifying and celebrating the presence of God in the world; if it brings nearer the hope of providing an imaginative framework within which Christian witness can transform human consciousness for today, then it has all the justification it needs.

On 21 January the Pope spoke of some of the difficulties in the way of reunion. Catholics for their part must first heal their own divisions. Orthodox and Protestants must accept the papal primacy. Intercommunion, however, is not 'the right way'.

> Unity is Christ's will. It will find its expression in one single Church. Religion's cause needs it. If this be the duty and the interest of Christians, unity must be re-established.

On 31 March 1970, the Pope issued the *Motu Proprio* entitled *Matrimonia Mixta*, revising the rules for marriages between Catholics and other Christians. Noting the growth in the number of such marriages due to the increased contact between Christians of different denominations, the Pope stated that mixed marriages 'do not, except in some cases, help in re-establishing unity among Christians'.

> There are many difficulties inherent in a mixed marriage, since a certain division is introduced into the living cell of the Church, as the Christian family is rightly called, and in the family itself the fulfilment of the Gospel teachings is more difficult because of diversities in matters of religion, especially with regard to those matters which concern Christian worship and the education of the children.

Consequently the Church discourages mixed marriages.

> However, since man has the natural right to marry and beget children, the Church, by her laws, which clearly show her pastoral concern, makes such arrangements that on the one hand the principles of divine law be scrupulously observed and that on the other the said right to contract marriage be respected.

He repeated the Church's teaching that a marriage between a Catholic and a baptized non-Catholic was a true sacrament; there is 'a certain communion of spiritual benefits which is lacking in a marriage entered into by a baptized person and one who is not baptized.' The Catholic partner, by 'divine law' and not only as a point of discipline, has a duty to preserve his or her own faith and 'as far as possible, to see to it that the children be baptized and brought up in that same faith'.

Thus the Church's attitude to mixed marriages was not fundamentally changed. While much is said of the Catholic partner's duties, there is no explicit recognition that the non-Catholic partner also has a duty to obey his or her conscience with regard to the baptism and unbringing of the child. However, respect is shown to the convictions of the non-Catholic partner in so far as he or she is no longer required to make any promise about the children's Church membership. Moreover, Catholic pastors are reminded

> to aid the married couple to foster the unity of their conjugal and family life, a unity which, in the case of Christians, is based on their baptism too. To these ends it is to be desired that those pastors should establish relationships of sincere openness and enlightened confidence with ministers of other religious communities.

The *Motu Proprio* repeats the affirmation of Vatican II that non-Catholics who 'believe in Christ and have been properly baptized are brought into a certain, though imperfect, communion with the Catholic Church.' Separated Eastern Christians have a special position: 'they possess true sacraments, above all the priesthood and the Eucharist, whereby they are joined to us in a very close relationship.'

At an audience held on 15 April 1970, the Pope spoke of misplaced appeals to conscience. The Protestant Reformation had given rise to the misconception that conscience could 'direct the mind of the believer by itself alone'. This view 'put every follower of Christ into direct contact with the Holy Scriptures and permitted its "free examination" to each of them.'

> Is this the way Christ wished his revelation to be passed on to believers, and was there no danger that the truth of the Holy Scriptures might lose its unique significance and crumble into a thousand different and contrasting interpretations? What has happened to the unity of the faith that was intended to unite Christians in this synthesis: 'one Lord, one faith, one baptism'?

Freedom of conscience, he said, was legitimate, 'if it is exercised to express the conscience's moral judgement regarding the single and immediate action to be accomplished', but it 'cannot, must not, leave out of consideration a higher and more general ruling that is called law'. In the sphere of faith conscience alone cannot suffice to guide the believer:

> Objective faith is not a personal opinion but an unshakeable and delicate doctrine, founded on the rigorous testimony of a qualified organ, the ecclesiastical magisterium, which is a scrupulous interpreter and transmitter of the faith – so much so that St Augustine said: 'I would not believe in the Gospel if the Church's authority did not induce me to do so.'

In May 1970 the Supreme Catholicos of all the Armenians, Vasken I, went to Rome to pay an official visit to the Pope. The Armenian Church, which is not in full communion with Rome, traditionally uses monophysite formulations of faith; that is to say, it speaks of a single nature in Christ, rather than the two natures of God and Man. Addressing the Catholicos on 9 May, the Pope spoke of the re-establishment of full communion between the two Churches from the twelfth to the fourteenth centuries, of the 'close ties' in the sixteenth and seventeenth, and of frequent expressions of 'deep agreement in the faith'. Pope Paul then turned to differences:

> If we have come to divergent expressions of the central mystery of our faith, because of unfortunate circumstances, cultural differences and the difficulty of translating terms worked out with much effort and given precise statement only gradually, then research into these doctrinal difficulties must be undertaken again in order to understand what has brought them about and to be able to overcome them in a brotherly way.

The Pope recalled how Pius XII had quoted the twelfth-century Armenian Catholicos Nerses IV to the effect that the truth about Christ can be expressed both in the terminology of 'one nature' and that of 'two natures'. Pope Paul himself spoke of the clearing up of misunderstandings, not the renunciation of traditional language:

> Has not the time come to clear up once and for all such misunderstandings inherited from the past, and this in a dialogue such as your Church, along with the other Churches meeting at Addis Ababa in 1965, has outlined in principle? The way that leads to agreement on these questions has already been cleared by the theologians in thorough studies and profitable meetings.

At another meeting on 11 May the Pope spoke of the 'profound and sacramental reality existing between our two Churches ... beyond the daily differences and the hostilities of the past'. The words implicitly reject the conception of the Church as a visible society coextensive with the Roman Catholic Church; he speaks rather of a 'reality' which is based on the sacraments (if this is what the word 'sacramental' is intended to convey), which is not yet, however, full unity.

Next day the two leaders signed a Joint Declaration, which stated that efforts for unity were likely to be sterile 'unless they are rooted in the whole life of the entire Church'. The 'search for a full unity . . . must be based on the mutual recognition of the common Christian faith and the sacramental life, on the mutual respect of persons and their Churches.'

The Pope and the Catholicos exchanged the kiss of peace.

At a consistory of Cardinals held on 18 May, the Pope declared his intention to canonise the Forty Martyrs of England and Wales in October, and touched upon some of the ecumenical implications of this act.

> It is far from our intention that this canonisation be an occasion of mutual accusation and recrimination. On the contrary, this event seems to offer an ideal opportunity for us all to acknowledge with humility our own shortcomings and to be sorry for them, as well as to express our deep gratitude to God that in our own day the work of reunion of all Christians has made great progress.
>
> Whereas four hundred years ago this slaying of brother by brother could be regarded as an action pleasing to him, today all men of good will, with the help of God's grace, turn with horror from such a course, and are strong in their determination that it should never be allowed to happen again that those who bear the name of Christ, the Prince of Peace and the Good Shepherd of our souls, should contaminate ourselves by such violence and bloodshed. For by no means can violence be thought to be a means to restore the desired unity, but only the humble and docile search for the Lord's will, a sincere regard for the truth and respect due to those who are baptized in water and the Holy Spirit, and who, moved by his grace, so ardently desire to be rid of all that unfortunately still divides, and thus to work together so that the Church that belongs to the Lord be one and undivided.

The Forty Martyrs, he said, could be of 'valuable assistance' along the road to union. They are 'examples of that loyal integrity which rejects false compromise'. But above all they 'give us ... an example of true Christian charity also towards those who do not profess the same Christian faith.'

> It is indeed most moving to see that in an age so prone to outright hostility in religious controversy, no trace of this hatred is to be found in these heroic men and women.

Finally, in our own time when 'growing materialism and naturalism tend to subvert the spiritual patrimony of our civilisation', the martyrs are a 'shining example of human dignity and liberty'.

The canonisation took place on 25 October. In the concluding section of his allocution at the ceremony (a section which he delivered in English), the Pope returned to the ecumenical significance of the event, praying that the blood of the martyrs might 'heal the great wound inflicted upon God's Church by reason of the separation of the Anglican Church from the Catholic Church'. Once again it is evident that Pope Paul is careful to avoid equating 'God's Church' with the Roman Catholic Church. His next remarks were of great importance, for they apply to the Anglican Communion the term 'sister Church' which up till now had been reserved for the Orthodox, and restate the conception of the Church of Christ as a family of sister Churches, each with its own 'typology' (to adopt Cardinal Willebrands's term).

Is it not one – these Martyrs say to us – the Church founded by Christ? Is not this their witness? Their devotion to their nation gives us the assurance that on the day when – God willing – the unity of faith and of Christian life is restored, no offence will be inflicted on the honour and sovereignty of a great country such as England. There will be no seeking to lessen the legitimate prestige and the worthy patrimony of piety and usage proper to the Anglican Church when the Roman Catholic Church – this humble 'Servant of the Servants of God' – is able to embrace her ever-beloved sister in the one authentic communion of the family of Christ: a communion of origin and of faith, a communion of priesthood and of rule, a communion of the Saints in the freedom and love of the Spirit of Jesus.

In the last months of 1970 the Pope undertook a demanding series of visits to Pakistan, South East Asia and Australia. Speaking at Rome airport as he set out on his tour, the Pope once more stated that the Church must not seek to impose a uniformity; rather it should be 'the point of convergence of multiple expressions in one faith. She must also be the starting point for those principles which ensure the Catholic dimension for each believer.' In Australia, speaking at a meeting of Oceanian bishops, the Pope reminded them of their 'obligation to take up a secure position on the teaching concerning the Church, and especially on her unity'. On 2 December Pope Paul took part in an ecumenical service held in Sydney, attended by representatives of the Catholic Church and ten other Churches. Ecumenism, he said, was a 'continuing and costly task'. Differences must be faced honestly.

History cannot be written off overnight, and the honest hesitations of sensitive consciences always demand our respect and understanding.
There is no easy way. The reconciling work of our Lord was achieved through suffering and the Cross. The unity which the ecumenical movement strives to serve must be bought at a similar price.

95

The reason why Christians were obliged to search for unity was not

> because we seek safety in a hostile world, nor because it is nice and comfortable to be together. It is rather a search for truth, a search for renewal, a search for obedience, that will lead us out into costly service.

The Pope's remarks had a special relevance as the Anglican Archbishop of Sydney and some of his clergy had felt themselves bound in conscience to absent themselves from the service.

1970 also saw the publication by the Secretariat for Unity of two important ecumenical documents. The first, published by order of the Pope, was the second part of the Ecumenical Directory; it dealt with ecumenism in higher education. Guidelines are laid down for ecumenical courses in non-theological institutions and faculties:

> The purpose of programmes of this type is to increase among students a deeper knowledge of the faith . . . , so that they may wisely and fruitfully take part in ecumenical dialogue . . . ; a further purpose is that teachers and students should learn more about other Churches and communities, and so understand better and assess more correctly what unites Christians and what divides them; finally, since these efforts are not to be mere intellectual exercises, the aim is that those taking part in them should better realise the obligation of fostering unity between Christians and so be led to apply themselves more effectively to achieving it.

The Directory goes on to discuss 'the ecumenical dimension of religious and theological education'. There is not space to summarise all the proposals; it must suffice to pick out some of the more important recommendations.

> To give adequate emphasis to the Catholic and apostolic character of the Church, the ecumenical spiritual life of Catholics should also be nourished from the treasures of many traditions, past and present, which are alive in other Churches and ecclesial communities.

(The implication seems to be the 'other Churches and ecclesial communities' are part of *the* Church.)

> Ecumenism should bear on all theological discipline as one of its necessary determining factors, making for the richer manifestation of the fullness of Christ.

96

There should also be lectures treating of ecumenism explicitly. Students should be led to understand that there is a 'hierarchy' in the truths of Catholic doctrine.

> Already from the time of their philosophical training students should be put in a frame of mind to recognise that different ways of stating things in theology too are legitimate and reasonable, because of the diversity of methods or ways by which theologians understand and express divine revelation. Thus it is that these various theological formulae are often complementary rather than conflicting. . . .
> Where it seems advisable and the Ordinary agrees, the Catholic clergy should be invited to attend special meetings with ministers of other Churches and communities – for the purpose of getting to know each other better and of solving pastoral problems by a joint Christian effort.

The Directory also has sections on co-operation between institutions of higher learning belonging to different denominations, the establishment of centres for ecumenical research, and inter-confessional institutes.

The second document was entitled 'Reflections and Suggestions concerning Ecumenical Dialogue'.

> Each of the parties to the dialogue is ready to clarify further his ideas and his ways of living and acting, if it appears that truth is leading him in this direction. . . .
> Christians are in a position to communicate to each other the riches that the Holy Spirit develops within them. . . .
> It is inside their Churches and ecclesial communities that Christians enjoy these spiritual goods. . . . Between them [the Churches and communities separated from Rome] and the Catholic Church therefore there is a certain communion already existing which must be the starting point for dialogue. This latter will tend towards a more perfect sharing by each Church and ecclesial community in the very mystery of Christ and his Church, which is the foundation of their communion among themselves.

The Catholic partner in dialogue must not discard or conceal his belief that 'the Lord has confided to the Catholic Church the fullness of the means of salvation and all truth revealed by God', but this conviction itself will form an object of dialogue. 'Catholics will take careful note of the legitimate diversity within the Church.' The commitment to dialogue can only be lived in a 'spirit of renunciation'.

Among fruitful lines of enquiry are:

truths which have been allowed to become obscured in this or that community as a result of divisions and historical circumstances, and which may be better preserved and sometimes better developed in some other community. . . .

In some countries, the questions raised during the crises of the eleventh and sixteenth centuries are today no longer the problem that they once were. Without forgetting historical origins, dialogue about such questions should focus attention on the way they pose themselves here and now. . . . It will be a fruitful exercise to begin from the ecclesial witness of those taking part, so as to obtain a clearer picture of how this faith is lived by them today within their communities.

Thus this document stresses the reciprocity of dialogue much more than Paul VI's 1964 encyclical *Ecclesiam Suam*.

6. LAST YEARS 1971-1978

IT may seem strange to refer to the last half of Pope Paul VI's reign as 'last years'. However, it seems reasonable to do so, at least as far as ecumenism is concerned, because the great steps had been taken and the great gestures made in those first seven and a half years. What remained was the patient and meticulous working out of the process which he, his predecessor John XXIII, and the Council had initiated. The Secretary of the Secretariat for Unity, Fr. Jérôme Hamer, O.P., spoke at the end of 1970 of 'ecumenical rhythm':

> The Council and the post-Council years were the periods of discovery, of acquisition. We have now reached a stage, that of *assimilation*, which is a slow process, but which goes deeper into the matter.

So too Pope Paul, speaking during the 1971 Church Unity Week, pointed out that 'slow and difficult' effort was required, 'even if consoling advances have been made'.

On 8 February 1971 the Pope received the Orthodox Metropolitan Meliton of Chalcedon, and handed him a letter in his own handwriting to be delivered to the Ecumenical Patriarch Athenagoras of Constantinople. In it Pope Paul spoke again of the 'almost full communion' which existed between the Catholic and Orthodox Churches.

> Although not yet perfect, this results from our common participation in the mystery of Christ and of his Church.
> Over the last few years the Spirit has enabled us to recapture an intense awareness of this fact and to translate the demands of that communion into action in the life of our Churches and their relationship. At the same time the Spirit inspired us with the firm will to do all that is possible to hasten the much desired day when at the end of a concelebrated Mass we can communicate together from the same chalice of the Lord.

This letter met with the usual generous response from the Ecumenical Patriarch. Addressing the Pope as 'elder brother', thus once more acknowledging some degree of papal primacy, he spoke of present unity and future hopes:

Actually, even if the Eastern Churches and the Western Church are separated, for causes known to the Lord, they are not divided, however, in the substance of communion in the mystery of Jesus, God made man, and of his divine-human Church.

We have broken away from mutual love and we are deprived of the boon of unanimous confession of Christ's faith; we have been deprived of the blessing of going up together towards the one altar for the sacrifice instituted by the Lord shortly before his passion; we have been deprived of the blessing of perfect and unanimous harmonious communion in the same precious eucharistic Body and Blood, even if we have never ceased to acknowledge that the apostolic priesthood and the sacrament of the divine Eucharist of each of us are both valid . . .

The Eucharist is ready in the Upper Room, and Our Lord wishes to eat the paschal supper with us. Shall we say no?

Perhaps an even more important response to the Pope's letter was expressed in a communiqué from the Patriarchal Office. The Pope's letter, it is said,

undoubtedly constitutes a historic and unprecedented change of attitude on the part of the Roman Catholic Church.

It is for this reason that it was hailed at Phanar [at Constantinople] and everywhere else as a great event which could serve as a basis for a very rapid development of relations, and notably for the meeting in the common cup of the Body and Blood of Christ.

The communiqué goes on to expound a conception of the five patriarchates, with the Bishop of Rome enjoying a primacy of honour:

It is not a question of unity, since we are united in the historical person of Christ; nor is it a question of organic union, since we have never been united in that way . . .

Up till the year 1054, when the schism occurred, there existed numerous differences between the two Churches, often expressed in a violent manner and going as far as a breaking-off of relations, as was the case under the Ecumenical Patriarch Saint Photios I. Nevertheless, unity in the sacraments, and notably in the Eucharist, the common cup, was undoubtedly preserved.

The schism of 1054 did not take place as the result of a decision by West and East; nor was it confirmed by decisions on the part of Rome and Constantinople; it imposed itself when the two Churches ceased to love one another.

Now the schism has been abolished [the communiqué referred to the events of 7 December 1965] . . . Things thus returned automatically to the state prior to 1054. Hence the question: why

100

do we not also automatically return to the common cup, given that since 1054 no more serious obstacle has presented itself, and given the fact that the existing differences are constantly diminishing? . . .

However, this constitutes the final stage; it is a step that is easy and difficult at the same time. The Patriarch regards it as easy, as a result, in particular, of the aforesaid letter of His Holiness Pope Paul VI of Rome. But this final stage is not a personal affair – like the meeting of the Pope and the Patriarch in Jerusalem on 5 January 1964 – nor an affair between the two Churches of Rome and Constantinople as when the anathemas were lifted, on 7 December 1965.

The ground has got to be prepared on both sides; the local situations and ensuing consequences have got to be well weighed up; above all it is necessary to reach a preliminary agreement and accord between the Orthodox Churches, while in the West the Pope has got to secure the assent of the episcopate around him.

In this communiqué the Patriarchal Office emphasises that the Patriarch's ecumenical acts were personal to himself, and do not commit his own Church of Constantinople, let alone the whole of Orthodoxy. On the other hand, it is significant that the communiqué does not fall far short of the Patriarch in enthusiasm for eucharistic communion with Rome, and concedes to the Bishop of Rome a primacy of honour.

On 29 August 1971 the Pope spoke to pilgrims at Castel Gandolfo about Christian divisions in Northern Ireland, and prayed that the people of that country, sharing as they do a common Christian faith that should unite them, 'may be able to return soon to the enjoyment of the great benefit of true peace in the mutual understanding and reciprocal collaboration which constitute the most sure conditions for the civil and moral progress of society'.

In October the Syrian Orthodox Patriarch of Antioch, Mar Ignatius Jacob III, paid an official visit to Rome. The Syrian Orthodox Church is known as Jacobite or Monophysite, as, like the Armenian Church, it rejected the definition of the two natures of Christ made at the Fourth Ecumenical Council at Chalcedon in 451, considering that the Chalcedonian formula fell into the Nestorian error of falsely separating the divine and the human Christ. Dialogue with the Orthodox Church of Antioch therefore posed special problems.

In welcoming the Patriarch on 25 October the Holy Father spoke of the improved relations between the two Churches.

The history of the relations between our Churches shows many lights and shadows. We recognise that difficulties which have

101

been created over centuries are not always easily overcome. Each of us is motivated by a sincere desire to be faithful to our Fathers in the faith and to the tradition they have handed down to us. Yet this very desire to be faithful to them impels us to search with ever greater zeal for the realisation of full communion with each other.

We share a common sacramental life and a common apostolic tradition, particularly as affirmed in what is popularly called the Nicene Creed. The dogmatic definitions of the first three Ecumenical Councils form part of our common heritage. Thus we confess together the mystery of the Word of God, become one of us to save us and to permit us to become in him sons of God and brothers of each other.

. . . Already theologians are working with renewed effort to throw new light on the mystery of the one Lord Jesus Christ. If they recognise that there are still differences in the theological interpretation of this mystery of Christ because of different ecclesiastical and theological traditions, they are convinced, however, that these various formulations can be understood along the lines of the faith of the early councils, which is the faith we also profess.

We, as pastors, can encourage the common efforts being made for a deeper and more comprehensive understanding of the mystery which, far from raising doubts about our two different ecclesiastical traditions, can reinforce them and show the basic harmony which exists between them.

The Pope's words show an acceptance of the doctrine of 'typologies' going so far as to allow the truth of an 'ecclesiastical and theological tradition' which rejected the Chalcedonian definition. Pope Paul practises here one of the principles of dialogue which he laid down in *Ecclesiam Suam*, namely that we need to try to understand what the other side is saying and look for the truth in it.

The Patriarch in his reply spoke of the meeting in 'an atmosphere of love and fraternity' after '1520 years of break, mutual anathemas and the like'. The Churches now recognise that the events at Chalcedon were 'a stab to the heart of Christianity'.

Thank God, those days of unhappy relations are now a thing of the past; and today there is real love and co-operation between our two Apostolic Sees, and Christian communion in general.

. . . We on our part look forward to the day when we will have even a greater visible unity and that too without sacrificing our individuality and the cultural contribution each of our Churches can make towards the speedy spreading of the Kingdom of God on earth.

102

On 27 October the Pope and the Patriarch issued a Common Declaration, which emphasised the traditions which the two Churches share:

The Pope and the Patriarch have recognised the deep spiritual communion which already exists between their Churches. The celebration of the sacraments of the Lord, the common profession of faith in the Lord Jesus Christ, the Word of God made man for man's salvation, the apostolic traditions which form part of the common heritage of both Churches, the great Fathers and Doctors, including Saint Cyril of Alexandria, who are their common masters in the faith – all these testify to the action of the Holy Spirit who has continued to work in their Churches even when there have been human weakness and failings. The period of mutual recrimination and condemnation has given place to a willingness to meet together in sincere efforts to lighten and eventually remove the burden of history which still weighs heavily upon Christians.

Progress has already been made and Pope Paul VI and the Patriarch Mar Ignatius Jacob III are in agreement that there is no difference in the faith they profess concerning the mystery of the Word of God made flesh and become really man, even if over the centuries difficulties have arisen out of the different theological expressions by which this faith was expressed. They therefore encourage the clergy and faithful of their Churches to even greater endeavours at removing the obstacles which still prevent complete communion among them. This should be done with love, with openness to the promptings of the Holy Spirit, and with mutual respect for each other and each other's Church. They particularly exhort the scholars of their Churches, and of all Christian communities, to penetrate more deeply into the mystery of Christ with humility and fidelity to the apostolic traditions so that the fruits of their reflections may help the Church in her service to the world which the Incarnate Son of God has redeemed.

Other important moves were taken in relations between Rome and the Orthodox. A joint working group of the two Churches had produced a collection of the documents exchanged between Rome and the Patriarch of Constantinople since 1958. The collection bore the apt title *Tomos Agapis* (The Volume of Love). In December 1971 the President of the Secretariat for Unity travelled to Constantinople to present the Ecumenical Patriarch with a copy autographed by the Pope.

In his Christmas address to the Cardinals, the Pope spoke cautiously of the 'silent but very profitable advance of ecumenical work'.

On 24 January 1972 the Metropolitan of Chalcedon, representing the Ecumenical Patriarch, presented the Pope with a jewelled cross bearing the inscription:

> To Paul VI Athenagoras I (offers) the precious cross which has united what was divided with the divine charity crucified upon it, on the occasion of offering 'Tomos Agapis'.

In his address the Metropolitan spoke of the *Tomos*:

> . . . what volume could ever describe the divine plan and the divine method by which the God of love, the God of our common Fathers, has stirred the hearts and minds, the lips and pens of East and West to formulate this new theology of unity, a theology penetrated by spiritual experience and based upon the facts of ecclesiastical life, a new theology which is at the same time as old as the united Church? . . .
>
> All these facts of lived experiences, moulded by God in the mystery of the divine economy, are stored up as organic elements in the life of the Church. They will one day find their expression in the joyful fulfilment of a perfect Eucharistic communion, of a unique witness in unity to the world, and of the eschatological restoration and fulfilment of all things in Jesus Christ.

Replying to the Metropolitan, Pope Paul spoke of the prayers of the Mass for Christian Unity in the new Roman Missal, especially the Preface:

> 'Through him [Christ] you have led us to acknowledge your truth, you have joined us in one faith and one baptism, and made us his Body. Through him you have poured out your Holy Spirit on all nations, a Spirit wonderful in the diversity of his gifts and the unity he creates, a Spirit who dwells in the sons you adopt, and fills and rules the whole Church.'

The Pope linked this Preface with the Council's words concerning 'the unity of the Church, in Christ and through Christ, under the action of the Holy Spirit who effects a variety of ministries' (Decree on Ecumenism n. 2). By apparently applying the words of the Preface to the existing relations between the Churches, the Pope seemed clearly to imply once more that Catholics and Orthodox already form legitimate diverse manifestations of the action of the Spirit within the 'whole Church'.

Later the same day the Pope preached at an ecumenical service held in the Lateran Basilica, in the presence of the Metropolitan and his delegation. Speaking of the baptism and the faith which the two Churches shared, the Pope commented:

Here we have already constituted the basis of that ecumenical unity which we are seeking passionately.

Those last two words sum up perfectly Pope Paul's ecumenical endeavour.

Rejoicing at having rediscovered that they are branches of the same tree, born of the same root, they are now suffering at not having yet been able to consummate, by drinking at the same mystical chalice, that perfect communion which sanctions between the two communities the organic and canonical union characteristic of the one Church of Christ.

Eucharistic sharing, then, is dependent upon 'organic' and 'canonical' union.

The Pope proceeded to give his fullest account of the role of the papacy in a united Church:

. . . kindly tell that saintly Patriarch [Athenagoras] and the venerated Brothers and faithful gathered round him, how this happy celebration, which took place in the Church that the historical and theological tradition of the Western Church calls 'omnium urbis et orbis ecclesiarum mater et caput' (mother and head of all the churches of the city and the world: Clement XII) because it is the cathedral of the Bishop of Rome, the successor of blessed Peter the Apostle, far from flattering our human ambition because of the pastoral office entrusted by Christ to be one who sits on this chair, namely, to act as 'the perpetual and visible source and foundation of the unity of the bishops and of the multitude of the faithful' (Vatican II, Decree on the Church, n. 23), has profoundly recalled to our conscience this weighty privilege of ours. Here, more than elsewhere, we feel ourselves 'a servant of the servants of God'. Here we think of ourselves as a brother with our brothers in the episcopate and in collegial solidarity with them. Here we think of the resolution of another great predecessor, Gregory the Great, who, while asserting his apostolic function (cf. Reg. 13,50), wished to consider the honour of the whole Church and the efficiency of the individual local bishops, his own honour (cf. Reg. 8,30: PL 77.933). Here we remember St Cyprian's conception of the unity of the Church: 'una Ecclesia per totum mundum in multa membra divisa' (one Church throughout the whole world divided into many members: Ep. 36, 4), that is, like a composite and articulated body, in which parts and groups can be modelled in particular typical forms, and functions can be distinct, though fraternal and converging. Here, in the heart of unity and at the centre of catholicity, we dream of the living beauty of the Bride of Christ, the Church, wrapped in her many-coloured garment (Ps 45:14), clothed, we mean, in a legitimate pluralism of traditional expressions. Here

105

we seem to hear the limpid echo of a distant voice of yours: 'O you, Peter, the foundation stone of faith!' (cf. Menei, v. 394).

In March 1972 a delegation of the Rumanian Orthodox Patriarchate visited the Holy See at the invitation of the Vatican Secretariat for Unity. Relations between the two Churches were especially delicate, for in 1948 the Rumanian government forced the members of the Catholic Eastern Rite Church to join the Rumanian Orthodox Church. These events formed the background to the Pope's words:

> Concerned only to carry out God's will for his Church, we must progress in mutual knowledge and reciprocal trust. The Lord will give us the strength and the generous wisdom to seek in good faith and with good will and finally to reach the solution of the difficulties that exist today between the Catholic Church and yours: whether they go back to past centuries or to more recent years and are thus even more keenly felt and more painful.
>
> These difficulties are well known, and we are just mentioning them here in order to say, at the same time, by what sentiments of brotherly love we are disposed to consider them and to envisage the possibilities of a just and charitable settlement.

The head of the Rumanian delegation, Bishop Antonie (who had studied for a doctorate in theology at Heythrop College in England with a scholarship from the Vatican), addressed the Secretariat for Unity, and spoke of that body's work for the unity of all Christians.

> This effort is based upon an openness to other Churches, an attitude adopted by the Roman Catholic Church after the Second Vatican Council. This advance towards unity is no longer thought of as the return of some to the bosom of certain others, nor as the renunciation by some of their independence, but rather as a shared aspiration, in equality and brotherhood, with each one bringing the contribution of his theology and tradition, and with all seeking together a unity in which will be respected the independence and the centuries-old treasury of traditions of each Church, in a 'unity of diversity' as it has been defined by His Beatitude the Patriarch Justinian [of Bucharest].

On 1 June 1972 the Secretariat for Unity with the 'approval' of the Pope and at his 'command', published an 'Instruction concerning Cases when other Christians may be Admitted to Eucharistic Communion in the Catholic Church'. The document reaffirms 'the strict relationship between the mystery of the Church and the mystery of the Eucharist'. Consequently non-

Catholics may be admitted to eucharistic communion only in the particular case

> of those Christians who have a faith in the sacrament in conformity with that of the Church, who experience a serious spiritual need for the eucharistic sustenance, who for a prolonged period are unable to have recourse to a minister of their own community and who ask for the sacrament of their own accord; all this provided that they have proper dispositions and lead lives worthy of a Christian.

The document points out that the Ecumenical Directory in this regard differentiated between the Orthodox Churches and other non-Catholic Churches.

> The reason is that the Eastern Churches, though separated from us, have true sacraments, above all, because of the apostolic succession, the priesthood and the Eucharist, which unites them to us by close ties, so that the risk of obscuring the relation between eucharistic communion and ecclesial communion is somewhat reduced. Recently the Holy Father recalled that 'between our Church and the venerable Orthodox Churches there exists already an almost total communion, though it is not yet perfect: it results from our joint participation in the mystery of Christ and of his Church.'
>
> With Christians who belong to communities whose eucharistic faith differs from that of the Church and which do not have the sacrament of Orders, admitting them to the Eucharist entails the risk of obscuring the essential relation between eucharistic communion and ecclesial communion. This is why the *Directory* treats their case differently from that of the Eastern Christians and envisages admission only in exceptional cases of 'urgent necessity'. In cases of this kind the person concerned is asked to manifest a faith in the Eucharist . . . as Christ instituted it and as the Catholic Church hands it on. This is not asked for an Orthodox person because he belongs to a Church whose faith in the Eucharist is conformable to our own.

(Presumably if the Anglican/Roman Catholic International Commission's Statement on the Eucharist is accepted by both Churches, the Anglican Communion will enter into such a degree of ecclesial communion with the Catholic Church that the true eucharistic faith of its members will be presumed; however the question of apostolic succession will still require to be solved.)

On 7 July 1972 Athenagoras I, the Ecumenical Patriarch of Constantinople, died. His name and his words have often figured in these pages. He has been described as a charismatic figure like

107

Pope John XXIII. The obituary in *The Tablet* spoke of the 'fresh vision' he acquired from his twenty years as Orthodox Archbishop of New York.

> He set himself to build up the unity of the Orthodox Churches and to promote Christian Unity as a whole; he saw the two halves of his vision as inseparable and succeeded in making changes in both despite, or rather because of, the poverty of the means at his disposal.

Pope Paul's affection and respect for him is apparent from his comments which followed the news of the Patriarch's death. In a telegram addressed to the Holy Synod of Constantinople, the Pope said:

> We have heard with great emotion of the death of our brother and dear friend in Christ, his holiness Patriarch Athenagoras. We send you our most sorrowful condolence on the loss which has struck the entire Orthodox Church, and we pray the Lord to receive into his heavenly Kingdom him who was the great protagonist of reconciliation between all Christians and between our two Churches in particular.

On 9 July, speaking before the Angelus, the Holy Father spoke of

> the reverence and admiration due to superior men who personify an idea which invests the destinies of history and tends to interpret the thoughts of God. Athenagoras, even in his exterior, majestic and hieratic appearance, revealed his inner dignity, and his grave and simple conversation had accents of simple evangelical goodness. He commanded reverence and sympathy. And we also are among those who greatly admired and loved him; and for us he had a friendship and trust that always moved us, the memory of which now increases our sorrow, and our hope is that we may still have him as a brother close to us in the Communion of Saints. . . .
>
> Three times we had the good fortune of meeting him personally, and a hundred times have we exchanged letters, always mutually promising to make every effort to re-establish perfect unity in faith and in the love of Christ among us, and he always synthesized his feelings in one supreme hope: that of being able to drink from the same chalice with us, that is, to celebrate the eucharistic sacrifice together, the synthesis and the crown of our common ecclesial identification with Christ. And this we too have so much desired.

On 16 July 1972, Patriarch Dimitrios was elected to succeed Athenagoras as Archbishop of Constantinople and Ecumenical

Patriarch. The Pope sent representatives to the ceremony, and in a telegram sent his prayers and best wishes, with the assurance that 'you will always find in the Bishop of Rome a loving brother eager to continue to progress towards the day so much desired by your great Predecessor when our unity, fully refound, will be sealed.'

In November 1972 the Pope addressed representatives of national ecumenical commissions who had come to Rome to study unity. He pointed out that contemporary atheism should stimulate Christians in their search for unity, which was a 'ministry of reconciliation'.

> The unbelief of many of our contemporaries should force us to a new awareness of the urgency of mending our present divisions. Surely the unity of Christ's disciples is the great sign that must evoke the world's faith. Surely it is the reason why the second Vatican Council required that ecumenical activity should be undertaken in such a way that the co-operation of Catholics and other Christians, in social and technical, in cultural and religious affairs, should take place not only between private individuals but, subject to the decision of the appropriate Ordinary, between Churches or church congregations and between their activities . . . In all cases, care must be taken to ensure that in the exercise of this common responsibility, there is only that spiritual competition proper among brethren moved by authentic charity . . . Between Christians animated by the truth, there is no rivalry, but only friendship.

On 24 January 1973, during Christian Unity Week, the Pope addressed an audience on the ecumenical movement. Speaking of the concept of Church unity, he said:

> As soon as this thought is grasped in its general significance, it takes hold of us, dominates us. Unity: immediately it imposes itself on account of its logical and metaphysical force. It refers to the Church, that is, to mankind called by Christ to be one thing only with him and in him. It holds us spellbound because of its theological depth. Then it torments us because of its historic aspect, yesterday and still today, bleeding and suffering like that of Christ crucified. It reproves us and awakens us, like the sound of a trumpet, calling us with the urgency of a vocation, which becomes relevant and characteristic in our times. The thought of unity irradiates over the world scene, scattered with the magnificent rent limbs and the ruins of so many Churches, some of them isolated as if self-sufficient, others broken into hundreds of sects. All of them are now invaded by two conflicting forces, in a moving tension: one centrifugal, fleeing, in its pursuit of autonomy, towards schismatic and heretical goals; the other

centripetal, demanding with reborn nostalgia the recomposition of unity. Motherly and fearless, Rome, certainly not faultless, and burdened on her own account with immense responsibility, stubbornly affirms and promotes this unity as her own duty, redolent of witness and martyrdom. It is the authentically ecumenical and unitarian force, which is seeking its principle and its centre, the base, which Christ, the real corner-stone of the ecclesial edifice, chose and fixed, in his stead to signify and perpetuate the foundations of his kingdom . . . And again it reverberates, this thought of unity, in the conscience of so many thoughtful, religious souls, raising in them a spiritual problem: how do I respond to this imperative of unity?

Pope Paul went on to speak of the role of 'particular communities' in putting into practice the principles of unity which Christ had enunciated.

Unity, which is a real gift from Christ, develops and grows in the concrete situation represented by the lives of the Christian communities. Understanding of the important role of the particular communities, of the particular churches, was clearly formulated by the Council: 'The individual bishop is the visible principle and foundation of unity in his particular church, fashioned after the model of the universal Church. In and from such individual churches there comes into being the one and only Catholic Church' (Constitution on the Church, n. 23).

Continuing his exposition, Pope Paul showed that he did not identify the unity of the Church with that of the Roman Church:

In fact the unity of the Church, which, as we said, in the historical charism of the whole Catholic Church and the Roman Church particularly, is already a reality, in spite of the deficiencies of the men composing it, is not, however, complete. It is not perfect in the statistical and social framework of the world, it is not universal. Unity and catholicity are not equal, either in the sphere that calls for this correspondence most, the sphere of the baptized and believers in Christ, or, even less, in that of the whole of mankind on earth, where most do not yet adhere to the Gospel. These are the two great problems of the Church, the ecumenical and the missionary, both dramatic.

Today we are speaking of the first one, that is, the union of Christians in one Church.

One means of solving the problem is 'the duty and the possibility of interesting the local churches in the ecumenical question, in harmony, of course, with the universal and central

Church (if we do not want to make the situation worse instead of better)'.

Through the particular church the Catholic Church is present in the same local and regional environment in which other Christian Churches and Communities also live and work. The establishment of contacts and brotherly relations often turns out to be easier in this context . . .

The catholicity and the unity of the Church are manifested in the capacity of the particular churches and of the whole to take root in different worlds, times and places; to find themselves in reciprocal fellowship in every world, time and place.

Unity at the local level is always a sign and manifestation of the mystery of the unity which is the Lord's gift to the Church. The particular churches can enrich the ecumenical movement as a whole with their experiences, can make a contribution fruitful for the whole Church. At the same time they will receive suggestions and directives coming from the centre of unity, that is the Apostolic See, 'universo caritatis coetui praesidens' (Ignatius, *Ad. Rom.*, inscript.) [the Pope's Latin translation of the original Greek means 'presiding over the universal assembly of love'; more literally, the Greek means 'presiding over love – or over the love-celebration'], to be helped in their problems and to be able to judge the validity and fruitfulness of their own experiences.

'I believe in one Church . . .' – this profession of faith urges us, therefore, to dedicate ourselves to the cause of the unity of Christians with all the ardour of which we are capable, and with all the possibilities that the life of the Church offers us at many levels.

Dear Sons, in this week of prayer for the unity common to all Christians, we all ask for forgiveness for the faults committed against this great gift, greater than any merits of ours.

At a general audience held on 21 February 1973, the Pope spoke of the relationship between the Holy Spirit and the institutional Church:

Has our religion lost some virtue proper to it of bearing witness, of preserving and renewing itself along traditional and normal paths? Is the Spirit breathing only outside the usual ambit of canonical structures? Has the Church of the Spirit left the institutional Church? Are the charismata of genuine, primitive, Pentecostal Christian spirituality only found with the so-called spontaneous groups?

We do not wish to discuss this theme at the present moment, though it well deserves to be examined with great respect, but will state two things instead, namely, that the normal and institutional structure of the Church is always the main channel by

111

which the Spirit reaches us still, and more than ever, today; but it is necessary that the idea of the Church, the 'sensus ecclesiae', be re-established and rectified and deepened within us.

In May the Holy Father received a visit from another Eastern Patriarch, the Coptic Orthodox Patriarch of Alexandria Amba Shenouda III. This visit presented similar problems to that of the Syrian Orthodox Patriarch of Antioch in October 1971, for the Orthodox Churches of Alexandria and Antioch both reject the Council of Chalcedon, which defined the two natures of Christ. Dialogue accordingly between Rome and these Monophysite (or 'non-Chalcedonian') Churches seeks to establish a unity of faith in Christ underlying the differences of terminology.

Greeting the Patriarch on 5 May, the Pope admitted that 'we do not expect to overcome immediately the difficulties that fifteen centuries of history have created for us. But we do hope to set out upon a way which will lead to our overcoming these difficulties . . .' Each Church tries to be faithful to its tradition.

> But that tradition is a living one . . . May God enlighten us and guide us and grant us new insights as we strive together to see how we may attain that full unity of the Spirit in the bond of peace which Christ asks of us and which is his gift.

On the following day the Pope in the presence of the Patriarch said Mass in celebration of the sixteenth centenary of the death of St Athanasius, the great Bishop of Alexandria who had struggled and suffered so much in defence of the Church's faith in the divinity of Christ. The festival provided an occasion for the Church leaders to recall the close links between Rome and Alexandria in the century before the Chalcedonian crisis, and to seek agreement in faith in terms of St Athanasius' belief. Speaking of the Saint, Pope Paul said:

> When we reflect on his life, we see a believer solidly founded on evangelical faith . . . and one who was ready to endure every calumny, persecution and violence. Of the forty-six years of his episcopate, he spent twenty in repeated exile; this very city of Rome gave him shelter for three years during his second exile . . .
>
> Always and everywhere and before all men, before the powerful and those in error, he professed faith in the divinity of Jesus Christ, true God and true man; therefore the Eastern liturgical tradition describes him as a 'column of the true faith' and the Catholic Church numbers him among the Doctors of the Church.

The Patriarch gave his reply after Mass was over.

We dare say our differences were for the sake of Christ's love, through which we love each other regardless of the differences. We meet today so that we may deepen our mutual love. Talks guided by the Holy Spirit in such an atmosphere should lead to unity of heart, mind and faith.

After speaking of 'many points of agreement in the principles of faith,' the Patriarch continued:

As for points of difference, there is no doubt that, after fifteen centuries of study, examination and controversy both on theological and public levels, we are undoubtedly on much nearer grounds than our ancestors of the fifth and sixth centuries. We all are readier and more intent to reach solutions for the differences and attain simpler and more practical forms of expression for the conceptions of faith that all would welcome. We are mindful that the tension of old philosophic and linguistic misunderstandings together with the political implications connected with the days of schism and the following centuries have been considerably reduced.

The Patriarch then spoke of the fifth-century Bishop of Alexandria, St Cyril, who, like St Athanasius,

became a point of agreement not only in his faith but also in the proper and definite expression of faith which exemplify clearly the word of truth precisely and effectively.
The common traditional theology of Athanasius and Cyril stands as a solid centre for the dialogue that we commit to a considerable number of theologians to go through in a spirit of faithful love. We expect them to agree on proper belief expressed in clear and uncomplicated language that all minds understand and consciences approve with comfort.

In answer the Pope spoke again of the way Pope Julius I welcomed St Athanasius as a 'champion of that faith which was being compromised and even denied by people who were stronger than he in political power but weaker in faith and understanding'.

He in turn recognised in the Church of the West a secure identity of faith despite differences in vocabulary and in the theological approach to a deeper understanding of the mystery of the Triune God.

Pope Paul alluded to the two Churches' common vocation

to bring to the world faith, reconciliation and peace. He recalled the extent of their sharing in the same faith and traditions.

> Yet in humility and sorrow we must recognise that in the history of our Churches we have experienced fierce disputes over doctrinal formulae by which our substantial agreement in the reality they were trying to express was overlooked . . .
>
> A new phenomenon is taking place, of which our meeting today gives eloquent testimony. In mutual fidelity to our common Lord, we are rediscovering the many bonds which already bind us together.

The same day, in his customary Sunday address before the *Regina Coeli*, the Pope explained to the crowd the significance of the Patriarch's visit.

> A symbol of the most firm fidelity and of witness heroically endured, he (St Athanasius) gives us the joy of having with us his Church, cut off from Catholic communion, also by political controversies no longer existing, after the Council of Chalcedon (451), which defined that in the unity of the Person, there are in Christ two natures, divine and human. This Church is now flourishing again and in an act of reflection, while now it is happy to proclaim with us the identical Nicene faith of Athanasius, champion of the unity of the East with the Latin West, himself a guest of the Roman Church for a long sojourn in 339, during the time of Pope Julius.
>
> You see, dear sons, how the memories of the past become a presage and a hope for the future; and for their fulfilment, let us now pray.

On 10 May the Pope and the Patriarch issued a Common Declaration, in which they professed a common faith in the One Triune God, and in the perfect humanity and divinity of Jesus Christ. In expressing their faith they adopted several expressions from the Council of Chalcedon, but not the 'two natures' formula. They acknowledged the same faith in the seven sacraments and agreed in venerating the Virgin Mary, 'the God-bearer, . . . the Theotokos', who intercedes for us. 'We have, to a large degree, the same understanding of the Church, founded upon the Apostles, and of the important role of ecumenical and local councils.' They recognised the authenticity of one another's spirituality. However,

> since the year 451 A.D., theological differences, nourished and widened by non-theological factors, have sprung up. These differences cannot be ignored. In spite of them, however, we are

rediscovering ourselves as Churches with a common inheritance and are reaching out with determination and confidence in the Lord to achieve the fullness and perfection of that unity which is his gift.

As a means to attaining that unity, the Churches would set up a joint theological commission, and rejected all forms of proselytism.

In the early summer of 1973 two documents were issued in Rome which accorded with the impressive number of recent papal statements concerning the admissibility of differing theological expressions of essential faith. The first, entitled 'Unity of the faith and theological pluralism', was composed by the International Theological Commission in October 1972, but not published until about nine months later. The Second was the declaration *Mysterium Ecclesiae*, published by the Congregation for the Doctrine of the Faith with papal confirmation on 24 June 1973. This second document was described as being 'in defence of the Catholic doctrine on the Church against certain errors of the present day'. Nevertheless it accepted the view that dogmas might contain elements expressed in 'the changeable conceptions of a given epoch', or might have been expressed 'incompletely (but not falsely)', so that 'at a later date, when considered in a broader context of faith or human knowledge,' they might receive 'a fuller and more perfect expression'.

On 26 November 1973, the President of the Secretariat for Unity, Cardinal Willebrands, visited Istanbul, on the occasion of the Feast of St Andrew, the patron saint of the Church of Constantinople. Cardinal Willebrands delivered to the Ecumenical Patriarch, Dimitrios I, a letter from Pope Paul. In it the Pope speaks of his wish to continue along the path to full communion which he had begun to walk with Dimitrios' predecessor, Athenagoras. Promising prayers for this intention, the Pope stated that 'we are ready to collaborate in all the initiatives at present judged possible, in the spheres of both study and action.'

In his reply, the Patriarch expressed the hope that

> the road once embarked upon, through the will and good pleasure of God, in these recent years, towards unity should not be limited to the mere rediscovery of communion of brotherly love, but should consist in a widening of encounters and collaboration and should be extended – having in common thoughts, dispositions and actions – to the entire field of the Churches of East and West, in holiness, fidelity and veneration towards the truth transmitted by the Apostles and towards the consciousness

of the structure of the Church, until we attain to full and perfect unity, unity in faith and in the truth of our common Saviour and Lord Jesus Christ, in the common profession of faith . . .

On 7 December the Patriarch and the Pope exchanged telegrams on the occasion of the seventh anniversary of the mutual lifting of the anathemas. The Pope's telegram contained these words:

With Your Holiness we give thanks to the Lord who has permitted us to cancel the memories of the past which hindered our common journey towards full communion. In obedience to the Holy Spirit we have also decided to continue through prayer, study and action our efforts for hastening the day when we shall be able to concelebrate the Divine Liturgy which will set a seal on the full reconciliation of our Churches.

On 2 February 1974, the Pope published the Apostolic Exhortation *Marialis Cultus* (English title: To Honour Mary). Since Catholic belief concerning Our Lady and devotion to her is often seen to be one of the most serious obstacles to reunion between Rome and the Churches of the Reformation, the Exhortation had an evident ecumenical importance. The Pope maintains that devotion to Mary, in forms approved by the Church, has 'developed in harmonious subordination to the worship of Christ,' and 'gravitated towards this worship' as to its 'natural and necessary point of reference'. Devotion to the Blessed Virgin 'is motivated by the Word of God and practised in the Spirit of Christ' (Introd.). Since, as Vatican II affirmed, Mary is 'a most excellent exemplar of the Church in the order of faith, charity and perfect union with Christ,' it follows that she is 'a model of the spiritual attitude' embodied in the liturgy (n. 16). 'In the Virgin Mary everything is relative to Christ and dependent upon him (n. 25). Devotion to the Blessed Virgin, like all Christian piety, 'should have a biblical imprint' (n. 30).

Christ is the only way to the Father (cf. Jn 14:4–11) . . . The Church has always taught this and nothing in pastoral activity should obscure this doctrine. But the Church, taught by the Holy Spirit and benefiting from centuries of experience, recognises that devotion to the Blessed Virgin, subordinated to worship of the divine Saviour and in connection with it, also has a great pastoral effectiveness and constitutes a force for renewing Christian living (n. 57).

On 5 April the Pope issued another Apostolic Exhortation, this time on the needs of the Church in the Holy Land. It is

116

notable that he appeals for financial aid for 'Christians' and not just for 'Catholics'. The different Christian communities there need to grow more closely together, so that 'the Christian presence in the Holy Land, alongside Jews and Muslims, could contribute to harmony and peace'.

The Bull of Indiction of the Holy Year 1975 was promulgated in June 1974. In it the Pope spoke of the ecumenical significance of the Year:

> Finally we wish to proclaim and preach that the reconciliation of Christians is one of the principal aims of the Holy Year. However, before all men can be brought together and restored to the grace of God our Father, communion must be re-established between those who by faith have acknowledged and accepted Jesus Christ as the Lord of mercy who sets men free and unites them in the Spirit of love and truth. For this reason the Jubilee Year, which the Catholic Church has accepted as part of her own custom and tradition, can serve as a most opportune period for spiritual renewal and for the promotion of Christian unity.

Vatican II had taught that

> all true ecumenism must necessarily start from an inner conversion of the heart, since the desire for Christian communion springs and grows from spiritual renewal, self-denial, the full exercise of charity and fidelity to revealed truth.
>
> It is here that there is to be found the full and proper realisation of the whole ecumenical movement, to which the Catholic Church adheres as far as she is able, and through which Churches and communities not yet fully in communion with the Apostolic See seek and desire the perfect unity willed by Christ. It is in fact the task and duty of the whole Church to re-establish this unity in full ecclesial communion. The year of grace, in this sense, provides an opportunity for doing special penance for the divisions which exist among Christians; it offers an occasion for renewal in the sense of a heightened experience of holiness of life in Christ; it allows progress towards that hoped-for reconciliation by intensified dialogue and concrete Christian collaboration for the salvation of the world: 'that they also may be one in us, so that the world may believe.'

On 16 June, in his usual Sunday address, the Pope called for a renewed concern for unity, both the unity of the Church as a whole, which was the object of ecumenism, and 'unity "within" the Church, that unity which is now being threatened by an exaggerated and false kind of pluralism, as well as by systematic and unreasonable principles of dissent from within'.

On 3 September 1974 the Holy Father received in audience the members of the Anglican/Roman Catholic International Commission. Pope Paul recalled his meeting with Archbishop Ramsey in 1966, and continued:

> The Fathers of the Second Vatican Council saw and expressed in the Decree on Ecumenism the 'special place' occupied by the Anglican Communion in relation to the Catholic tradition. The dedication and the depth manifested in your work during these recent years testify to and strengthen that special relationship. This is so not only because of your own industry and achievements, but also because of the collaboration you have been able to enlist in many parts of the world, showing how widespread is the impulse towards that reconciliation in Christ which strives to perfect the unity which he wills.
>
> You interrupt a difficult phase of your work to come to visit us. At such a moment there is no need for us to remind you of the obstacles that remain to be overcome. Let us rather dwell on hope and encouragement. What you seek to do is God's work – an indispensable aspect in our time of the ministry of Christ, which is a ministry of reconciliation. As you do so, our thoughts, our gratitude, our fervent prayers are with you. We pray that you will have the spirit of knowledge and of prophecy, and the faith that moves mountains, but remembering Saint Paul's scale of values, we pray above all that you will have love, which 'bears all things, believes all things, hopes all things, endures all things' and leads us from partial knowledge to full understanding (cf. 1 Cor 13 : 7).

In October 1974 the seventh centenary of the Council of Lyons was celebrated in that city. Orthodox, Anglican, Lutheran and Reformed representatives took part. In a letter appointing Cardinal Willebrands to represent him, Pope Paul recalled the motives which had led Pope Gregory X to call the Council in 1274.

> Chief among these was 'that all who take pride in being called Christian, out of deep sorrow for the insults offered to their Redeemer, might rise up with more power and with patience for the defence of the Holy Land, the assistance of God's cause'. This undertaking, however, was only part of a larger spiritual programme which included the reformation of life in the Church, unity between Greeks and Latins, and peace among nations.

However, several factors prejudiced the aims of the Council:

> There was the growth of the nation states; political affairs in Europe were taking new roads; the treatment of the Orientals by

Christian princes was ruinous for their mutual relations; many who worked for the unity of the Churches were ignorant of the realities of the situation among the Orientals and did not take into account the mentality and the traditions of the Greek Church.

Pope Paul gave reasons why the reconciliation brought about between Rome and the Orthodox in 1274 had been unlikely to last:

> The reconciliation between the two Churches was brought about by the supreme authorities. It was ratified by the Emperor Michael VIII Palaeologus without giving the possibility to the Greek Church of expressing itself freely in this matter. On the other hand, the Latins chose texts and formulae expressing an ecclesiology that had been conceived and developed in the West. These were proposed to the Emperor and the Greek Church to be accepted simply without discussion. It is understandable then that, no matter what may have been the sincerity of its authors, a unity achieved in this way could not be accepted completely by the mentality of the Eastern Christians, and therefore, when the first difficulties arose, it was unhappily broken again.

The Pope then indicated the different mode of proceeding at the present time:

> In our days we see more clearly that an indispensable condition accompanying any effort towards Christian unity is dialogue. . . . However this dialogue demands of those engaged in ecumenical work that 'they give due consideration to these special aspects of the origin and growth of the Churches of the East and to the character of the relations which obtained between them and the Roman See before the separation' (Decree on Ecumenism, (n. 14). Finally whether it be concerned with doctrinal matters or with the more urgent pastoral necessities of our time, this dialogue must be characterised by a fraternal spirit (ibid. n. 18).

Pope Paul was confident that

> the conversations of a truly new kind which have been already begun between ourselves and our brothers of the Orthodox Churches of the East will, with the help of God, permit us to overcome the obstacles with which the Christians of the thirteenth century were faced. Surely this dialogue will not limit itself to the more than thousand-year-old controversy concerning the theology of the Holy Spirit. Rather, in a spirit of patience and mutual love, it will take up again other controverted points of doctrine which Gregory X and the Fathers of Lyons had thought were resolved.

119

The Holy Father thanked God that in seven centuries many obstacles to reconciliation had been removed, and promised:

We shall not hesitate to pursue this work in this age of ours which offers the Church new opportunities. We make our own the almost prophetic words of that Pontiff [Gregory] as we beg 'with much intensity and many tears the Giver of all good gifts, that he in whose unity is founded the unity of faith, the foundation of unity, as the Apostle tells us: "One Lord, one faith", may unite his holy catholic Church by recomposing it and recompose it by uniting it'.

Cardinal Willebrands's sermon, preached in Lyons on 20 October, contained a sensitive account of the reasons why Pope Gregory's efforts failed:

He did not seem to suspect the formidable wave of opposition caused by the diversion of the Fourth Crusade and the conquest of Constantinople, with all its violence and pillage. The attempt to revive Roman imperium in feudal form, known as Rumania, and forced latinisation for some sixty years had caused to take deep root in people's minds and still more in their hearts an invincible hostility to any idea of unity, which, at that time, meant for each and every person in Constantinople submission and unconditional alignment with the theology and usages of the Latins.

Today, however, the Cardinal said, 'we have a healthy plurality necessary for unity'. Pope Paul had spoken to Patriarch Athenagoras of 'the identity of belief lying beyond different vocabularies, beyond different theologies, beyond even the different expressions of this belief'. There is 'respect for different mentalities and cultures... expressed at the level of the customs that have progressively constituted the different canonical traditions of the Churches.... But this diversity can only blossom in full freedom if identity of faith is ensured within full communion.'

That same month the Secretary General of the World Council of Churches, Dr Philip Potter, came to Rome to address the Synod of Bishops. Welcoming Dr Potter, Pope Paul spoke of the aim of the ecumenical movement

in faithfulness to the Lord's prayer, to recompose the ecclesial unity of all those who believe and are baptized in Christ. It finds on its way difficulties and obstacles that go beyond human forces. We warmly encourage and bless efforts in the service of unity, placing our hope 'entirely in the prayer of Christ for the Church, in the love of the Father for us, and in the power of the Holy Spirit.

"And hope does not disappoint, because the charity of God is poured forth in our hearts by the Holy Spirit who has been given to us" (Rom 5:5)' (Decree on Ecumenism, n. 24).

In December 1974, as the Holy Year was about to begin, the Pope issued an Apostolic Exhortation on Reconciliation within the Church. The Church, he said, is the sacrament of God's work of reconciliation between God and man and between man and man. Therefore the Church must itself be reconciled as well as reconciling; 'there must be realised and verified in her that harmony and consistency of doctrine, life and worship which marked the first days of her existence and which ever remain her essential element.' Although the Pope's main concern is the Roman Catholic Church's internal reconciliation among its members, he does not forget the reconciliation of all Christians with one another.

In order to co-operate with God's plans in the world, all the faithful must persevere in fidelity to the Holy Spirit, who unifies the Church in 'fellowship and service' and 'by the power of the Gospel . . . makes the Church grow, perpetually renews her, and leads her to perfect union with her Spouse' (Vatican II, Dogmatic Constitution on the Church, n. 4). This fidelity cannot fail to have happy ecumenical effects upon the quest for the visible unity of all Christians, in the manner laid down by Christ, in one and the same Church; and this Church will thus be a more effective leaven of fraternal oneness in the community of the peoples.

On 10 January 1975 Pope Paul addressed the Liaison Committee between the Catholic Church and World Judaism, following the publication by a Catholic Commission of guidelines to be applied to Jewish/Catholic relations. That document, the Pope stated, 'evoked the difficulties and confrontations . . . which have marked relations between Christians and Jews over the past two thousand years'. This reminder is 'salutary and indispensable', but is only one side of the picture, as the efforts of the Catholic Church on behalf of the Jews under the leadership of Pius XII show. There have been mutual borrowings between Jewish and Christian thought.

We hope that this dialogue, conducted with great mutual respect, will help us to know one another better and will lead us all better to know the Almighty, the Eternal One, to follow more faithfully the ways that have been traced out for us by him who, in the words of the prophet Hosea (11:9) is in our midst as the Holy One, who takes no pleasure in destroying.

121

Preaching on 25 January the Pope spoke again of the dangers and the hopes of ecumenism:

> The heart that loves is always hasty. If our haste is not heeded, love itself makes us suffer. We are conscious of the inadequacy of our efforts. We are aware of the laws of history, which call for a longer period of time than that of our human existence: and it is understandable that the slowness in reaching solutions should seem to make our desires, our attempts, our efforts and our prayers vain. Let us accept this economy of the divine plan; and let us resolve humbly to persevere. But is not perseverance also suffering? Is it not understandable that we should feel a sentiment which consumes itself in expectancy, whose duration is unknown? Ecumenism is a most difficult undertaking. It cannot be simplified to the detriment of faith and of the plan of Christ and of God for the authentic salvation of mankind.
>
> But there is another sentiment that fills our heart with its life-giving breath in regard to ecumenism, that ecumenism which really strives for the re-establishment of unity among all Christians. It is hope. Is it not prayer that nourishes hope? And does not St Paul assure us that 'hope is not deceptive'? (Rom 5:5).

In June theological talks took place between representatives of the Roman Catholic Church and the Russian Orthodox Church. On 3 July the leader of the Russian delegation, Metropolitan Nikodim of Leningrad, was received in audience by the Pope. Greeting the Metropolitan, the Holy Father said:

> It is our ardent prayer that these joint efforts may bear lasting fruit. We pray that the divisions of centuries will be overcome in the truth and charity of Christ, and that the Holy Spirit will bring to completion a work that has been begun under his inspiration – a work that is indeed manifested among the signs of the times.

On 20 November 1975 the Pope wrote to the General Secretary of the World Council of Churches on the occasion of the Fifth Assembly of that body at Nairobi. The letter recalled that Pope Paul was sending sixteen Catholic observers 'because your desire for unity and reconciliation coincides with my own'. He expressed the hope that

> the efforts which the Catholic Church has made and will continue to make to promote the ecumenical movement and, wherever possible, to collaborate with the World Council of Churches will continue and grow even greater with God's help. May the assurance of our fraternal solidarity hearten you for the years ahead.

7 December 1975 was the tenth anniversary of the mutual lifting of the anathemas by the Pope and the Ecumenical Patriarch of Constantinople. Celebrations took place simultaneously on the following Sunday in the Sistine Chapel and in the Church of St George in the Phanar, Constantinople. At the Sistine celebration the leader of the Orthodox delegation, Metropolitan Meliton of Chalcedon, recalled the events of ten years ago, at which Pope Paul had told this anecdote:

'A certain man approached a sage of Greek antiquity and offered him a large reward to teach him the art of remembering. The sage replied that he was willing to give him a reward twice as large in exchange for the art of forgetting.' And Your Holiness added: 'A few minutes ago, we celebrated, in St Peter's Basilica, the act of forgetting a distressing event of the past.'
Today, Your Holiness, we come back to celebrate, this time, an act of memory: memory of the forgetting of the past.

The Metropolitan brought with him a letter from the Ecumenical Patriarch of Constantinople, Dimitrios, in which the Patriarch reiterated 'the ultimate, perfect aim, that is, unity in love, confession of the one Faith in our Lord Jesus Christ, and, by this confession, the attainment of communion in the Holy Eucharist'. The letter is important, because the Patriarch makes it clear that he is speaking 'after consulting our Holy Synod', and not simply for himself as his predecessor had sometimes been criticised for doing. It puts forward the system of the pentarchy (the five patriarchates of Rome, Constantinople, Antioch, Alexandria and Jerusalem) acknowledging to the Bishop of Rome a presidency of love and honour (but not 'of order', as Athenagoras had said):

It is in the Word of God that our Holy Church of Christ in Constantinople embraced the Bishop of Rome and the Holy Church of Rome, in an act which is like a perfume of praise rising towards God from the pentarchy of the One, Holy, Catholic and Apostolic Church, in which the Bishop of Rome is designated to preside in love and honour; it embraces him, rendering him all the honour that is due to him through his designation.

The Patriarch promised 'in all simplicity of heart, but also with austere respect for the ancient Tradition of the One Church ... to promote Christian unity in the framework of the principles that have always been lived by the One, Holy, Catholic and Apostolic Church'. Accordingly 'after an inter-Orthodox consultation', the 'Pan-Orthodox decision' had been taken to initiate theological dialogue with Rome.

The Holy Father in his reply also recalled the act of ten years ago:

> The enthusiasm and piety with which this action was received by the praying congregation in St Peter's Basilica showed us clearly that this event was really desired by the Lord. In fact the Council Fathers, who were finishing their conciliar work with God's blessing, were present on that occasion, as were the religious families and an immense multitude of laymen from various parts of the world.
>
> The conscience of the faithful of the Church saw in this act a sign of atonement for regrettable acts on both sides and the manifestation of a determination to construct together, in obedience to the Lord, a new era of brotherhood, which should lead the Catholic Church and the Orthodox Church, 'with the help of God, to live once more, for the greater good of souls and the coming of the kingdom of God, in the full communion of faith, brotherly concord and sacramental life which existed between them in the course of the first millenium of the Church's life' (Joint Declaration of 7 December 1965).
>
> Ten years after this event, we renew to the Lord our fervent and humble gratitude, now enriched with new and even more important reasons. This act has, in fact, set free so many hearts which, up till then, had been prisoners of their bitterness, locked in reciprocal distrust. Mutual charity has found its intensity again and has become active once more. All of us, at the same moment, heard the voice of the Lord, asking each of us: 'Where is your brother?' (Gen 4:9) . . .
>
> The Holy Spirit has enlightened our intelligences and has brought us to see with increased lucidity that the Catholic Church and the Orthodox Church are united by such a deep communion that very little is lacking to reach the fullness authorising a common celebration of the Lord's Eucharist 'by which the unity of the Church is both signified and brought about' (Vatican II, Decree on Ecumenism, n. 2). . . .
>
> It is charity that has enabled us to become aware of the depth of our unity. In the course of recent years, we have also seen the development of a sense of joint responsibility as regards the preaching of the Gospel to every creature, which is seriously harmed by the persisting division among Christians (Decree on Ecumenism, n. 1).

Pope Paul went on to announce the beginning of theological dialogue both with all the Orthodox Churches and with the Patriarchate of Constantinople individually.

> In this way, in respect of a legitimate liturgical, spiritual, disciplinary and theological diversity (cf. Decree on Ecumenism, nn.

124

14–17), may God grant us to construct, in a stable, certain way, full unity between our Churches!

This dialogue, long before arriving at its final purpose, must aim at influencing the life of our Churches, reviving common faith, increasing mutual charity, drawing closer the bonds of communion, bearing joint witness that Jesus Christ is the Lord and that 'this alone of all the names under heaven has been appointed to men as the one by which we must needs be saved' (Acts 4:12).

It is the divine Spirit himself who asks us to carry out this task. And does not the unbelief that seems to be spreading in the world and to tempt even the faithful of our Churches, does it not call too for a better testimony of faith and unity on our side?

At the same time a similar exchange was taking place at the Phanar. The Archbishop of Naples, who led the Catholic delegation, brought to the Patriarch a letter from Pope Paul, in which the Holy Father spoke of his pleasure 'at the possibility of creating new instruments of theological dialogue'.

In this way (the Pope wrote), in charity, in mutual trust, in reciprocal respect, animated by the one desire to serve the Church of Christ, One and Holy, greater light will be shed on everything that is lived in common in our Churches. In addition, we will have the possibility of discussing in a brotherly way and overcoming wisely the difficulties that still prevent us from celebrating the Lord's Eucharist together.

In his reply the Ecumenical Patriarch spoke of the effects of the lifting of the anathemas.

Starting from different ecclesiologies – different because of negative historical incidents – but led by the same Paraclete and in full awareness of their responsibility for unacceptable faults in the past – the distant as well as the recent past – our two Churches found themselves in agreement concerning the joint step to be taken – in the name of Lord, 'in nomine Domini' – in undertaking the specific step of revoking those actions which at the time had caused so much harm.

This action of revoking the anathemas was 'an ecclesial act which furnishes an example of the new ecclesiastical and theological way of approaching the subject of Church unity'. The Patriarch had, on his own responsibility, 'set in motion the recognised procedural machinery for obtaining a unanimous decision of the Orthodox sister Churches' to undertake theological dialogue with Rome. This dialogue would deal with remaining differences concerning dogma and 'historical-canonical impediments to unity'.

> On the other hand, this dialogue must also direct its attention to the major problem of man today, those contemporary problems which more than ever call for constant attention, problems where it is the duty of our sister Churches, serving and witnessing to the same Lord, to offer their joint service.

At the end of the celebrations at Rome, Pope Paul kissed the feet of Metropolitan Meliton, as the representative of the Ecumenical Patriarch. Patriarch Dimitrios was much moved by this totally unexpected gesture, taking the Metropolitan as the representative of 'the whole of Orthodoxy'. In a statement he said of this act:

> We characterize this great act of His Holiness as a continuation of the tradition of the Bishop Fathers of the undivided Church, who constructed very great things by means of humility.
> By this manifestation the most venerable and our most beloved brother the Pope of Rome Paul VI has excelled himself and has shown to the Church and the world who the Christian bishop and above all the first bishop of Christendom is and can be, namely, a force of reconciliation and unification of the Church and the world.

The phrase 'first bishop' is significant. The impact of the Pope's actions suggests once more that the subject-matter of this book must be papal gestures as well as papal words.

On 8 December 1975, Pope Paul promulgated his Apostolic Exhortation *Evangelii Nuntiandi* (Evangelisation in the Modern World). The subject of the Christian duty to proclaim the Gospel to the world was one which corresponded with the ideals of the Churches of the Reformation. For this reason alone the document was of ecumenical importance. Moreover, the Pope's development of his theme inevitably led him into the consideration of the relations between the Roman Catholic Churches and the other Churches. The 'adherence' which evangelisation aims at arousing in listeners 'cannot remain abstract and unincarnated', but 'reveals itself concretely by a visible entry into a community of believers' (n. 23). 'The Church also has a lively solicitude for the Christians who are not in full communion with her'. This involves 'preparing with them the unity willed by Christ . . . in order to realise unity in truth'. Nevertheless the Church has the consciousness that she would be gravely lacking in her duty if she did not give witness before them of the fullness of the revelation whose deposit she guards (n. 54).

The Pope goes on to consider the relation between the universal Church and the local Churches in terms which envisage great diversity.

Nevertheless this universal Church is in practice incarnate in the individual Churches made up of such or such an actual part of mankind, speaking such and such a language, heirs of a cultural patrimony, of a vision of the world, of an historical past, of a particular human substratum. Receptivity to the wealth of the individual Church corresponds to a special sensitivity of modern man.

Let us be very careful not to conceive of the universal Church as the sum, or, if one can say so, the more or less anomalous federation of essentially different individual Churches. In the mind of the Lord the Church is universal by vocation and mission, but when she puts down her roots in a variety of cultural, social and human terrains, she takes on different external expressions and appearances in each part of the world.

Thus each individual Church that would voluntarily cut itself off from the universal Church would lose its relationship to God's plan and would be impoverished in its ecclesial dimension. But, at the same time, a Church *toto orbe diffusa* (scattered over the whole world) would become an abstraction if she did not take body and life precisely through the individual Churches (n. 62).

As history in fact shows, whenever an individual Church has cut itself off from the universal Church and from its living and visible centre – sometimes with the best of intentions, with theological, sociological, political or pastoral arguments, or even in the desire for a certain freedom of movement or action – it has escaped only with great difficulty (if indeed it has escaped) from two equally serious dangers. The first danger is that of a withering isolationism, and then, before long, of a crumbling away, with each of its cells breaking away from it just as it itself has broken away from the central nucleus. The second danger is that of losing its freedom when, being cut off from the centre and from the other Churches which gave it strength and energy, it finds itself all alone and a prey to the most varied forces of enslavement and exploitation.

The more an individual Church is attached to the universal Church by solid bonds of communion, in charity and loyalty, in receptiveness to the Magisterium of Peter, in the unity of the *lex orandi* (law of praying) which is also the *lex credendi* (law of believing), in the desire for unity with all the other Churches which make up the whole – the more such a Church will be

127

capable of translating the treasure of faith into the legitimate variety of expressions of the profession of faith, of prayer and worship, of Christian life and conduct and of the spiritual influence on the people among which it dwells (n. 64).

In this sense, the Pope said, he had insisted on 'the role of Peter's Successor as a visible, living and dynamic principle of the unity between the Churches and thus of the universality of the one Church' (n. 65). Pope Leo I had accordingly attributed to the Bishop of Rome 'the primacy of the apostolate'; later councils had placed him 'at the highest point of the apostolate' (n. 67).

The chapter entitled 'The Spirit of Evangelisation' devotes several pages to the search for unity.

> The power of evangelisation will find itself considerably diminished if those who proclaim the Gospel are divided among themselves in all sorts of ways. Is this not perhaps one of the great sicknesses of evangelisation today? Indeed, if the Gospel we proclaim is seen to be rent by doctrinal disputes, ideological polarisations or mutual condemnations among Christians, at the mercy of the latter's differing views on Christ and the Church and even because of their different concepts of society and human institutions, how can those to whom we address our preaching fail to be disturbed, disoriented, even scandalised?
>
> The Lord's spiritual testament tells us that unity among his followers is not only the proof that we are his but also the proof that he is sent by the Father. It is the test of the credibility of Christians and of Christ himself. As evangelisers, we must offer Christ's faithful not the image of people divided and separated by unedifying quarrels, but the image of people who are mature in faith and capable of finding a meeting-point beyond the real tensions, thanks to a shared, sincere and disinterested search for the truth. . . .
>
> And it is with a strong feeling of Christian hope that we look to the efforts being made in the Christian world for this restoration of the full unity willed by Christ.

The Pope spoke of his desire

> for a collaboration marked by greater commitment with the Christian brethren with whom we are not yet united in perfect unity, taking as a basis the foundation of baptism and the patrimony of faith which is common to us. By doing this we can already give a greater common witness to Christ before the world in the very work of evangelisation (n. 77).

The ecumenical significance of *Evangelii Nuntiandi* was

128

indicated by Dr Donald Coggan, who had succeeded Dr Michael Ramsey as Archbishop of Canterbury, when he was preaching at an Anglican Church in Rome in April 1977:

> It has commanded the assent, in the main thrust of its argument, of millions not only of our Roman Catholic brethren but of a great number of members of the Anglican Communion and of others besides.

On 26 May 1976 the Holy Father addressed the non-Catholic delegates taking part in a Roman Catholic/Pentecostal Dialogue in Rome, telling them:

> you have been dealing with spiritual resources of which the whole human family has urgent need. Your exchanges have been a testimony to the living power of the Spirit of God experienced in the lives of Christians and offered to all who will accept it. You have spoken together of how faithful souls participate in the reality of God. We believe this is a reality which establishes itself among the faithful as a visible communion, so that they are united not only by a spiritual relationship on the level of mystery and the invisible, but also on the visible level of human realities transformed by the Spirit. It is a communion expressed in the fellowship of the Church which seeks always, according to our Lord's will, to become perfect in unity.

On 25 October 1976, the Pope met a delegation of the Lutheran World Federation. In addressing them as 'Brothers in Christ', he recalled that Cardinal Bea had used this form of words in speaking to the observers at the Council 'in order to underline the unity that all Christians have: a unity which Christ created in baptism itself. In using this very same title now, we wish to communicate to you our joy and gratitude for your visit, which has for its purpose the further advancement of that mutual understanding which is so basic in the movement towards the re-establishment of full ecclesial communion.'

The Pope made special mention of the joint work on Scripture; differences remained, but

> it is nevertheless always true that the Word of God in the Holy Scriptures 'is living and active' (Heb 4:12) and is able to build up and to give the inheritance among all those who are sanctified (cf. Acts 20:32; Vatican II, Dogmatic Constitution on Divine Revelation, n. 21).
>
> And we are likewise convinced of the need for authentic Christian living in accordance with the Gospel, if there is to be hope for the re-establishment of full ecclesial communion. The

Second Vatican Council warned against the idea of limiting ecumenism to doctrinal conversations and practical collaboration, when it stated with profound insight: 'Let all Christ's faithful remember that the more purely they strive to live according to the Gospel, the more they are fostering and even practising Christian Unity' (Decree on Ecumenism, n. 7). And since the full unity of Christians has its highest exemplar and source in the mystery of the Holy Trinity itself (ibid, n. 2), Christians can therefore more deeply and easily grow in mutual fraternal relations to the extent that they enjoy profound communion with the Father, the Word, and the Holy Spirit (ibid. n. 7).

On 13 November 1976, Pope Paul delivered an address to the Plenary Session of the Secretariat for Christian Unity which one Catholic journal suggested might be felt by ecumenists as a 'life-saving shot in the arm'. Speaking of the initial rediscovery of 'bonds of communion that united us in spite of our divergences', the Pope tried to remove the sense of discouragement that some people felt:

The joy of meeting again in this way made many people think, perhaps, that we were on the eve of reaching the goal of refound full communion. Hence their disappointment, their impression of marking time when the theological dialogue was started and developed. Wishing to cure ourselves of the disease of our divisions, it was necessary for us, in a common effort of brotherly lucidity, to discern its real causes and discover its roots. It is inevitable that the progress made in this field should be less perceptible to the general public. It is a question of an effort of renewed and deepened faithfulness to the Word of God, understood and lived in the great multiform tradition of the Church, One Holy, Catholic and Apostolic.

Convergences assert themselves; agreements are outlined on the fundamental realities of baptism, the Eucharist, the ministry of unity in the Church. Studies begin or are continued on the authority of the Church in her teaching. The Catholic Church is determined to continue and intensify her contribution to this common effort of all Christians. It is furthermore 'a requirement of the work of preaching and of the witness to be borne to the Gospel', as we stated in our recent Exhortation on Evangelisation in the modern world (cf. n. 77). . . . And we must all collaborate in promoting this 'civilisation of love', which seems to us to be more and more a necessity of the action of Christians in this world.

The fact that we have not yet arrived at the goal, that serious obstacles are still to be overcome, must not discourage or stop us. . . .

130

We would also like to recall emphatically the fundamental importance of spiritual ecumenism. Change of heart, renewal of the spirit, renunciation of self, the free outpouring of charity, that is the soul of the ecumenical movement (cf. Vatican II, Decree on Ecumenism, nn. 7–8), for which, under this aspect, one and all of the faithful are responsible. . . .

The seeking of unity also calls for complete loyalty to all the demands of truth. This loyalty does not oppose the effort, here and now, to bear witness together with our brothers, to all that we profess in common. But what we must avoid is acting now 'as if' we had reached the goal. This would be to render a very bad service to our march forward. It would delay it considerably by leading it into blind alleys.

From 21 to 30 November 1976 there took place the first Pan-Orthodox Conference in preparation for the Great Holy Council of the Orthodox Churches. The Pope sent a message to Metropolitan Meliton of Chalcedon, the President of the Conference, expressing 'brotherly wishes for complete success', and prayers for the guidance of the Holy Spirit.

We ask the Lord that this Conference may also contribute to preparing the re-establishment of full communion among our Churches and that it will hasten the day when, all obstacles being overcome, we will at last be able to celebrate his one Eucharist together.

The Metropolitan replied on behalf of the Conference, thanking Pope Paul for his 'brotherly sentiments'.

At a general audience held on 19 January 1977, Pope Paul spoke of the week of prayer for Christian unity. He saw the increase in the number of people of all traditions who took part in this prayer as 'an evident sign that people are gaining new awareness of the importance of unity for the life of the Church and for her mission in the world. In this way the deep ties which still unite Christians are becoming more manifest.'

But our supplication to God cannot and must not be limited to one rapidly passing week a year. Prayers are offered incessantly for the unity of Christians in the various Churches also during the whole year. It is necessary to do so every day, since the problem of division is so serious that it undermines Christ's own work. . . . But this week remains the highlight and the moment most pregnant with meaning. It produces, in fact, a communion of spirits, which gives us a foretaste of the day when all Christians, fully united, will glorify God's name with one voice and one heart and will bear concordant and faithful witness to him before the world (cf. Phil 2 : 15).

131

The Pope turned to the subject proposed for the 1977 Week, namely hope, quoting a favourite text: 'hope does not disappoint us' (Rom 5: 5).

> How opportune this appeal is, so that we do not fall into disappointment, so that we do not remain caught up in the web of habit and stop half way. Hope is the moving spirit of the ecumenical cause. It is the star that directs our steps towards the place where the Lord certainly is. St Paul reminds those who, from the first hour, have committed themselves to the search for unity and who, perhaps with a touch of sadness, observe that the desired unity is not yet reached, that 'hope does not disappoint us' and that perseverance is necessary. He reminds those whose interest in this work may now be a matter of routine, no longer creative, that 'hope does not disappoint us' and that it is necessary to strain towards the future and race towards the goal (cf. Phil 3 : 13). He reminds those who are tempted to be satisfied with the positive results already reached in the relations between Christians and who therefore run the risk of stopping at a stage of peaceful coexistence, but not of complete unity, that it is necessary to carry out the work right to the end, attaining finally the goal indicated by the Lord himself, which is that of being 'consecrated in truth' (Jn 17 : 19) and 'perfect in unity' (Jn 17 : 23). And to those who, at the last minute, are in doubt whether to take their place in this movement, St Paul announces with ardent conviction that 'hope does not disappoint us' and that, united with the Lord, it is possible to defeat all resistance and overcome every difficulty.

Christians are already united by their common baptism;

> but they are also called to draw the due ecclesial consequences from the requirement of common baptism, so that Christ may also become 'our peace', in a mutual and ecumenical way (Eph 2 : 14) . . . So there is still a path to be traversed, before we can find ourselves united at last in joint participation in the one Eucharist, which we cannot realise today owing to the lack of full unity in faith.

The Pope recalled that 'Peter's See' should be seen as 'a particular form of service for the unity of the Church'.

> We wish to conclude by stressing again that the search for unity is not just the task of special groups, such as our special Secretariat, but the responsibility of all the baptised and of all Catholics in particular.

On 27 April 1977, retracing the steps that his predecessor

had trodden eleven years previously, the Archbishop of Canterbury paid a three-day visit to Rome. Welcoming the Anglican
delegation, the Pope recalled the 'special place' which Vatican II
had attributed to the Anglican Communion. Recalling the recent
feast of St Anselm of Canterbury, Pope Paul continued:

> At such moments it is natural to think of full communion be-
> tween our Churches. However, we must not see such a celebration
> as mere nostalgia for the past, but rather as a spiritual reality.
> For the liturgy also prophesies what is to come; it is the first-
> fruits, pointing to what is to come.

Referring to recent advances in the relations between the two
Churches, Pope Paul stated:

> The pace of this movement has quickened marvellously in recent
> years so that these words of hope 'the Anglican Church united
> but not absorbed' [words of Dom Lambert Beauduin, adopted by
> Cardinal Mercier] are no longer a mere dream.

In a reference to Dr Coggan's evangelical spirituality, the Pope
observed:

> You yourselves, Brethren, are concerned that the Gospel should
> be translated into deeds, and renew its significance for a society
> of Christian tradition. As our predecessor Pius XI put it, 'the
> Church civilises by evangelising'.
> That Gospel is the heart and soul of your Christian living
> and it is equally our inspiration. The civilisation of love is our
> shared hope – something which is utopia for the worldly-wise, but
> prophecy for those who live in truth.

Two days later the Pope and the Archbishop attended a joint
service in the Sistine Chapel, exchanging addresses and the kiss
of peace. In his discourse Pope Paul spoke of Dr Coggan's
'desire for common witness to Christian faith and hope'.

> It is the experience of all of us today that the world desperately
> needs Christ. The young, in whose aspirations good is often seen
> most vividly, feel this need most strongly. Secular optimism does
> not satisfy them. They are waiting for a proclamation of hope.
> Now is our chance to bear witness together that Christ is indeed
> the way, and the truth and the life, and that he is communicated
> through the Holy Spirit.

The Pope recalled that when he had met Dr Ramsey, they had
given a 'pledge to a serious dialogue which, founded on the

133

Gospels and on the ancient common traditions, may lead to that perfect unity in truth for which Christ prayed'.

It is good that, while our experts continue their work, we should meet humbly to encounter our Lord in prayer. Indeed we might think of the example of Moses, supported by Aaron and Hur, holding up his arms in supplication for Israel (cf. Ex 17:10–13). . . .

We know that a long road remains to be travelled. But does not one of the most moving accounts of the Risen Christ in Saint Luke's Gospel tell us how, as two of the disciples travelled a road together, Christ joined them and 'interpreted to them in all the Scriptures the things concerning himself'? (Lk 24:27).

The Archbishop in his discourse, after speaking of the world 'still dark in larger part where the Gospel has not penetrated', continued:

Let us pray also for ourselves, that, as we are united by baptism and by a living faith, so, strengthened by the word of God's grace and by the Body and Blood of Christ, we may reach out in joint evangelistic action to those for whom our Saviour Christ was contented to be betrayed and given up into the hands of sinful men.

. . . And may we, in the intimacy of an increasingly deep communion, together be the agents of God's love and peace in the power of the Holy Spirit.

At the end of the service, the Pope and the Archbishop issued their Common Declaration. It began by speaking of the achievements of the eleven years that had elapsed since Dr Ramsey's visit, making special mention of the three documents produced by the Anglican/Roman Catholic International Commission.

We now recommend that the work it has begun be pursued, through procedures appropriate to our respective Communions, so that both of them may be led along the path towards unity.

The moment will shortly come when the respective Authorities must evaluate the conclusions.

The response of both communions to the work and fruits of theological dialogue will be measured by the practical response of the faithful to the task of restoring unity, which, as the Second Vatican Council says, 'involves the whole Church, faithful and clergy alike' and 'extends to everyone according to the talents of each' (Decree on Ecumenism, n. 5) . . .

In mixed marriages between Anglicans and Roman Catholics,

where the tragedy of our separation at the sacrament of union is seen most starkly, co-operation in pastoral care (*Matrimonia Mixta,* n. 14) in many places has borne fruit in increased understanding. Serious dialogue has cleared away many misconceptions. . . .

The Declaration affirms that the goal of dialogue was 'the restoration of complete communion in faith and sacramental life'; we must 'move forward resolutely to the communion of mind and heart for which Christ prayed'.

It is this communion with God in Christ through faith and through baptism and self-giving to him that stands at the centre of our witness to the world, even while between us communion remains imperfect. Our divisions hinder this witness, hinder the work of Christ (*Evangelii Nuntiandi,* n. 77) but they do not close all roads we may travel together. In a spirit of prayer and of submission to God's will we must collaborate more earnestly in a 'greater common witness to Christ before the world in the very work of evangelisation' (ibid.). It is our desire that the means of this collaboration be sought: the increasing spiritual hunger in all parts of God's world invites us to such a common pilgrimage.

This collaboration, pursued to the limit allowed by truth and loyalty, will create the climate in which dialogue and doctrinal convergence can bear fruit. While this fruit is ripening, serious obstacles remain both of the past and of recent origin. Many in both communions are asking themselves whether they have a common faith sufficient to be translated into communion of life, worship and mission. Only the communions themselves through their pastoral authorities can give that answer. When the moment comes to do so, may the answer shine through in spirit and truth, not obscured by the enmities, the prejudices and the suspicions of the past.

To this we are bound to look forward and to spare no effort to bring it closer: to be baptised into Christ is to be baptised into hope – 'and hope does not disappoint us because God's love has been poured into our hearts through the Holy Spirit which has been given us' (Rom 5:5).

Christian hope manifests itself in prayer and action – in prudence but also in courage. We pledge ourselves and exhort the faithful of the Roman Catholic Church and of the Anglican Communion to live and work courageously in this hope of reconciliation and unity in our common Lord.

During his visit, Dr Coggan preached at the American Episcopalian Church of St Paul's Within-the-Walls. In the course of his sermon he showed that, unlike the Pope and the Orthodox leaders, he did not believe that shared communion need wait for total agreement in faith. In the light of the Agree-

135

ments of the Anglican/Roman Catholic International Commission, and of the shared commission to preach Christ to 'a world of doubt and cynicism, and, very frequently, of wistful searching', he asked:

> Has not the time now arrived when we have reached such a measure of agreement on so many of the fundamentals of the Gospel that a relationship of shared communion can be encouraged by the leadership of both our Churches? I would go further and ask whether our work of joint evangelisation will not be seriously weakened until we are able to go to that work strengthened by our joint participation in the Sacrament of Christ's Body and Blood? The day must come when together we kneel and receive from one another's hands the tokens of God's redeeming love and then directly go, again together, to the world which Christ came to redeem.

On 26 May 1977 Cardinal Villot, the Pope's Secretary of State, wrote in Pope Paul's name to the President of the Faith and Order Commission on the occasion of that Commission's fiftieth anniversary. Speaking of the Holy Father's interest in their work, the Cardinal wrote:

> The visible organic unity willed by Christ among all the members of his body is the object of your research and your efforts. It is the goal of the ecumenical movement. Of course different ways should be used at the same time in working towards this goal, but the Catholic Church has a particular interest in the one which is proper to your Commission, because the Church is convinced that unity in the faith, in 'the Apostles' teaching' (Acts 2:42), is the fundamental element of the communion which we ask God to re-establish among us. . . . It is urgent, as a matter of fact, that Christians be all together (cf. Acts 5:12) concerning the content of their witness because their unity is the sign which should bring the world to believe (cf. Jn 17:21), and their division is a scandal which hampers evangelisation.

At the end of June 1977, a delegation from the Ecumenical Patriarchate of Constantinople paid its now customary annual visit to Rome. The Patriarch Dimitrios, in a message conveying to Pope Paul 'our brotherly greeting and our warm wishes', concluded with the hope that

> Christ, our true God who, in his ineffable love for man, has given us the strength and the joy of reconciliation, will bless our effort in the future until we arrive at perfect communion in the same chalice of the Lord . . .

Replying to the Ecumenical Patriarch, the Pope wrote that the presence of the Orthodox delegation

> shows clearly that the bonds of brotherhood which are being woven anew, more and more closely, between the old and the new Rome, are now such that everything that concerns the life of one of the two sister Churches is also lived by the other in communion in the same Spirit.

Pope Paul reiterated his 'unshakeable decision to go forward, in full harmony with you, along the road that must lead us to celebrate the Lord's Eucharist together'.

On 27 June the head of the Orthodox delegation, Archbishop Meliton, in addressing Pope Paul, spoke of the Orthodox tradition of 'lived theology' which 'expresses itself in ecclesiastical deeds'. Thus, by sending a delegation to Rome for the Feast of SS Peter and Paul, the Orthodox were *doing theology*: 'until recently these were internal affairs of the Roman Church; today in the new structure of our church life in common they are a matter of *pietas* also for the Orthodox Church'. So too the Pope's visit to Constantinople ten years ago

> was no ordinary visit but a visit in the biblical sense. Hence it is not a matter of simply recalling a historical fact or estimating it as a past event: rather of understanding the theological and ecclesiological import of the visit in the sacred cause of unity.

The Metropolitan in conclusion spoke of the work of the inter-Orthodox theological commission which was preparing for theological dialogue with the Church of Rome.

In his reply, the Pope, after recalling his meetings with Patriarch Athenagoras, continued:

> During these last years, the good relations between our Churches have deepened and multiplied. As a result, we now have, twice each year, an exchange of delegations. This permits fruitful reciprocal information which is indispensable for harmonising our efforts in the progress towards a regained full communion.

During 1977, in a series of addresses delivered to national groups of bishops paying their *ad limina* visits, Pope Paul referred to the duty of ecumenism. The fullest treatment of the subject was contained in the words with which he greeted the Scandinavian bishops on 2 May:

> Above all, however, you with your communities are faced with the delicate problem of religious relations with Christian brothers

separated from us. The fact of finding yourselves side by side with them cannot prevent you, but on the contrary urges you, to form ties of sincere friendship in the name of our one Saviour and Lord Jesus Christ; this is possible, without, however, going too far, adopting an ambiguous ecumenism which renounces its own orginal context and is passively ready to let itself be absorbed. Catholics, in your countries, have values of their own to guard: the riches of the doctrinal deposit, faithfulness to it while duly updating it as the Council desired, the duty of evangelisation in conviction and joy, communion with the universal Church, obedience to the successor of Peter and union with his ministry which guarantees ecclesial unity, respect for the wholesome values of culture and progress, sincere and constructive brotherhood. These are all *tesserae* of a splendid mosaic, which gives an extraordinarily beautiful and persuasive image of Catholicism in your lands. This may lead to a fruitful rapprochement with other brothers of Christian denomination on the way to the recomposition of unity in the Lord Jesus.

On 30 November, receiving a delegation sent by the Orthodox Patriarch Pimen of Moscow, the Pope spoke of his appreciation of such visits, which deepened 'our relations, for people love each other more ardently when they know each other better'.

And we have much to learn from one another in order to make the Gospel heard by a world in which both individuals and peoples have so much need of reconciliation and peace.

The same day, a Catholic delegation under Cardinal Willebrands visited Constantinople. The delegation attended the Orthodox Eucharist at the Phanar (a significant gesture). At the end of the liturgy, addressing the Ecumenical Patriarch, the Cardinal spoke of the 'signs of ecclesial communion' between the two Churches, founded on a 'common patrimony' of Scripture, transmitted through tradition, illuminated through the reflection of the Fathers, defended and proclaimed in seven Councils'.

Is it not the sacramental reality which makes this communion solid and substantially unalterable? We believe, in effect, Catholics and Orthodox, that the Church is the great sacrament of salvation, the pillar and foundation of truth. This profound conviction is the fundamental reality on which the relations between our two Churches, the relations between sister Churches, are based.

The Cardinal read out a message sent by Pope Paul to the Patriarch, in which the Pope recalled the tenth anniversary of the last Patriarch's visit to Rome, and the ikon the Patriarch gave the Pope, depicting

> Peter and Andrew [the patron saint of Constantinople] embracing with the blessing of Christ the Lord. This gesture betokens the programme to be carried out through an ever greater sharing in the truth, until the day comes – so greatly to be longed for – when the bishop of Rome and the bishop of Constantinople will be able to exchange the kiss of peace in the concelebration of the most Holy Eucharist. For this it is necessary that the obstacles that still exist between us should be surmounted. . . .
>
> On this unity depends the credibility of the witness we have to give to Christ in the world today.

Patriarch Dimitrios in reply stated his views on the direction that the coming dialogue between the two Churches should take.

On 7 December 1977 the Pope received a letter from the Ecumenical Patriarch, and a present of a lamp from his private chapel in honour of his eightieth birthday, 'as a humble expression of love, brotherly honour and our gratitude to your venerated person as the first Bishop of Christendom in the world' – a significant term. The occasion of the visit was the twelfth anniversary of the lifting of the anathemas. Pope Paul, in replying, connected the visit with the Advent season, and spoke of 'the bracing wind of messianic hope'. In words echoing those of Cardinal Willebrands, the Pope said:

> the dialogue between our Churches, based on the sacramental reality itself, benefits from a solid foundation which holds out the hope of overcoming the difficulties which do not yet permit a concelebration of the Eucharist.

Speaking at a general audience on 18 January 1978, during what was to be his last Week of Prayer for Christian Unity, Pope Paul spoke of 'this ever pressing question of ecumenism, that is, the recomposition of the real union, in faith and in discipline, of those who believe in Jesus Christ'.

> It is, in fact, a duty, a constitutional one, we may say, for all Christians to be united with one another, to be, according to Jesus Christ's will, 'one single thing' (Jn 17:11–23). It is a duty that the centuries of divisions among Christians do not weaken, but make more appreciable, while our times impose with even clearer awareness the necessity that Christians be unified!
>
> The first thing to do is to be aware of this duty! It is Christ's solemn will! We have become accustomed to a paradoxical situation, that of thinking that we are real Christians even though

the divisions among those who call themselves Christians exist in fact, and are serious, multiple and deep-rooted. . . . But the difficulties of re-establishing a real unitarian fusion of the various Christian denominations are such as to paralyse all human hope that it can be realised historically. The ruptures that have taken place have ossified, solidified and organised themselves in such a way that one may characterise as utopian all attempts to reconstruct in dependency on Christ, the head, 'a body', as St Paul describes it, 'joined and knit together by every joint with which it is supplied, when each part is working properly', so that it builds itself up in charity (Eph 4 : 16).

The problem of the unity of Christians seems insoluble, moreover, also because of the fact that it is a question of real unity. It is impossible to admit any unauthorised pluralistic interpretation of this sacred word 'unity', which is illustrated by the example of the ineffable unity of the heavenly Father and the divine Son (Jn 17:22). The city of the Mystical Body of Christ, which is the Church, admits, nay more demands, a multiplicity of functions (Eph 4 : 11-15), but always in the organic union of one faith and one charity.

And this requirement, compared with the concrete and historical conditions of the various segments of faithful belonging to the various Christian denominations, seems to discourage all ecumenical hope; history does not turn back! Yet this cannot be so. Christ's saying: 'Let them all be one!', is not only a precept for us, but it is also a prophetic promise. . . . It cannot remain unfulfilled!

The Week of Prayer, therefore, prompts 'two positive conclusions'. The first was that 'You are no longer strangers'.

This is another saying of St Paul which teaches us that there is already in progress a communion, a charity, which enables us to call 'brothers' also those Christians who are, unfortunately, still divided from true Christian unity. . . . There already exist bonds of union that we cannot ignore or underestimate; bonds that are not perfect; bonds which still show the laceration suffered by the whole organic structure of the Mystical Body; bonds which demand from the mother Church that they should be rejoined with immense patience and exemplary humility, but which are still capable of new and worthy vitality; shattered bonds, which must not be, today, a motive of inextinguishable polemics, but a motive of increased love if they still favour a return to the ancestral house.

So the second conclusion is: 'we must pray.'

What can prayer not obtain? Here is the secret hope for the re-establishment of unity among Christians.

On 15 July 1978 Pope Paul sent his last message to the Ecumenical Patriarch of Constantinople. The exchange of delegations to Rome and Constantinople for the feasts of SS Peter and Paul and St Andrew, he said,

> concretise and reinforce the spiritual links uniting Catholic and Orthodox. These celebrations permit us to renew before the Lord our common involvement in the search for full unity. For the People of God, and in front of the world, they provide a witness to charity and they constitute the pledge of the hope that animates us to celebrate one day together the one Eucharist of the Lord.

On 18 July he sent a message to the Anglican Lambeth Conference.

On 6 August Pope Paul died. It was said that his gestures were the beautiful thing about him, and many of those gestures concerned unity. In his Testament he wrote:

> As regards ecumenism: the approach to the separated Brethren must go on, with great understanding and patience, with great love; but without deflecting from the true Catholic doctrine.

POPE JOHN PAUL I

7. TOO SHORT A CHAPTER

THE election of Cardinal Albino Luciani, Patriarch of Venice, as Paul VI's successor surprised the world. He at once impressed himself on the Romans, and through television on the world, as a warm-hearted, modest man who liked a joke, practised a cheerful informality, and appeared to be taken completely by surprise by his sudden elevation. Instead of an aura of other-worldly dedication, people felt they could recognise in him human feelings like their own. He was the son of a Venetian glass-worker. As Patriarch he had taken to journalism in order to reach a larger audience; his letters to characters of real life or fiction (including Christopher Marlowe, G. K. Chesterton, the Pickwick Club and Pinocchio), later collected under the title *Illustrissimi*, were not only humorous and self-mocking *jeux d'esprit*, but showed skill in the communication of a serious and topical religious message in a light-hearted and imaginative way. What would this unassuming, laughing, original mind make of the papacy? He had had contact, as Patriarch, with the sessions of dialogue between Catholics and Anglicans, and Catholics and Orthodox that had taken place in Venice.

He was elected, after only one day of conclave, on 26 August 1978. That Saturday night he spent on his inaugural address to be delivered to the cardinals after Mass in the Sistine Chapel the following day. In it he spoke of the Church's call 'to give the world that spiritual injection that is required from so many areas and which alone can give assurance of salvation'. He needed, he said, the memory of his predecessors to help him, especially that of Paul VI, a 'great and humble man' of 'extraordinary scope', whose 'prophetic gestures ... marked his unforgettable pontificate'. He then set out the policy he intended to follow in his pontificate, continuing the programme of Paul VI, 'in the path already indicated by the great heart of John XXIII'. The 'first duty' of the Church was evangelisation, from which he turned to the subject of ecumenism:

> We wish to continue our ecumenical effort which we consider the ultimate task of our immediate predecessors, watching with unchanging faith, with lively hope, and with never ending love for the realisation of the great command of Christ: 'That all may be one,' in which we see vibrating the anxiety of his heart on the eve of his sacrifice on Calvary.

The mutual relationships between the Churches of various denominations have achieved constant and extraordinary progress, and this is before everyone's eyes. But the division does not, however, cease to cause perplexity, contradictions and scandal in the eyes of non-Christians and non-believers.

And to this end we intend to dedicate our prayerful attention, to all that can favour unity without yielding doctrinally but also without hesitation.

We wish to continue with patience and firmness that peaceful and constructive dialogue that Paul VI, whom we can never mourn too much, placed as a foundation and as a programme of his own pastoral actions, giving the major lines in his great encyclical *Ecclesiam Suam*.

These lines call for a reciprocal knowledge between men, even those who do not share our faith, always ready to give them the testimony to the faith that is in us, and to the mission that Christ has given us.

This statement of John Paul I's ecumenical programme nowhere goes beyond the views that Paul VI had already expressed; indeed, the note of pluriformity, which Paul had struck so repeatedly, is missing here. However, it is not the details of the statement which are important, for it was, after all, put together without preparation in the small hours of the night. What is significant is the weight which the new Pope attached to the reunion of Christians: of the space which John Paul devoted to the setting out of his policy, a third is given over to ecumenism and dialogue.

Paul VI's pontificate had shown the close connection which existed in his mind between the two questions of the papacy and of ecumenism. Accordingly the indications which John Paul gave as to his conception of the papal office are important for our purposes. In his inaugural address he spoke of his desire 'strongly to emphasise' the collegiality of the bishops, and to 'make use of their efforts in the government of the universal Church'. He chose not to receive the papal tiara; he decided to call the ceremony of 3 September the 'inauguration of his ministry as Supreme Pastor', rather than his 'coronation' or 'enthronement' as Vicar of Christ, Supreme Pontiff or Head of the Church. He abolished many of the ceremonial accompaniments of the papacy. These were the signs that John Paul I might have shown other Churches that the papacy could work as the servant of unity within collegiality without threatening their traditions or authority.

At the Mass of his inauguration, Pope John Paul addressed the delegations sent by other Churches as follows:

In this way we greet affectionately and with gratitude the delegations from other Churches and Ecclesial Communities present here. Brethren not yet in full communion, we turn together to Christ our Saviour, advancing all of us in the holiness in which he wishes us to be and also in the mutual love without which there is no Christianity, preparing the paths of unity in faith, with respect for his Truth and for the Ministry that he entrusted, for his Church's sake, to his Apostles and their Successors.

On 5 September the Pope received in audience the Orthodox Metropolitan Nikodim of Leningrad, who, in the pontificate of Paul VI, had shown himself a great friend of unity with Rome. The Metropolitan had attended the Pope's inauguration. While in conversation with the Holy Father, he was struck by a heart attack and died immediately. The Pope at once sent a telegram of condolence to the Patriarch of Moscow, Pimen, promising prayers for the repose of the soul of 'this devoted servant of his Church and constructor of deepening relations between our Churches'.

On the night of 28–29 September Pope John Paul himself succumbed to a massive heart attack, and was found dead in his bed next morning. What might a pontificate which started with such promise have achieved for the reunion of Christians?

POPE JOHN PAUL II

8. BEGINNINGS

ON 16 October 1978, Karol Wojtyla, Archbishop of Krakow, was elected Pope, and showed his intention of following the lines of his predecessors by choosing the title John Paul II. He had attended all the sessions of the Council, and therefore the conciliar debates which contributed to the evolution of the Decree on Ecumenism. But the challenges which had helped to shape his strong character had little to do with Christian reunion. The preoccupation of Catholics in Poland had been to survive and safeguard Christian and human liberties, in the face first of the Nazis and then of the Communists. Before ordination he had shown his capabilities as poet and actor. He then studied for the priesthood in the shelter of the residence of the Archbishop of Krakow under the Nazi occupation. After ordination he turned to moral philosophy, and eventually became professor of that subject at the Catholic University of Lublin. His approach has in some respects remained that of a philosopher rather than a theologian. His method has been said to be deductive, in that he is never content simply to restate or even reinterpret tradition, but seeks to rethink the human implications of a question. His favourite theme is the dignity of the human person. His ecumenical experience scarcely extended beyond contact with the small Polish Orthodox Church. How would this original and tough-minded man build on the ecumenical foundations laid by his predecessors?

In 1972, while still Archbishop of Krakow, Cardinal Wojtyla had published a commentary on the documents of Council, which was published in English translation in 1980 under the title *Sources of Renewal*. Although much of the work consists of quotations from the conciliar documents, the future Pope showed his own convictions not only by his comments on these quotations, but also by his choice of passages to cite and emphasise. He devotes more than one chapter of the book to ecumenism.

> The true ecumenical attitude . . . is the expression of a profound love for man and respect for his inner liberty (p. 313).
> Members of 'separated Christian communities' are 'with good reason accepted as brothers by the children of the Catholic Church' (Decree on Ecumenism, n. 3; p. 315).

The ecumenical attitude must be marked in the first place by full respect for human beings, by readiness to meet and co-operate with them, and by a 'dialogue' or exchange of opinions on doctrinal matters, which of course presupposes adequate theological preparation (p. 318).

It is not only a question of praying for the separated brethren but also of praying with them so that the Church may become one (p. 318).

The Council is well aware that the schisms that have taken place through history have left a deep mark on human souls and the organisation of the separated communities. Humanly speaking they appear irreversible and insurmountable; but it must be remembered that ecumenical action and a truly ecumenical attitude can be born only of the hope, based on faith, that, although the Church is divided by men, in the mind and will of Christ it is one and undivided (p. 319).

It is an attitude . . . that, far from avoiding the 'test' of dialogue, manifests in dialogue its own spiritual maturity (p. 32).

The path of ecumenical cooperation seems closer and more accessible than that of theological dialogue (p. 325).

There is 'a certain duality in the authentic ecumenical attitude'.

It involves the aspiration to unity and a tendency to claim that that unity is already stronger than any division; but we must not forget to respect the discipline of faith and obedience to the truth already possessed by various communities. Without such recognition we may do a disservice to the true progress of unity. The discipline of faith and loyalty to professed truth does not conflict with the Augustinian principle: *in necessariis unitas, in dubiis libertas, in omnibus caritas* (in necessary things unity, in doubtful things liberty, in all things charity: p. 326).

The day after his election, Pope John Paul II, like the pope he succeeded, in his address to the cardinals made special mention of collegiality and ecumenism. On the latter subject he said:

At this point we cannot forget our brothers of other Churches and Christian confessions. The cause of ecumenism is in fact so great and so delicate that we cannot now let it go unmentioned. How many times have we meditated together on the last will of Christ, who asked the Father for the gift of unity for his disciples. And who does not recall St Paul's insistence on the 'communion of the spirit' (Phil 2: 1), which unites people in love with a common purpose and a common mind, in imitation of Christ the Lord? It does not seem possible that the drama of the division among Christians should still remain – a cause of confusion and perhaps even of scandal. We intend, therefore, to proceed along the way already mapped out, by encouraging those initiatives which serve to remove obstacles, in the hope that, thanks to a common effort, we might finally achieve full communion.

On collegiality, after speaking of the links that join the bishops to the Pope and to one another, he spoke suggestively of the 'appropriate development of those bodies, sometimes new, sometimes updated, which can secure a better union of heart, will and initiative in building up the Body of Christ which is the Church'.

On 22 October, following the precedent set by John Paul I, he celebrated the 'inauguration of his ministry as Supreme Pastor', with a great reduction in external pomp. In his homily he spoke of his decision, like his predecessor, to dispense with the tiara. His text was Peter's confession of faith: 'You are the Christ, the Son of the living God' (Mt 16: 16); his theme was: 'Open wide the doors for Christ'. At the end of his homily he addressed these words to the representatives of other Churches:

I open my heart to all my brothers of the Christian Churches and communities, and I greet in particular you who are here present, in anticipation of our coming personal meeting: but for the moment I express to you my sincere appreciation of your having wished to attend this solemn ceremony.

The central emphasis on Christ, and the reference to the non-Catholics as 'brothers' were likely to be well received by those outside the Roman Catholic Church.

The Pope received the delegates of the other Churches later the same day. In his address he once more referred to divisions among Christians as an 'intolerable scandal, hindering the proclamation of the good news of salvation given in Jesus Christ, and the announcement of this great hope of liberation which the world needs so much today'.

At this first meeting, we are anxious to tell you of our firm resolution to go forward along the way to unity in the spirit of the Second Vatican Council and following the example of our predecessors. A fine stretch has already been covered, but we must not stop before arriving at the goal, before realising this unity which Christ wishes for his Church and for which he prayed.

The will of Christ, the witness to be borne to Christ, that is the motive that incites one and all of us not to tire or become discouraged in this effort. We are confident that he who began

153

this work among us, will give us abundantly the strength to persevere and carry it out successfully.

Please say to those whom you represent, and to everyone, that the commitment of the Catholic Church to the ecumenical movement, such as it was solemnly expressed in the Second Vatican Council, is irreversible.

We rejoice at your relations of brotherly trust and collaboration with our Secretariat for Unity. We know that you are searching patiently, along with it, for the solution of the differences that still separate us, and the means of progressing together in more and more complete faithfulness to all aspects of the truth revealed in Jesus Christ. We assure you that we will do everything to help you.

May the Spirit of love and truth grant that we may meet often and in increasing closeness, more and more in deep communion in the mystery of Christ our one Saviour, our one Lord. May the Virgin Mary be for us an example of this docility to the Holy Spirit which is the deepest centre of the ecumenical attitude; may our answer always be like hers: I am your servant, let it be to me according to your word (Lk 1 : 38).

The Council had made Mary the model of the Church; John Paul was now making her the model of ecumenism.

On 18 November 1978, Pope John Paul addressed a plenary session of the Secretariat for Unity. He repeated his pledge to carry out the directives of the Council with regard to Christian Unity, 'seeing this as one of my first duties'.

A movement does not stop, should not stop before reaching its goal. We have not reached it, even though we have to thank God for the road we have covered since the Council. . . . But our haste to get there, the eagerness to put an end to the intolerable scandal of Christian divisions, means that we must avoid 'all superficiality, all rash enthusiasms which might hinder the progress towards unity' (Decree on Ecumenism, n. 24). You do not heal a sickness by giving painkillers but by attacking its causes.

The Pope recalled that the Church, according to the Council, is chiefly manifested in the assembly of all the people with the priests and ministers round the bishop for the celebration of the Eucharist. 'In every Eucharist it is the whole faith of the Church that comes into play; it is ecclesial communion in all its dimensions that is manifested and realised.'

We cannot arbitrarily separate its component parts. To do so would be to fall into that superficiality the Council tells us to guard against. It would be a failure to perceive the close relations between Eucharist and church unity, their richness, the

154

demands they make on us. I know that the more we find that we are brothers in the charity of Christ, the more painful it is for us not to be able to take part together in this great mystery. Have I not said that the divisions between Christians are becoming intolerable? This suffering should incite us to overcome the obstacles which still hold us back from unanimous profession of the same faith, from the reunification of our divided communities by means of the same sacramental ministry. We cannot escape the obligations of solving together those questions which have divided Christians.

The Pope quoted Cardinal Bea's principle: 'seek the truth in charity', and recalled that the Secretariat for Unity throughout the thirteen years of its existence had not only searched for agreement with other Christians, but had also tried to 'promote throughout the Catholic Church a mind and spirit loyally at one with the wishes of the Council – something without which the positive results achieved in the various dialogues could not be received by the faithful.' Hence the importance of taking account of ecumenism 'in teaching theology and forming the outlook of future priests'

> Indeed there should be no loosening of the bond, still less opposition, between the deepening of the Church's unity by renewal and the search for restoration of unity among divided Christians. Both are aspects of the same unity for which Christ prayed and which is brought about by the Holy Spirit; there should therefore be an unceasing interaction between them as between two manifestations of a single pastoral effort which must come from the whole Church.

It was evident from this speech that Pope John Paul, while committed to the ecumenical aims of Vatican II and Paul VI, was prepared to think out traditional positions in his own terms. This was, for example, probably the most reasoned exposition of the case against intercommunion that a Pope had ever made. Moreover, it was evident that the Pope was aware of the need for what is sometimes called 'grass-roots' ecumenism, i.e. the fostering of ecumenical attitudes in the minds of the faithful.

Pope John Paul II continued the half-yearly exchange of visits with the Orthodox Patriarchate of Constantinople which had become the custom during the pontificate of Paul VI. The Catholic delegation which visited Constantinople for the feast of St Andrew, 30 November 1978 brought to the Patriarch Dimitrios a letter from the Pope. The Holy Father thanked the Patriarch for the letters and representatives he sent in connection with the deaths of the last two popes and the inauguration of their successors. He expressed his hopes for the planned theological dialogue. He went on to speak of the papal office:

> The particular ministry which I have just assumed in the Church has for its foundation the confession of faith of the apostle Peter. 'Thou art the Christ, the Son of the living God' (Mt 16:16). Christ is the centre of our faith. . . . He is the ultimate goal of all our striving. . . .
> To serve unity is an essential part of my new ministry. It is a service which conforms to the will of Christ for his Church. It is also a response to the world of today to which all Christians should give a single witness of their faith in Christ 'who came that they might have life and have it more abundantly' (Jn 10:10).

So the Holy Father at once brings the papal ministry into his exchange of greetings with the Orthodox; but it should be noticed that he speaks in terms, not of authority or jurisdiction, but of ministry and service.

The Ecumenical Patriarch in his reply spoke, in the now familiar language, of 'the election of the new head of the sister Church of Rome'.

> We ardently desire Dialogue and Unity. . . . We believe in the force of the word and of dialogue. . . .
> We have already by our common efforts travelled a long and arduous road in preparing for our theological dialogue, both on the Pan-Orthodox and the Roman Catholic side. . . .
> . . . With common and parallel decisions and action, between you and us, between Western and Eastern Orthodoxy in equality and reciprocally.

On 17 January 1979 the Pope spoke at a general audience on the Week of Christian Unity which was about to begin. It was an 'important subject which commits every baptized person, pastors and faithful, each according to his own capacity, his function, and the place he occupies in the Church'. It placed a special obligation on the Pope: 'service of unity is the primary duty of the Bishop of Rome.' Consequently in the diocese of Rome, as throughout the world, the Week of Prayer was intended to involve everyone; 'the attempt is being made to organise also common prayers with the other brother Christians.'

Prayer for unity was 'the soul of the whole ecumenical movement' (Vatican II, Decree on Ecumenism, n. 8).

> Prayer puts us, first and foremost, before the Lord, purifies us in intentions, sentiments, in our heart, and produces that 'interior conversion', without which there is no real ecumenism (cf. ibid. n. 7).

156

Prayer, furthermore, reminds us that unity, ultimately, is a gift of God, a gift for which we must ask and for which we must prepare in order that we may be granted it.

But 'the action of God requires our answer', an answer which is shown especially in 'prayer, mutual love, service of one another', which 'construct fellowship among Christians and put them on the way to full unity'.

'In this week our prayer for the unity of Christians must be, above all, prayer of thanks and supplication'. God should be thanked for planting among Christians the desire for unity, for the progress in official dialogue with other Churches, and for the 'brotherly relations' existing between the Catholic Church and other Churches – an attitude existing not only among leaders, but which was 'gradually penetrating into the local Churches; for a change of relations on the local plane is indispensable for all further progress.'

> So let us renew our prayer to the Lord, in order that he may give Christians light and strength to do everything possible to obtain full unity in truth as soon as possible, so that 'speaking the truth in love, we (shall) grow up in every way into him who is the head, into Christ . . .' (Eph 4 : 15–16).

In the address he put especial emphasis (as had Pope Paul VI) on relations with the Orthodox, with whom 'the dialogue of charity has made us rediscover a communion that is almost full, even if still imperfect'. He spoke of the 'theological dialogue' about to open between these two Churches with the aim of eliminating 'those difficulties which still prevent eucharistic concelebration and full unity'.

In the same month the Pope addressed the Italian Bishops' Conference, and spoke of the principles of collegiality. Just as the Pope is the visible source of unity in the Church as a whole, so the individual bishop is the visible source of unity in his local church. He spoke of the need to 'bring back to the fullness of ecclesial communion those movements, organisations and groups',

> which, born of a desire for generous and meaningful commit-ment to the Gospel, do not yet fall within that community perspective which is necessary for an ever more conscious living out of the common responsibility of the people of God.

In one of his first references to pluriformity, he continued:

157

The balance between institutional unity and pastoral pluralism is a difficult goal, and one that is never definitely achieved; it depends on the concerted and constant efforts of all members of the ecclesial body and must be sought in the light of the always relevant maxim, *in necessariis unitas, in dubiis libertas, in omnibus caritas* (in necessary things unity, in doubtful things liberty, in all things charity).

In January 1979 the Pope flew to Mexico to address the General Assembly of the Latin American Bishops meeting at Puebla. One section of his address of 28 January he devoted to the subject of unity. His words referred principally to the need for Catholics to be united in their efforts to repair the social injustices of the subcontinent, but he did have this to say about ecumenism: 'we must safeguard the precious gift of ecclesial unity between all those who form part of the pilgrim people of God.'

On 23 February 1979 Pope John Paul sent a message to the Joint Working Group of the World Council of Churches and the Secretariat for Unity. In it he spoke of his 'desire that efforts to hasten the re-establishment of unity among all Christians should be intensified'.

> For it is a matter of urgency that we should be able to bear witness to our faith in Christ and his saving work with complete accord. Yet even now, even before this unity of faith, sacramental life and hierarchical bonds is re-established, it is our duty, while honestly recognising our actual situation today, to find ways whereby we may bear witness to the faith we already share and to the real though incomplete fellowship which already unites us in Christ and in the mystery of his Church.

This was perhaps John Paul's first indication that the Church in his conception was not simply identical with the Roman Church, but included other Christians in a 'real though incomplete fellowship'.

On 12 March the Holy Father welcomed representatives of several Jewish organisations. In his address he affirmed:

> I believe that both sides must continue their strong efforts to overcome the difficulties of the past so as to fulfil God's commandment of love, and to sustain a truly fruitful and fraternal dialogue that contributes to the good of each of the partners involved and to our better service of humanity.

The Pope published his first encyclical, *Redemptor Hominis*, on 15 March 1979. One section of it deals explicitly with Christian unity and reveals the Holy Father's own deep convictions on the subject, for it appeared that the Pope drafted the text himself, after months of deliberation. This section (6) is entitled 'The road to Christian unity'.

What shall I say of all the initiatives that have sprung from the new ecumenical orientation? The unforgettable Pope John XXIII set out the problem of Christian unity with evangelical clarity as a simple consequence of the will of Jesus Christ himself our Master, the will that Jesus stated on several occasions but to which he gave expression in a special way in his prayer in the Upper Room the night before he died: 'I pray . . . Father . . . that they may all be one' (Jn 17:21; cf. 17:11, 22–23; 10:16; Lk 9:49, 50, 54). The Second Vatican Council responded concisely to this requirement with its Decree on Ecumenism. Pope Paul VI, availing himself of the activities of the Secretariat for Promoting Christian Unity, began the first difficult steps on the road to the attainment of that unity. Have we gone far along that road? Without wishing to give a detailed reply, we can say that we have made real and important advances. And one thing is certain: we have worked with perseverance and consistency, and the representatives of other Christian Churches and Communities have also committed themselves together with us, for which we are heartily grateful to them. It is also certain that in the present historical situation of Christianity and the world the only possibility we see of fulfilling the Church's universal mission, with regard to ecumenical questions, is that of seeking sincerely, perseveringly, humbly and also courageously the ways of drawing closer and of union. Pope Paul VI gave us his personal example for this. We must therefore seek unity without being discouraged at the difficulties that can appear or accumulate along that road otherwise we would be unfaithful to the word of Christ, we would fail to accomplish his testament. Have we the right to run this risk?

The Pope then sought to reassure those who were discouraged by the results of the ecumenical movement.

There are people who in the face of the difficulties or because they consider that the first ecumenical endeavours have brought negative results would have liked to turn back. Some even express the opinion that these efforts are harmful to the cause of the Gospel, are leading to a further rupture in the Church, are causing confusion of ideas in questions of faith and morals and are ending up with a specific indifferentism. It is perhaps a good thing that the spokesmen for these opinions should express their fears. However, in this respect also, correct limits must be maintained. It is obvious that this new stage in the Church's life demands of us a faith that is particularly aware, profound and

159

responsible. True ecumenical activity means openness, drawing closer, availability for dialogue, and a shared investigation of the truth in the full evangelical and Christian sense; but in no way does it or can it mean giving up or in any way diminishing the treasures of divine truth that the Church has constantly confessed and taught. To all who, for whatever motive, would wish to dissuade the Church from seeking the universal unity of Christians the question must once again be put: Have we the right not to do it? Can we fail to have trust – in spite of all human weakness and all the faults of past centuries – in our Lord's grace as revealed recently through what the Holy Spirit said and we heard during the Council? If we were to do so, we would deny the truth concerning ourselves that was so eloquently expressed by the Apostle: 'By the grace of God I am what I am, and his grace towards me was not in vain' (1 Cor 15:10).

The title of Section 11 of the encyclical was 'The mystery of Christ as the basis of the Church's mission and of Christianity'. In it the Pope spoke of religion as 'a universal phenomenon linked with man's history from the beginning'. But

in Christ and through Christ God has revealed himself fully to mankind and has definitely drawn close to it; at the same time, in Christ and through Christ man has acquired full awareness of his dignity, of the heights to which he is raised, of the surpassing worth of his own humanity, and of the meaning of his own existence.

This thought leads the Pope back to the subject of Christian unity.

All of us who are Christ's followers must therefore meet and unite around him. This unity in the various fields of the life, tradition, structures and discipline of the individual Christian Churches and ecclesial Communities cannot be brought about without effective work aimed at getting to know each other and removing the obstacles blocking the way to perfect unity. However, we can and must immediately reach and display to the world our unity in proclaiming the mystery of Christ, in revealing the divine dimension and also the human dimension of the Redemption, and in struggling with unwearying perseverance for the dignity that each human being has reached and can continually reach in Christ, namely, the dignity of both the grace of divine adoption and the inner truth of humanity, a truth which – if in the common awareness of the modern world it has been given such fundamental importance – for us is still clearer in the light of the reality that is Jesus Christ.

On 29 March 1979 Pope John Paul addressed the Board of Directors of the 'Pro Oriente' Foundation, a charity founded in Vienna in the early 'sixties for the fostering of dialogue between the Orthodox and non-Chalcedonian Churches and Rome. In the course of his address the Pope spoke appreciatively of Eastern traditions:

> . . . you have contributed to better reciprocal acquaintance, to a deeper understanding of the different historical developments and traditions of the individual Churches of the East and of the West, and to a more conscious recognition of the rich common heritage which already exists.

On 5 May 1979 the Pope received the Bishops of the Antilles (Carribbean), who were making their *ad limina* visit. 'Communion and ministry,' he told them, 'are indeed two great aspects of the Church's unity, of which we are the servants and guardians.' Communion is the heart of the mystery of the Church, a communion which is a communion of faith with God. Pope John Paul recalled that in his address to the Secretariat for Unity he had promised to make Christian reunion 'one of my first duties'. He recalled the Council's phrase 'spiritual ecumenism' (Decree on Ecumenism, n. 8), and the need for fidelity to Christ and of 'conversion or change of heart'.

The Pope drew attention to his remarks to the Secretariat concerning the 'pain' of divisions, which is to be healed not by 'painkillers but by attacking its causes'. He repeated that eucharistic sharing presupposes unity in faith.

> Intercommunion between divided Christians is not the answer to Christ's appeal for perfect unity. God has set an hour for the realisation of his salvific design for perfect unity. As we yearn for this hour, in common prayer and dialogue, and endeavour to offer an ever more purified heart to the Lord, we must also wait for the Lord's action. It must be said and said again that the restoration of Christian unity is above all a gift of God's love. Meanwhile, on the basis of our common baptism and the patrimony of faith that we already share, we must intensify our common witness to the Gospel and our common service to humanity.

On 19 May 1979 the Holy Father received a group of Orthodox theological students who had been invited by the Catholic Committee for Cultural Collaboration to attend courses in Catholic institutions. He pointed out that the students had the chance to get acquainted with the new spirit of the Catholic Church, the great effort of theological reflection and pastoral renewal carried out at all levels of the life of the Catholic Church, especially after the recent Council. An effort of spiritual deepening, purifying tension towards what is essential, increasingly dynamic and consistent faithfulness to our one Lord and to all aspects of his message of salvation, which we must announce to the men and women of today.

The Pope went on to speak of 'the possibilities of collaboration between the Catholic Church and the venerable Orthodox Churches', which 'spring from the communion which, although not yet full, already unites us'.

This collaboration is not only possible immediately, but it is necessary, if we really wish to be faithful to Christ. . . . Today more than ever, in a world that demands authenticity and consistency, our division is an intolerable counter-testimony. It is as though we denied in our lives what we profess and proclaim.

I wished to communicate these thoughts to you, on receiving you here for the first time, to ask you to tell your Bishops and your Patriarchs my firm determination to collaborate with them to progress towards full unity, manifesting in the life of our Churches that unity that already exists among us. That charity without deception, in which we have found ourselves again and met again in recent years, must become inventive and courageous to find safe and rapid paths which will lead us to that full communion which will seal our faithfulness to our one Lord.

On 21 May 1979 Pope John Paul addressed a group of Superiors General of non-Catholic religious orders of men and women who were in Rome for a series of ecumenical meetings on the religious life. He spoke first of religious life as 'the practical recognition of the absolute primacy of Christ in the Church and in the world', and as 'a new and special title of fulfilling the universal call of all God's people to holiness'. He then considered the 'ecclesial aspects of religious life'; it received the guarantee of ecclesiastical authority, and bore a relationship to the entire Body of Christ. Therefore religious life was relevant to the question of Church unity.

Who more than religious should experience in prayer the urgency, not only of manifesting unity, but also of living it in the fullness of truth and charity? And as we experience this urgency – an experience which is itself a gift of God – do we not likewise experience the need for that increased personal purification, for that ever greater conversion of heart that God seems to be requiring as a prerequisite for the restoration of the corporate

162

unity of all Christians? And does not the spiritual freedom that religious endeavour to acquire in adhering totally to the Lord Jesus bind them ever more closely, in love, to pursue to the end the will of Christ for his Church? Are religious not called in a special way to give expression to the yearning of Christians that the ecumenical dialogue – which by its nature is temporary – should be brought to term in that full ecclesial fellowship which is 'with the Father and with his Son Jesus Christ' (1 Jn 1:3)? Should religious not be the first to pledge the fullness of their generosity before God's salvific plan, each one repeating with Saint Paul: 'What am I to do, Lord?' (Acts 22:10).

On 23 June 1979, Pope John Paul received a delegation from the Coptic Orthodox Church of Alexandria. The Patriarch had visited Paul VI in Rome, when the Pope and the Patriarch had issued a joint declaration of faith in Christ. The importance of that declaration can hardly be exaggerated, for it showed both Churches willing to discover their identity of faith which was obscured by the fact that the Catholic Church was committed to the validity of the description of the humanity and divinity of Christ as two 'natures', while the Coptic Church was equally committed to the rejection of this formulation. This was a very clear case of diversity permissible even in formulations of essential doctrine.

Pope John Paul's words showed that he also could find unity in faith under differing expressions:

> How marvellous are the ways of the Lord! He permits us to profess today our common faith in Jesus Christ, his divine Son, true God and true man ... We rejoice together that the doubts and suspicions of the past have been overcome so that with full hearts we can proclaim together once again this fundamental truth of our Christian faith.

> From the very first days of my election as Bishop of Rome, I have considered as one of my principal tasks that of striving to bring about the unity of all those who bear the holy name of Christian. The scandal of division must be resolutely overcome, so that we may all fulfil in the lives of our Churches and in our service to the world the prayer of the Lord of the Church 'that all may be one'. I have stressed this on a number of occasions already. I repeat it to you now, since what is involved here is the communion between two apostolic Churches such as ours.

The Holy Father then referred to the position of the papacy in a united Church.

> I know that one of the fundamental questions of the ecumenical movement is the nature of that full communion we are seeking with each other and the role that the Bishop of Rome has to

play, by God's design, in serving that communion of faith and spiritual life, which is nourished by the sacraments and expressed in fraternal charity. A great deal of progress has been made in deepening our understanding of this question. Much remains to be done. I consider your visit to me and to the See of Rome a significant contribution towards resolving this question definitively.

Pope John Paul then treated explicitly of diversity, without however saying expressly that this permissible diversity could include statements of faith.

Fundamental to this dialogue is the recognition that the richness of this unity in faith and spiritual life has to be expressed in diversity of forms. Unity – whether on the universal level or the local level – does not mean uniformity or absorption of one group by another. It is rather at the service of all groups to help each live better the proper gifts it has received from God's Spirit. This is an encouragement to move ahead with confidence and reliance upon the guidance of the Holy Spirit.

The Pope then spoke of the need to overcome long-standing mistrust, especially at the level of the local churches.

Whatever may be the bitterness inherited from the past, whatever may be the present doubts and tensions that may exist, the Lord calls us to move forward in mutual trust and in mutual love. If true unity is to be achieved, it will be the result of cooperation among pastors on the local level, of the collaboration at all levels of the life of our Churches so that our people may grow in understanding of each other, in trust and love of each other. With no one trying to dominate each other but to serve each other, all together will grow into that perfection of unity for which Our Lord prayed on the night before he died (Jn 17) and for which the Apostle Paul exhorted us to work with all diligence (Eph 4 : 11–15).

The Coptic Patriarch, Shenouda III, had sent with the delegation a letter to the Pope in which he spoke of the improved relations between the two Churches, mentioning especially the return of the relics of St Mark in 1968, the Joint Declaration of the two Popes of Rome and Alexandria in 1973, and the progress made in theological dialogue.

It became clear that our two Churches confess and profess in essence almost the same teaching that Christ our Lord is God Incarnate, who is perfect in his Divinity, meantime he is perfect in his Humanity. His Godhead and his Manhood are united together inseparably and unconfusedly. In Ecclesiology only very little real progress has been reached.

The usual delegation came from Constantinople to Rome to celebrate the feast of SS Peter and Paul. Its customary leader, the Metropolitan Meliton, gave to the Pope a letter from the Patriarch of Constantinople. In it the Patriarch recognised Pope John Paul's 'brotherly sentiments for us', so that 'we are in the communion of charity'. Once more Dimitrios acknowledged in the Bishop of Rome one 'who lovingly presides within the whole of Christendom'. He recalled that the custom of exchanging visits

> has already been inaugurated between our two Churches by your great predecessor of blessed memory Pope Paul VI in the reality of our refound brotherhood, and in joint witness to the fact that, from the Apostles, in a continual succession, we have maintained the service of the apostolicity of the Church in the East as well as in the West.

Pope John Paul, addressing the delegation, also alluded to the custom of exchanging visits.

> These contacts, which are being increasingly intensified, bring us closer and closer to the full unity that is so much desired. In the past, time, adverse circumstances, the weaknesses and faults of men, drove our Churches to ignorance of each other, sometimes even to hostility. Today, by the grace of God and by virtue of the good will of men attentively listening to the Lord, there is a firm resolution on both sides to do everything to re-establish full unity. The contacts between the Churches, between those who bear special responsibilities in them as well as among their faithful, contribute to teaching us to live together in prayer, in consultation in view of common solutions to give to the problems that are raised for the Churches today, in mutual aid, in brotherly life.

The Holy Father, like the Patriarch and the Metropolitan, spoke of the theological dialogue between the two Churches, for which the preparations had been completed.

> I can assure you that the Catholic Church tackles this dialogue with a fervent desire for the re-establishment of full unity, in all frankness and honesty with regard to her Orthodox brothers, in a spirit of obedience to the Lord, who founded his Church as one and who wants her to be fully united so that she may be a

sign and means of deep union with God and of the unity of the whole of mankind, and an effective instrument of the preaching of the Kingdom of God among men.

As the first year of the new pontificate drew to its end, it was possible to compare John Paul II's understanding of ecumenism with that of Paul VI. Pope John Paul was evidently as passionately devoted to the reunion of Christians as his predecessor; both saw ecumenism as an essential Christian duty. Both popes aimed at perfect unity, and ruled out intercommunion until this perfect unity, especially unity in faith, was established. Both insisted on the need for conversion of heart before Christians could be ready to receive God's gift of unity. Pope Paul worked out in greater detail the steps involved in the process of dialogue, and gave more explicit attention to the Church's need of diversity, even in doctrine. Pope John Paul, on the other hand, placed greater stress on the need and the possibility of immediate pastoral co-operation among the Churches, especially at the local level. Both Popes saw the need to overcome mutual irrational suspicions.

9. IRELAND, AMERICA, CONSTANTINOPLE

THE autumn of 1979 saw the Pope engaged on a series of visits, during which the issue of ecumenism was never far from the centre of attention. In Ireland, however polite the relations between the leaders of the main churches, talk about reunion among Christians was conducted in the shadow of the gunman, against an accompaniment of ranting speeches by demagogic politicians intent on keeping open the old wounds of hatred and suspicion. On his arrival at Dublin on 29 September, Pope John Paul proceeded at once to Drogheda. Politics and violence prevented him from getting any closer to the historic primatial see of Armagh, which is in the North. There at Drogheda, in his first speech, the Pope referred to the invitations he had received to visit Armagh, from Protestant leaders as well as from the Catholic Primate:

> For all these invitations I am particularly grateful.
> These invitations are an indication of the fact that the Second Vatican Council is achieving its work and that we are meeting our fellow-Christians of other churches as people who together confess Jesus Christ as Lord, and who are drawing closer to one another in him as we search for unity and common witness.
> This truly fraternal and ecumenical act on the part of representatives of the churches is also a testimony that the tragic events taking place in Northern Ireland do not have their source in the fact of belonging to different churches and confessions; that this is not – despite what is so often repeated before world opinion – a religious war, a struggle between Catholics and Protestants. On the contrary, Catholics and Protestants, as people who confess Christ, taking inspiration from their faith and the Gospel, are seeking to draw closer to one another in unity and peace. When they recall the greatest commandment of Christ, the commandment of love, they cannot behave otherwise.

The Pope then spoke at some length of justice, peace and the dignity of man. 'On his knees' he pleaded with men and women engaged in violence to 'return to the ways of peace'. He urged those 'who are called to the noble vocation of politics to have the courage to face up to your responsibility'. In conclusion he addressed an appeal directly to Protestants:

167

May no Irish Protestant think that the Pope is an enemy, a danger, or a threat. My desire is that instead Protestants would see in me a friend and a brother in Christ. Do not lose trust that this visit of mine may be fruitful, that this voice of mine may be listened to. And even if it were not listened to, let history record that at a difficult moment in the experience of the people of Ireland, the Bishop of Rome set foot in your land, that he was with you and prayed with you for peace and reconciliation, for the victory of justice and love over hatred and violence. Yes, this our witness finally becomes a prayer, a prayer from the heart for peace for the peoples who live on this earth, peace for all the people of Ireland.

Returning to Dublin, Pope John Paul celebrated and preached at an open-air Mass for a vast crowd in Phoenix Park. Later that evening he met forty representatives of other Christian Churches. In his address to them, the Pope told them how happy he was 'to come together with you in the holy name of Jesus and pray with you'. Many of his familiar themes appeared in the speech: it was a gift of God that Christians had come to realise more clearly the need to be 'perfectly one in Christ and in his Church'; the desire for Christian unity springs from fidelity to Christ's will; 'it determines the credibility of our witness before the world'. He then continued:

Today has indeed been a memorable day in my life: to have embraced in the love of Christ my separated Christian brethren and to confess with them 'that Jesus Christ is the Son of God' (1 Jn 4:15); that he is 'the Saviour of all men' (1 Tim 5:10); that he is 'the one Mediator between God and men, the man Christ Jesus' (1 Tim 2:5). From Drogheda this afternoon I appealed for peace and reconciliation according to the supreme will of Christ, who alone can unify the hearts of men in brotherhood and common witness.

Pope John Paul went on to reaffirm the Catholic Church's ecumenical commitment:

Let no one ever doubt the commitment of the Catholic Church and of the Apostolic See of Rome to the pursuit of the unity of Christians. Last November, when I met the members of the Secretariat for Promoting Christian Unity, I spoke of the 'intolerable scandal of division between Christians'. I said that the movement towards unity must not stop until it has reached its goal; and I called for an energetic commitment by Catholic bishops, priests and people to forward this movement, I said on that occasion: 'The Catholic Church, faithful to the direction taken at the Council, not only wants to go forward on the way that leads to the restoration of unity, but is anxious, according to its means and in full submission to the promptings of the Holy Spirit . . . to strengthen at every level its contribution to this great movement of all Christians' (Address of 18 November 1978). I renew that commitment and that pledge today here in Ireland, where reconciliation between Christians takes on a special urgency, but where it also has special resources in the tradition of Christian faith and fidelity to religion which marks both the Catholic and the Protestant communities.

The work of reconciliation, the road to unity, may be long and difficult. But, as on the way to Emmaus, the Lord himself is with us on the way, always making 'as if to go on' (Lk 24 : 28). He will stay with us until the longed-for moment comes, when we can join together in recognizing him in the Holy Scriptures and 'in the breaking of the bread' (Lk 24 : 35).

Meanwhile, the internal renewal of the Catholic Church, in total fidelity to the Second Vatican Council, to which I pledged all my energies at the beginning of my papal ministry, must continue with undiminished vigour. This renewal is itself an indispensable contribution to the work of unity between Christians. As we each, in our respective Churches, grow in our searching of the Holy Scriptures, in our fidelity to and continuity with the age-old tradition of the Christian Church, in our search for holiness and for authenticity of Christian living, we shall also be coming closer to Christ, and therefore closer to one another in Christ.

It is he alone, through the action of his Holy Spirit, who can bring our hopes to fulfilment. In him we place all our trust : in 'Jesus Christ our hope' (1 Tim 1 : 1). Despite our human weakness and our sins, despite all obstacles, we accept in humility and faith the great principle enunciated by our Saviour : 'What is impossible with men is possible with God' (Lk 18 : 27).

May this day truly mark, for all of us and for those whom we serve in Christ, the occasion for ever greater fidelity, in prayer and penance, to the cause of Jesus Christ, and to his message of truth and love, of justice and peace. May our common esteem and love for the holy and inspired word of God unite us ever more, as we continue to study and examine together the important issues affecting ecclesial unity in all its aspects, as well as the necessity for a united service to a world in need.

In his homily at his Mass in Phoenix Park earlier that day, Pope John Paul spoke of the erosion of the traditional moral standards of Irish life, and the temptations to 'materialism', 'self-indulgence and consumerism', and false attitudes to life and sexuality. Now he appealed to all Christians to join in safeguarding spiritual and moral values:

169

Ireland, dear brothers in Christ, has special and urgent need for the united service of Christians. All Irish Christians must stand together to defend spiritual and moral values against the inroads of materialism and moral permissiveness. Christians must unite together to promote justice and defend the rights and dignity of every human person. All Christians in Ireland must join together in opposing all violence and all assaults against the human person – from whatever quarter they come – and in finding Christian answers to the grave problems of Northern Ireland. We must all be ministers of reconciliation. We must by example as well as by word try to move citizens, communities and politicians towards the ways of tolerance, co-operation and love. No fear of criticism, no risk of resentment, must deter us from this task. The charity of Christ compels us. Precisely because we have one common Lord, Jesus Christ, we must accept together the responsibility of the vocation we have received from him.

Dear brothers: with a conviction linked to our faith, we realise that the destiny of the world is at stake, because the credibility of the Gospel has been challenged. Only in perfect unity can we Christians adequately give witness to the truth. And so our fidelity to Jesus Christ urges us to do more, to pray more, to love more.

May Christ the Good Shepherd show us how to lead our people along the path of love to the goal of perfect unity for the praise and glory of the Father, and of the Son, and of the Holy Spirit. Amen.

Next day the Holy Father addressed the Irish bishops, stressing the idea of collegiality:

I come also as your brother bishop from Rome, and I have greatly looked forward to this day: so that we may celebrate together the unity of the episcopate of our Lord Jesus Christ, so that we may give public expression to a dimension of our episcopal collegiality. . . .

Later in his speech the Pope turned directly to ecumenism:

I recall with deep satisfaction a significant feature in the series of events connected with my journey to Ireland. It is highly significant that the invitation from the episcopate, through its four archbishops, was followed by invitations from other churches, especially from Irish Anglicans. I take the opportunity to stress this once again and to express my renewed thanks and appreciation to them. I see in this circumstance a very promising sign of hope.

The witness of faith in Christ which we share with our brethren must continue to find expression not only in prayer for full unity but also in prayer and sustained effort for reconciliation and peace in this beloved land.

Pope John Paul flew on from Ireland to the United States on 1 October. It was not until the last day of his visit that he devoted an address expressly to the subject of ecumenism, but several of his other speeches during the six days touched on the subject in passing. At New York on 3 October he addressed some words to the Jewish community:

Several common programmes of study, mutual knowledge, a common determination to reject all forms of anti-Semitism and discrimination, and various forms of collaboration for human advancement, inspired by our common biblical heritage, have created deep and permanent links between Jews and Catholics. As one who in my homeland has shared the suffering of your brethren, I greet you with the word taken from the Hebrew language: Shalom!

On 5 October he devoted a section of an address to the bishops in Chicago to the subject of ecumenism:

The will of Christ impels us to work earnestly and perseveringly for unity with all our Christian brethren, being mindful that the unity we seek is one of perfect faith, a unity in truth and love. We must pray and study together, knowing, however, that inter-communion between divided Christians is not the answer to Christ's appeal for perfect unity. And with God's help we will continue to work humbly and resolutely to remove the real divisions that still exist, and thus restore that full unity in faith which is the condition for sharing in the Eucharist.

On 7 October the Holy Father met more than five hundred representatives of different Christian Churches in Washington. He began by recapitulating some of his earlier statements so as to show that 'since the inception of my pontificate, almost a year ago, I have endeavoured to devote myself to the service of Christian unity'.

With great satisfaction and joy I welcome the opportunity to embrace you, in the charity of Christ, as beloved Christian brethren and fellow disciples of the Lord Jesus. It is a privilege to be able, in your presence and together with you, to give expression to the testimony of John, that 'Jesus Christ is the Son of God' (1 Jn 4:15), and to proclaim that 'there is one Mediator between God and men, the man Christ Jesus' (1 Tim 2:5).

In the united confession of faith in the divinity of Jesus Christ, we feel great love for each other and great hope for all humanity. We experience immense gratitude to the Father, who has sent his Son to be our Saviour, 'the expiation for our sins, and not for ours only but for the sins of the whole world' (1 Jn 2:2).

By divine grace we are united in esteem and love for Sacred Scripture, which we recognise as the inspired word of God. And it is precisely in this word of God that we learn how much he wants us to be fully one in him and in his Father. Jesus prays that his followers may be one 'so that the world may believe . . .' (Jn 17:21). That the credibility of evangelisation should, by God's plan, depend on the unity of his followers is a subject of inexhaustible meditation for all of us.

The Pope went on to refer in detail to the many theological dialogues which the Roman Catholic Church in America was carrying on with other Christian communions.

My gratitude goes to all who collaborate in the matter of joint theological investigation, the aim of which is always the full evangelical and Christian dimensions of truth. It is to be hoped that, through such investigation, persons who are well prepared by a solid grounding in their own traditions will contribute to a deepening of the full historical and doctrinal understanding of the issues.

The particular climate and traditions of the United States have been conducive to joint witness in the defence of the rights of the human person, in the pursuit of goals of social justice and peace, and in questions of public morality. These areas of concern must continue to benefit from creative ecumenical action, as must the fostering of esteem for the sacredness of marriage and the support of healthy family life as a major contribution to the well-being of the nation. In this context, recognition must be given to the deep division which still exists over moral and ethical matters. The moral life and the life of faith are so deeply united that it is impossible to divide them.

Much has been accomplished but there is still much to be done. We must go forward, however, with a spirit of hope. Even the very desire for the complete unity in faith – which is lacking between us, and which must be achieved before we can lovingly celebrate the Eucharist together in truth – is itself a gift of the Holy Spirit, for which we offer humble praise to God. We are confident that through our common prayer the Lord Jesus will lead us, at a moment dependent on the sovereign action of his Holy Spirit, to the fullness of ecclesial unity.

Faithfulness to the Holy Spirit calls for interior conversion and fervent prayer . . . It is important that every individual Christian search his or her heart to see what may obstruct the attainment of full union among Christians. And let us all pray that the genuine need for the patience to await God's hour will never occasion complacency in the *status quo* of division in faith. By divine grace may the need for patience never become a substitute for the definitive and generous response which God asks that there be given to his invitation to perfect unity in Christ.

And so, as we are gathered here to celebrate the love of God that is poured out in our hearts by the Holy Spirit, let us be conscious of the call to show supreme fidelity to the will of Christ, let us together perseveringly ask the Holy Spirit to remove all divisions from our faith, to give us that perfect unity in truth and love for which Christ prayed, for which Christ died: 'to gather together in unity the scattered children of God' (Jn 11:52).

The same day Pope John Paul made this prayer to the Blessed Virgin in the National Shrine of the Immaculate Conception in Washington:

I entrust to you the great work of ecumenism here, in this land, in which those who confess Christ belong to different Churches and communions. I do this in order that the words of Christ's prayer may be fulfilled: 'That they may be one.' I entrust to you the consciences of men and women and the voice of public opinion, in order that they may not be opposed to the law of God but follow it as the fount of truth and good.

Pope John Paul's Apostolic Exhortation on catechesis, *Catechesi Tradendae*, published on 16 October 1979, contained two sections (32-33) on the ecumenical dimension of catechesis, and ecumenical collaboration in catechesis. 'Catechesis,' he wrote, 'cannot remain aloof from this ecumenical dimension, since all the faithful are called to share, according to their capacity and place in the Church, in the movement towards unity.' This dimension will be present if three conditions are fulfilled. First, 'while not ceasing to teach that the fullness of the revealed truths and of the means of salvation instituted by Christ is found in the Catholic Church', catechists must do so 'with sincere respect, in words and in deeds, for the ecclesial communities that are not in perfect communion with this Church'. Consequently 'it is extremely important to give a correct and fair presentation of the other Churches and ecclesial communities that the Spirit of Christ does not refrain from using as means of salvation . . . This presentation will help Catholics to have both a deeper understanding of their own faith and a better acquaintance with and esteem for their other Christian brethren, thus facilitating the shared search for the way towards full unity in the whole truth.' Secondly, catechesis should create and foster a true desire for unity, so as to inspire

173

serious efforts – including the effort of self-purification in the humility and the fervour of the Spirit in order to clear the ways – with a view not to facile irenics made up of omissions and concessions on the level of doctrine, but to perfect unity, when and by what means the Lord will wish.

Thirdly, catechesis must 'prepare Catholic children and young people, as well as adults, for living in contact with non-Catholics, affirming their Catholic identity while respecting the faith of others'.

> In situations of religious plurality, the bishops can consider it opportune or even necessary to have certain experiences of collaboration in the field of catechesis between Catholics and other Christians, complementing the normal catechesis that must in any case be given to Catholics. Such experiences have a theological foundation in the elements shared by all Christians. But the communion of faith between Catholics and other Christians is not complete and perfect; in certain cases there are even profound divergences. Consequently, this ecumenical collaboration is by its very nature limited; it must never mean a 'reduction' to a common minimum. Furthermore, catechesis does not consist merely in the teaching of doctrine: it also means initiating into the whole of Christian life, bringing full participation in the sacraments of the Church. Therefore, where there is an experience of ecumenical collaboration in the field of catechesis, care must be taken that the education of Catholics in the Catholic Church should be well ensured in matters of doctrine and of Christian living.

On 26 October the Holy Father addressed the members of the International Theological Commission. In what was probably the most explicit statement yet of his pontificate on doctrinal diversity, he stated that theological pluralism was legitimate so long as it did not detract from the purity of the deposit of faith. The Pope asked the theologians not to confine themselves to a repetition of dogmatic formulations, but rather to help the Church to deepen its understanding of Christ.

On 23 November Pope John Paul gave an address to delegates representing fifty-eight countries taking part in a conference for representatives of National Ecumenical Commissions. The Pope spoke of 'the close collaboration that must exist between the local churches and the Holy See' in this matter.

> Some years ago the Secretariat in its document on ecumenical collaboration emphasised, on the one hand, the proper initiative of the local Church in ecumenical work at the local level and,

on the other hand, the need to take care that such initiatives are undertaken within the limits of the doctrine and discipline of the whole Catholic Church. These principles are clearly reflected in the character and composition of your present meeting.

Pope John Paul then put forward his reflections on the theme of the conference: 'Ecumenism as a pastoral priority in the Church's work'.

You are here to discuss *ecumenism*. This word should not evoke that false fear of the adjustments necessary to any genuine renewal of the Church (cf. Ecumenical Directory 1, 2). But still less is ecumenism a passport to indifferentism or to neglect of all that is essential to our sacred tradition. Rather it is a challenge, a vocation to work under the guidance of the Holy Spirit for the visible and perfect oneness in faith and love, in life and work, of all who profess faith in our one Lord Jesus Christ. Despite the rapid progress of recent years, much remains to be done.

Two aspects of this work were theological dialogue, and co-operation with other Christians 'in work for social justice, human rights, development and the relief of need'. But there was another, 'equally vital, aspect'.

One of the principal tasks of ecumenical commissions at every level is to promote unity by placing before the Catholic people the aims of ecumenism, aiding them to respond to this urgent vocation which they should see as integral to their baptismal calling. This vocation is a call to renewal, to conversion, to that prayer which can alone bring us nearer to Christ and to each other, which the Council so rightly calls 'spiritual ecumenism', and 'the soul of the ecumenical movement' (Vatican II, Decree on Ecumenism, n. 8). Every Christian is called to serve the unity of the Church. Two tasks are particularly urgent today. One is that of aiding priests and students for the priesthood to appreciate this ecumenical dimension of their mission and to convey it to the people entrusted to their care. The other . . . concerns the ecumenical dimension of catechesis.

He recalled his statement in *Catechesi Tradendae* to the effect that catechesis should foster the desire for unity, excluding 'facile irenics', and requiring self-purification and humility.

The Pope then turned explicitly to the pastoral quality of ecumenism.

For these very reasons the task of promoting unity must be seen as an essentially *pastoral* task. It is pastoral in that the bishops are the principal ministers of unity within the local churches and therefore 'have a special responsibility for promoting the ecumenical movement' (Ecumenical Directory II, 65). It is pastoral also in that all who are entrusted with this work must see it as primarily ordered to the building up of the Body of Christ and the salvation of the world. As long as Christians are divided, so long will the work of preaching the Gospel be hampered: divisions among Christians impair the credibility of the Gospel, the credibility of Christ himself (cf. *Evangeli Nuntiandi*, n. 77). This service of unity is a service of Christ, of the Gospel, and of all humanity. It is, then, a truly pastoral service.

A high *priority* attaches to this truly pastoral work. The Vatican Council clearly stated the urgency of the ecumenical task. Disunity is a scandal, a hindrance to the spread of the Gospel; it is our duty to strive by God's grace to overcome it as soon as we can. The inner renewal of the Catholic Church is an indispensable contribution to the work of Christian unity. We must therefore present this call to holiness and renewal as central to the Church's life. Let no one delude himself that work for perfect unity in faith is somehow secondary, optional, peripheral, something that can be indefinitely postponed. . . . You, then, who are charged with particular responsibility for the Catholic Church's ecumenical work in your own lands must always look upon this as one of the main priorities in the Church's mission today.

For it is the work of the *Church*. The Vatican Council's commitment of the Catholic Church to work for ecumenism has been frequently reaffirmed by both Paul VI and myself. To work for unity is not simply to follow one's own fancy, one's personal preference; it means being faithful to and truly representative of the position of the Catholic Church.

The third ecumenical journey that the Holy Father undertook that autumn was to Constantinople. Since the pontificate of Paul VI it had become the custom that a delegation from Rome should attend the celebrations at Constantinople in honour of St Andrew. On this occasion Pope John Paul decided to go himself. He announced his intention in his regular Sunday Angelus message on 18 November.

This visit is an important one. It shows in a practical way the Pope's decision, already stated several times, to continue with the effort for the unity of all Christians. This was one of the main purposes of the Council. Today it is a more urgent need than ever. Great progress has been made, but we cannot yet be content. We must carry out Christ's will fully. With the Venerable Orthodox Churches we are on the eve of beginning a theological dialogue, with a view to overcoming together the divergences that still exist between us. With this visit I wish to show the importance that the Catholic Church attaches to this dialogue. I wish to express my respect, my deep brotherly charity, for all these Churches and their Patriarchs, but above all for the Ecumenical Patriarchate to which the Church of Rome is bound by so many centuries-old bonds which have taken on new force and relevance in the last few years, thanks to the wise and courageous action of the great and venerated Patriarch Athenagoras and of my great and beloved predecessor, Pope Paul VI.

He intended also to visit Ephesus, where the Council of 431 proclaimed the Virgin Mary 'Theotokos: Mother of God'.

I would also like this journey of mine to remind all, each one of you, and every member of the faithful of the Church, of the sacred duty of working for union. Every Catholic must do so at least with prayer and with conversion of the heart, as the Council requested.

Pope John Paul arrived at Ankara on 28 November 1979, and at once exchanged greetings with the Turkish authorities, and then addressed the small Catholic community in that city, choosing as his main theme their relations with Moslems. The 'golden rule' was given by St Peter: 'Always be prepared to make a defence to anyone who calls you to account for the hope that is in you, yet do it with gentleness and reverence; and keep your conscience clear' (1 Pet 3: 15-16). Quoting his own encyclical *Redemptor Hominis* and the Council's Declaration on the Relation of the Church to Non-Christian Religions, the Pope spoke of the Catholic Church's esteem for the 'religious values' of Islam.

When I think of this spiritual heritage and the value it has for man and for society, its capacity of offering, particularly to the young, guidance for life, filling the gap left by materialism, and giving a reliable foundation to social and juridical organisation, I wonder if it is not urgent, precisely today when Christians and Moslems have entered a new period of history, to recognise and develop the spiritual bonds that unite us, in order to preserve and promote together for the benefit of all men, 'peace, liberty, social justice and moral values' as the Council calls upon us to do (Declaration on Non-Christian Religions, n. 3).

Faith in God, professed by the spiritual descendants of Abraham – Christians, Moslems and Jews – when it is lived sincerely, when it penetrates life, is a certain foundation of the dignity, brotherhood and freedom of men and a principle of uprightness for moral conduct and life in society. And there is more: as a result of this faith in God the creator and transcendent, man finds himself at the summit of creation. He was created, the Bible teaches, 'in the image and likeness of God' (Gen 1: 27); for the

177

Koran, the sacred book of the Moslems, although man is made of dust, 'God breathed into him his spirit and endowed him with hearing, sight and heart", that is, intelligence (Sura 32 : 8).

For both Christian and Moslem, the universe is subject to man as God's representative; man has inviolable rights, but is bound to the moral order established by God, and must never put an idol in God's place. The Pope accordingly invited his hearers

> to consider every day the deep roots of faith in God in whom also your Moslem fellow citizens believe, in order to draw from this the principle of a collaboration with a view to the progress of man, emulation in good, the extension of peace and brotherhood in free profession of the faith peculiar to each one.

But Catholics should remember the riches of their own faith:

> Always have courage and pride in your own faith. Study it more deeply. Draw constantly nearer to Christ, the corner-stone, like living stones . . . Draw joyfully upon the gushing spring of his Eucharist. May he fill you with his charity!
> Have also the sentiment of being in communion with the universal Church, which the Pope represents before you, in his humble person. Your witness is all the more precious in that it is limited in number, but not in its quality.

On 29 and 30 November the Pope and the Patriarch exchanged five discourses before they issued their final Joint Declaration. As many of the themes of the declaration were anticipated in the preceding addresses, it seems best to give an account of the declaration first, so as to assign to it the prominence it deserves. After thanking God for their meeting, the leaders continued:

> Seeking only the glory of God through the accomplishment of his will, we affirm again our resolute determination to do everything possible to hasten the day when full communion will be re-established between the Catholic Church and the Orthodox Church and when we will at last be able to concelebrate the divine Eucharist.

The statement then officially announces the beginning of theological dialogue between the Catholic and Orthodox Churches, aiming

> not only at progressing towards the re-establishment of full communion between the Catholic and Orthodox sister Churches, but also at contributing to the multiple dialogues that are developing in the Christian world in search of its unity.

The essential preparation had been made by the 'dialogue of charity'. This had

> opened up the way to better understanding of our mutual theological positions and, thereby, to new approaches to the theological work and to a new attitude with regard to the common past of our Churches. This purification of the collective memory of our Churches is an important fruit of the dialogue of charity and an indispensable condition of future progress. . . .
>
> We want the progress in unity to open up new possibilities of dialogue and collaboration with believers of other religions, and with all men of good will, in order that love and brotherhood may prevail over hatred and opposition among men.

Let us now go back to trace the exchange of speeches that preceded this Joint Declaration. At the Patriarchal residence at the Phanar, the Pope spoke of his joy at the meeting, and greeted not only the Patriarch but also 'all the Churches that you represent'.

> I cannot hide my joy to be in this land of very ancient Christian traditions and in this city rich in history, civilisation and art, which make it figure among the most beautiful in the world. Today as yesterday. . . .
>
> The fundamental dogmas of Christian faith . . . were defined by the Ecumenical Councils which were held in this city or in neighbouring cities. The very formulation of our profession of faith, the *credo*, took place in these first Councils celebrated together by the East and the West. Nicaea, Constantinople, Ephesus, Chalcedon, are names known to all Christians. They are particularly familiar to those who pray, who study and who work in different ways for full unity between our sister Churches.
>
> Not only have we had in common these decisive Councils, pauses, as it were, in the life of the Church, but for a millenium these two sister Churches have grown together and developed their great vital traditions.
>
> The visit I am paying today is intended to signify a meeting in the common apostolic faith, to walk together towards this full unity which sad historical circumstances have wounded, especially in the course of the second millenium. How could I fail to express our firm hope in God in order that a new era may dawn?

Perhaps the most remarkable feature of this address is the Pope's adoption of the Orthodox conception of sister-Churches, rather than describing the Church as a body of Christians with the Pope as its head.

In reply the Ecumenical Patriarch thanked the Pope for the 'greatness' of his step.

We believe that at this moment the Lord is present among us here, and that the Paraclete is upon us – that the two brothers Peter and Andrew are rejoicing with us – that the spirits of the common Fathers and Martyrs are hovering over us to inspire us. But at the same time we feel arriving right in front of us, right in front of our responsibility, the anxious expectation of the divided Christians, the anguish of the man without recognised human rights, without freedom, without justice, without bread, without medical care, without education, without security and without peace.

It is for this reason that we consider the blessed presence of Your Holiness here and our meeting an expression of God's will, a challenge and an invitation of the world to which we must respond.

That evening Pope John Paul celebrated Mass in the Catholic Cathedral, in the presence of the Ecumenical Patriarch, the Armenian Patriarch, and other religious leaders. During the Mass the Pope and the two Patriarchs exchanged the Kiss of Peace, in Orthodox eyes a ceremony which, when performed in the liturgy, expresses ecclesial unity.

In his homily at the Mass, the Holy Father spoke of his joy at the presence of the 'venerated brothers who have wished to join in this celebration and in this way do honour to us and to the whole of our local community'. He spoke again of the history associated with Constantinople and its neighbouring cities, then considered the imminent feast of St Andrew.

Let us now extend our meditation to the mystery of the Church. St Andrew, the first one called, the Patron Saint of the Church of Constantinople, is the brother of St Peter, the leader of the apostles, the Founder with St Paul of the Church of Rome and its first Bishop. On the one hand, this fact recalls to us a drama of Christianity, the division between the East and the West, but it also recalls the deep reality of the communion that exists, in spite of all divergences, between the two Churches.

How we must thank the Lord for having brought forth, in the course of the last few decades, enlightened pioneers and indefatigable architects of unity, such as Patriarch Athenagoras, of venerated memory, and my great predecessors, Pope John XXIII – whose memory this city and this Church treasure – and Pope Paul VI who came to meet you before me! Their actions were fruitful for the life of the Church and for the pursuit of full unity between our Churches, which rest on the one cornerstone, Christ, and are built on the foundation of the apostles.

The Pope recalled the 'more and more intense contacts in the last few years' which 'have caused us to discover again the brotherhood between our two Churches and the reality of a communion between them, even if it is not perfect'. He referred to the impending theological dialogue, and the bi-annual exchange of visits between Rome and Constantinople.

Communion in prayer will lead us to full communion in the Eucharist. I venture to hope that this day is near. Personally, I would like it to be very near. Have we not already in common the same eucharistic faith and the true sacraments, by virtue of the apostolic succession? Let us hope that complete communion in faith, especially in the ecclesiological field, will soon permit this full 'communicatio in sacris'. . . .

And now, dear brothers and sisters, I ask you to pray fervently, in the course of this eucharistic sacrifice, for the full communion of our Churches. Progress in unity will be based on our efforts, on our theological work, on our repeated steps, and especially on our mutual charity; but it is at the same time a grace of the Lord. . . . Beseech him that we ourselves, pastors of the sister Churches, may be the best instruments of his plan, we whom Providence has chosen, at this hour of history, to govern these Churches, that is, to serve them as the Lord wishes, and thus serve the one Church, which is his Body.

In the course of the second millennium, our Churches had become petrified, as it were, in their separation. Now the third millenium of Christianity is drawing near. May the dawn of this new millennium rise on a Church that has found again her full unity, in order to bear witness better, in the midst of the exacerbated tensions of this world, to God's transcendent love, manifested in his Son Jesus Christ.

On the following day, the feast of St Andrew, the Holy Father returned to the Phanar to take part in the Orthodox liturgy, where another exchange of addresses took place. Pope John Paul again took the feast as the starting-point for his reflections:

Certainly, all the apostles are bound to one another by the new brotherhood that unites all those whose hearts are renewed by the Spirit of the Son (cf. Rom 8:15) and to whom the ministry of reconciliation is entrusted (cf. 2 Cor 5:18), but that does not suppress, far from it, the special bonds created by birth and upbringing in the same family. Andrew is Peter's brother. Andrew and Peter were brothers and, within the apostolic college, a greater intimacy must have bound them, a closer collaboration must have united them in the apostolic task.

Here again today's celebration reminds us that special bonds of brotherhood and intimacy exist between the Church of Rome

181

and the Church of Constantinople, that a closer collaboration is natural between these two Churches.

Peter, Andrew's brother, is the leader of the apostles. Thanks to the inspiration of the Father, he fully recognised, in Jesus Christ, the Son of the living God (cf. Mt 16:16); owing to this faith, he received the name of Peter, in order that the Church may rest on this rock (cf. Mt 16:18). He had the task of ensuring the harmony of apostolic preaching. A brother among brothers, he received the mission of strengthening them in the faith (cf. Lk 22:32); he is the first to have the responsibility of watching over the union of all, of ensuring the symphony of the holy Churches of God in faithfulness to 'the faith which was once for all delivered to the saints' (Jude 3).

It is in this spirit, animated by these sentiments, that Peter's successor has wished on this day to visit the Church whose patron saint is Andrew, to visit its venerated pastor, all its hierarchy and all its faithful. He has wished to come and take part in its prayer. This visit to the first see of the Orthodox Church shows clearly the will of the whole Catholic Church to go forward in the march towards the unity of all, and also its conviction that the re-establishment of full communion with the Orthodox Church is a fundamental stage of the decisive progress of the whole ecumenical movement. Our division may not, perhaps, have been without an influence on the other divisions that followed it.

In these paragraphs the Holy Father, by accurately analysing the place of St Peter among the apostles, as a brother who has the responsibility of safeguarding the unity of his brothers, and by referring to himself as Peter's successor, delicately hints at his understanding of the position of the Bishop of Rome in a reunited Church. He then turned to the history of the relations between the two sister Churches, as two 'complementary traditions'.

For nearly a whole millennium, the two sister Churches grew side by side, as two great vital and complementary traditions of the same Church of Christ, keeping not only peaceful and fruitful relations, but also concern for the indispensable communion in faith, prayer and charity, which they did not at any cost want to question, despite their different sensitivity. The second millennium, on the contrary, was darkened, apart for some fleeting bright intervals, by the distance which the two Churches took in regard to each other, with all the fatal consequences thereof. The wound is not yet healed. But the Lord can cure it and he bids us do our best to help the process. Here we are now at the end of the second millennium: is it not time to hasten towards perfect brotherly reconciliation, so that the dawn of the third millennium may find us standing side by side, in full communion, to bear witness together to salvation before the world, the evangelisation of which is waiting for this sign of unity?

Pope John Paul then spoke of the official theological dialogue between the two Churches which was about to commence. He spoke too of the 'habits of isolation' which had to be overcome 'in order to collaborate in all fields of pastoral action in which this collaboration is made possible by the almost complete communion that already exists between us'.

> We must not be afraid to reconsider, on both sides, and in consultation with one another, canonical rules established when awareness of our communion – now close even if it is still incomplete – was still dimmed, rules which, perhaps, no longer correspond to the results of the dialogue of charity and to the possibilities they have opened. It is important in order that the faithful on both sides realise the progress that has been made, and it would be desirable that those who are put in charge of the dialogue should be concerned to draw the consequences, for the life of the faithful, of future progress.

The impending theological dialogue would have the task

> of overcoming the misunderstandings and disagreements which still exist between us, if not at the level of faith, at least at the level of theological formulation.

This would require charity. Moreover,

> it is only in worship, with a keen sense of the transcendence of the inexpressible mystery 'which surpasses knowledge' (Eph 3 : 19), that we will be able to size up our divergences and to lay 'no greater burden than these necessary things' (Acts 15 : 28) to reestablish communion.

Then came the most dramatic sentences of the whole very significant speech:

> It seems to me, in fact, that the question we must ask ourselves is not so much, whether we are able to re-establish full communion, but whether we still have the right to remain separated. We must ask ourselves this question in the very name of our faithfulness to Christ's will for his Church, for which constant prayer must make us both more and more available in the course of the theological dialogue.

In reply the Patriarch Dimitrios spoke of the progress the two Churches had already made towards unity. 'During this march it was the Risen Christ who was present, walking with us and leading us even to the breaking of bread . . . Today we are entering a new phase of our co-fraternisation, . . . the phase of the official dialogue'.

> Christians of other Churches and confessions have been wondering if this dialogue between the Roman Catholic Church and the Orthodox Church, the beginning of which we bless today, is our final purpose. We could both answer this question in the negative, and we could add at once that our further and principal aim is not just the unity of the two Churches, but the unity of all Christians in the one Lord and in participation in the same chalice.
>
> To those non-Christians who might be wondering what significance Christian unity would have for them, if it would constitute a coalition and front of Christians against non-Christians, we could answer that the Christian unity pursued is not turned against anyone, but that it rather constitutes a positive service for all men, regardless of their sex, race, religion and social class – in accordance with the fundamental Christian principle that 'there is neither Jew nor Greek, there is neither slave nor free, there is neither male nor female' (Gal 3 : 28).

The Patriarch then spoke of obstacles to unity, in the first place the theological problems which the dialogue was designed to solve.

> But at the same time there are obstacles coming from mistrust, irresponsibility, fear – like that of the disciples in the garden of Gethsemane – non-theological factors concerning Christian differences, intolerance and fanaticism which set Christians and religions against one another – in one word all the obstacles that come from the arms of Lucifer.

It was not only with the Orthodox that the Pope exchanged ecumenical greetings. On 29 November he paid a visit to the Patriarch of the Armenian Church. Paul VI had received the Supreme Catholicos of the Armenian Church in 1970, when the Pope and the Catholicos had been able to profess a shared faith in Christ, even though the Armenian Church does not recognise the Council of Chalcedon, and therefore does not regard as binding that Council's affirmation of Christ's two natures. Addressing the Patriarch, Pope John Paul spoke of his visit as 'a testimony of the unity which already exists between us, and a testimony of my firm decision to pursue with God's grace the aim of attaining full communion between our two Churches'. He explained why 'the Bishop of Rome so naturally links his commitment to the pastoral care of the Catholic Church with his responsibility for the unity of all Christians' – namely, Christ's prayer for unity. There was a second reason for the visit: 'we are encouraged by what has already been achieved in the quest for the restoration of full Christian unity.'

In reply the Patriarch affirmed: 'There are far stronger and greater ties of unity, than differences, between our Churches.' With great courtesy, he chose to express the belief in Christ which both Churches share in the words of St Peter's confession: 'Thou art the Christ, the Son of the living God.' The two Churches accept the same Scriptures, and have 'one Lord, one faith, one baptism'; there is 'one Body and one Spirit' (Eph 4:3–6).

> We are united at least in the first three Ecumenical Councils, which laid the fundamental and essential points of the Common Creed. Moreover, we share so much in common with the Sacraments of the Church. The rest is secondary and not worthy of creating separation within the one body of Christ.

On 30 November, after his meeting and prayer with the Ecumenical Patriarch Dimitrios, Pope John Paul visited Ephesus, the site of the third Ecumenical Council of 431, which, in order to clarify the Church's understanding of Christ, defined Mary's role in salvation history as that of 'Theotokos: God-bearer or Mother of God'. There the Holy Father preached a homily on Our Lady. In the course of it he alluded to the 'great stress' laid by Eastern theologians on the '*katharsis*' (purification) 'that takes place in Mary at the moment of the Annunciation'. The Pope's purpose was presumably to show that this belief did not necessarily contradict the Catholic doctrine of the Immaculate Conception.

> Let it suffice to recall here the moving comment of St Gregory Palamas in one of his homilies: 'You are already holy and full of grace, O Virgin, says the angel to Mary. But the Holy Spirit will come to you again, preparing you, through an increase of grace, for the divine mystery' (Homily on the Annunciation: PG 151.178).

At the end of the homily the Holy Father spoke explicitly of ecumenism:

> There is one thing, in particular, that we wish to undertake today at the feet of her who is our common Mother: namely the commitment to push forward, with all our energy and in an attitude of entire availability to the inspiration of the Spirit, along the way that leads to the perfcct unity of all Christians. Under her motherly gaze, we are ready to recognise out mutual faults,

our selfishness and delays: she gave birth to one Son; we, unfortunately present him to her divided.

Pope John Paul, recalling the mutual revocation of the anathemas, continued:

A long way has been covered since that day; but other steps remain to be taken. We entrust to Mary our sincere resolution not to rest until the end of the way is reached. We seem to hear from her lips the Apostle's words: let there be no 'quarrelling, jealousy, anger, selfishness, slander, gossip, conceit and disorder' among you (2 Cor 12:20). Let us accept open-heartedly this motherly admonition and let us ask Mary to be close to us to guide us, with a gentle and firm hand, along the ways of complete and lasting brotherly understanding.

The Holy Father flew back to Rome the same day. Next day he sent a telegram to the Ecumenical Patriarch expressing his thanks for the visit:

Just arrived in Rome and still moved by the experience of the celebration in your Cathedral, I went to the tomb of the Apostle Peter to give thanks to the Lord for our brotherly encounter and pray the Apostle for his guidance in this new and decisive stage of our road towards unity.

In his Sunday Angelus message on 2 December, the Pope gave an account of his visit to 'the sister Church of Constantinople'. In it he spoke again of diversity in the Church's traditions as something to be welcomed:

The Church, in her bimillenary history, has developed from her primordial cradle along the way of great and distinct traditions: the Eastern and the Western. For many centuries these two traditions manifested the common riches of the Body of Christ, completing one another in the heart of the People of God and also in hierarchical institutions, in liturgical rites and in the doctrine of the Fathers and the theologians.

The Second Vatican Council pointed out to us that these riches and this tradition do not cease to be a common good of the whole of Christianity and that – on the basis of this good and under the action of the Holy Spirit – we must overcome the division that has weighed upon us since the eleventh century and seek rapprochement and unity again.

In this connection I am happy to recall here what the Council Fathers recognised, pointing out that 'from their very origins the Churches of the East have had a treasury from which the

Church of the West has drawn largely for its liturgy, spiritual tradition and jurisprudence' (Decree on Ecumenism, n. 14) and, especially, in the field of devotion to the Blessed Virgin, to whom 'the Eastern Christians pay high tribute, in beautiful hymns of praise' (ibid. n. 15) and in that of monastic spirituality, 'a source from which Latin monastic life took its rise and has often drawn fresh vigour ever since' (ibid.).

The Easterrn Churches, therefore, the Council Fathers concluded authoritatively, 'although separated from us, yet possess true sacraments, above all – by apostolic succession – the priesthood and the Eucharist, whereby they are still joined to us in closest intimacy' (ibid.).

Finally the Pope thanked 'my beloved brother, His Holiness Dimitrios I' and the members of his Church 'who treated me with exquisite and moving charity'. He also thanked the Armenian community, with their Patriarch Shnorhk Kalustian.

At a General Audience held on 5 December, the Holy Father returned to the same topic. Speaking again in terms of Andrew and Peter, he said:

. . . the successor of Peter in the Roman See wishes today to express his satisfaction at having heard the call coming from the East, from that See which surrounds with special veneration Andrew, the brother of Peter, for having followed that call. Thanks to that, he found himself, again, before Christ, who confirmed the vocation of Simon Peter on the basis of the brotherly tie with Andrew.

The 'culminating moment' of the meeting with the Ecumenical Patriarch, he said, was

the common prayer by means of mutual participation in the eucharistic liturgy, even though we were not yet able to break Bread together and drink at the same Chalice. . . We solemnly exchanged the brotherly kiss of peace, imparting the blessing together, at the end. And later, on the solemnity of the Apostle in the patriarchal church, where it was granted to me, together with the whole Delegation of the Apostolic See, to assist at the splendid liturgy of St John Chrysostom, to renew, with the same joy as those gathered there, the kiss of peace with my Brother of the See in the East, to speak and, above all, to listen to his address.

Now, together with the 'theological dialogue', the *dialogue of brotherly love and mutual rapprochement*', which had already been going on for some years, must be strengthened and deepened. The Holy Father told his audience of the gift he left with the Ecumenical Patriarch:

an Icon of the Mother of God: she with whom I became familiar at Jasna Gora and Czestochowa from my earliest youth. Making this gift, I let myself be guided not only by reasons of a personal nature, but above all by the particular eloquence of history. The Icon of Jasna Gora contains the symptomatic feature which speaks to the soul of the Christian of the East and of the West. It also comes from that land [Poland] in which the meeting of those two great traditions of the Church took place, in the course of the whole of history. My country, it is true, received Christianity from Rome and, at the same time, also the great heritage of Latin culture, but also Constantinople became the source of Christianity and of culture, in their Eastern form, for many Slav peoples and nations.

Speaking of the historic Church of Santa Sophia at Constantinople, now a mosque, the Holy Father said:

We are and must remain with our eyes fixed on that image of Wisdom, which speaks to us from the top of the great monument at the Bosphorus.

10. AFRICA, FRANCE, BRAZIL

THE theme of the Week of Prayer for Christian Unity in 1980 was the prayer: 'Thy kingdom come!' In his Sunday Angelus message on 20 January, the Holy Father spoke of this theme:

> The unity of all of us who have welcomed Christ as Lord, who have been incorporated into him and clothed in him in baptism, is closely linked with the demands of the Kingdom of God.
>
> Christians who wish to be coherent with their calling and mission should therefore strain and collaborate for the remaking of unity. To this end the quest for unity 'should in a certain sense become a necessary component in the pastoral programmes' of the Catholic Church and of other Christian Churches (General Audience, 5 December 1979).
>
> The prayer raised up to God throughout the whole world during this Week for Christian Unity will reaffirm the commitment of each one according to his own function and the gifts he has received. It will warm hearts and hopes anew so as to enable men to pursue with joy and confidence the ways of the Lord, who will most certainly lead us to full unity and to his Kingdom.

At the General Audience held three days later the Pope developed these thoughts further.

> (Christ) founded the Church in unity in order that she may be a sign and instrument of the Kingdom of God.
>
> The division between Christians is contrary to the requirements of the Kingdom of God, opposed to the very nature of the Church which is the beginning and instrument of this Kingdom. Furthermore, division dims the proclamation of the Kingdom of God, it hinders its efficacy, making its witness weaker. . . .
>
> Division comes from the fact that traces of sin remain among Christians, that the requirements of the Kingdom are not fully realised.

Hence ecumenism requires 'interior conversion, renewal of the mind, holiness of life, public and private prayer, and . . . the renewal of the Church'.

> We who believe in Jesus Christ, in whom the Kingdom of God is manifested, are called to become architects of reconciliation, pacification and brotherhood among men. We are called to be

heralds of the Kingdom of God. But precisely for this reason there is felt more deeply the urgent necessity of the re-establishment of full unity among Christians, which will make them able to bear a more and more effective witness and to proclaim the coming of the Kingdom with greater credibility.

Whenever we recite the 'Our Father' we ask: 'Thy kingdom come.' As the coming of the Kingdom is closely connected, as I said, with the cause of the union of Christians, then the daily and repeated recitation of the 'Our Father' can become an intention of prayer for unity.

We must daily ask the Lord for unity until all Christians, having overcome their divergences and reached full unity of faith, will be able to celebrate and take part together in the one Eucharist of the Lord, the sacrament of the coming of God's Kingdom.

On 25 January the Holy Father celebrated Mass with the members of the Dutch Synod, which was meeting in Rome. The Synod was discussing ecumenism, and the Pope took ecumenism as the subject of his homily. He drew some lessons from the feast of the day, which was the Conversion of St Paul.

Unity can only be the fruit of a conversion to Christ . . . Saint Paul met the Lord and gave himself wholly to him. . . . We in our turn must progress in a unity which depends ultimately on Christ and so on our adherence to him, for it is in him that we constitute the Church. . . .

. . . This celebration of 25 January makes us aware . . . that conversion, and therefore unity, is possible 'to God' even if it may seem impossible 'to men'.

To illustrate this for us we have the example of Saul of Tarsus who became Saint Paul. A mortal enemy of Christ and of Christians, one who, as he said of himself, 'was convinced I ought to do many things in opposing the name of Jesus of Nazareth' (Acts 26 : 9), he met the Lord and became 'Apostle of the nations', and the love of Christ became his whole life (cf. Phil 1 : 21).

So deep and radical a transformation is then possible through the grace of the Lord.

On 8 February the Pope addressed the plenary session of the Secretariat for Promoting Christian Unity. He recalled that the Council had said that:

the unity of all Christians was one of its principal aims (cf. Decree on Ecumenism, nn. 1 and 16); it remains an important part of my ministry, as of the pastoral action of the Church.

Unity calls for a fidelity that is continually deepened through listening to one another. With brotherly freedom partners in a true dialogue challenge one another to a more and more exacting faithfulness to God's plan in its entirety.

. . . They continually oblige themselves to go beyond the limits that the religious history of each one may have entailed in order to open up more and more to the 'breadth and length and height and depth' of God's mysterious plan which surpasses all knowledge (cf. Eph 3 : 18–19).

Such dialogue must be carried out 'in truth and faithfulness'.

It then becomes an indispensable means of balance which should make it unnecessary for the authority of the Church to be obliged to declare that certain members have embarked on a way that is not the real way to renewal. If the authority is obliged to intervene, it does not act against the ecumenical movement but makes its contribution to this movement by letting it be known that certain paths or certain short cuts do not lead to the goal sought.

Referring to his meeting with the Ecumenical Patriarch at Constantinople, the Pope spoke of his own 'impatience for unity', and the 'deep spiritual emotion' with which he was present at the Patriarch's eucharistic liturgy there; he expressed his pain and regret that concelebration was not yet possible. Recalling the imminent beginning of theological dialogue with the Orthodox Church, Pope John Paul stated his conviction

that a rearticulation of the ancient Eastern and Western traditions and the balancing exchange that will result when full communion is found again, may be of great importance to heal the divisions that came about in the West in the sixteenth century.

Pope John Paul spoke in detail about various discussions in progress between the Catholic and other Churches. Recalling the 450th anniversary of the Augsburg Confession, he continued:

In our dialogue with the Lutheran World Federation we have begun to rediscover the deep bonds which unite us in faith and which were masked by the polemics of the past. If after four hundred and fifty years, Catholics and Lutherans could arrive at a more exact historical evaluation of this document and establish better its role in the development of ecclesiastical history, it would be a considerable step forward in the march towards unity.

Theological dialogue would be fruitless 'unless, at the same time, everywhere in the Catholic Church, people realise more and more clearly the necessity of ecumenical commitment as defined by the Council'. The purpose of dialogue and collaboration is 'the witness to be borne to Christ today'.

This common witness is limited and incomplete as long as we disagree about the content of the faith we have to proclaim. Hence the importance of unity for evangelisation today. . . .

I hope that this reflection and this effort will take place everywhere in the Church under the direction of the bishops and Episcopal Conferences. In all situations, according to circumstances, it would be necessary to endeavour, with great pastoral wisdom, to discover the possibilities of joint witness of Christians. Doing so, we will come up against the limits that our divergences still impose on this witness and this painful experience will stimulate us to intensify the effort towards a real agreement in faith.

On 23 February the Holy Father addressed these words to a group of students from the Ecumenical Institute at Bossey, near Geneva:

. . . I am confident that you have come to a greater knowledge of and respect for the variety of traditions existing among Christians. You have developed a new awareness of the necessity of striving, with sincerity and fidelity to truth, to overcome those differences which still prevent Christians from expressing fully the faith and communion which are the Lord's will for them. In prayer, moreover, you will have gained new insights into just how much perfect Christian unity is a gift of God's grace – a gift to be sought humbly and perseveringly in the name of Jesus.

At the end of February, the Presbyterian Church in Ireland received from Pope John Paul a reply to a letter they had sent him asking him to give a fresh impetus to the ecumenical movement in their country. The sectarian killings taking place intermittently in Northern Ireland gave urgency to their request. In his letter the Holy Father praised the efforts at dialogue which had already taken place, and spoke of the planning of 'the next stages in our necessary dialogue'.

For such dialogue is indeed essential if we are to begin to overcome our doctrinal differences and the tragic social conditions with which they are sometimes linked, and thus to commence bearing a united witness to the presence of Christ in the Church and in the world and thereby to come nearer to that unity of faith and communion in Christ which we all earnestly desire. . . .

Inevitably such dialogue must first involve a small group of qualified representatives of either Church, but, once they arrive at consensus, it remains difficult to translate words into action until the results of the dialogue have been assimilated and communicated to the members of our Churches at every level, often by a process which is itself a form of dialogue. Dialogue alone is not enough. If our people are to listen to one another and to understand one another there is a long and sad history of mutual suspicion and distrust to be overcome.

I therefore wish to encourage as warmly as I can every effort that is being made by the people of your island to overcome, by God's grace, these prejudices and to facilitate and further a truly serious dialogue, for, as you say in your message, 'to find a way through this calls for real sustained discussion, for real prayer, dedication and sacrifice, not just for easy gestures.'

On 19 March 1980, Pope John Paul addressed a group from the British Council of Christians and Jews, praising them for their efforts 'to overcome prejudice, intolerance and discrimination, and to work for the betterment of human relations'. The following day he received the Editorial Committee of the Italian Interconfessional Translation of the Bible, and congratulated them on what the publication of their edition signified.

For it is a comforting sign of that 'hunger and thirst for the word of God' of which the prophet Amos spoke (Amos 8:11) and which is always a sure guarantee of renewal and strengthening in the faith. Moreover, in this fact there is also a broad approval of the ecumenical effort which has gone into your initiative; for the Word of the Lord is one for all the Churches and these can draw ever nearer to each other to the extent to which they can come together in 'hearing with reverence' (Vatican II, Constitution on Revelation, n. 1) that Word itself.

Ecumenism featured in the Pope's Easter *Urbi et Orbi* address on 6 April. Speaking of Christ as the cornerstone, he said:

In virtue of this cornerstone which unites, let us build our common hope with our brothers in Christ of East and West, with whom we are not yet in full communion and perfect unity.

Accept from us, dear brothers, the Easter kiss of peace and love. May the risen Christ awaken in us a still greater desire for this unity for which he prayed on the evening of his passion.

Let us not cease to implore this together with him. Let us place our trust in the power of the cross and the resurrection; this power is stronger than the weakness of any human division!

On 2 May 1980 Pope John Paul set out on a ten-day visit to six African countries. On 3 May, addressing leaders of other Churches at Kinshasa, he spoke of the joy of 'being together, united by our love for the Lord', and continued:

We must thank the Lord that the conflicts of the past have made way for an effort of meeting based on mutual esteem, and pursuit of truth and charity. Our meeting this evening is a sign of this. However, as we know, . . . the magnificent aim that we are pursuing to obey the Lord's command is not fulfilled. To reach it, there is required, with the grace of God, 'change of heart and holiness of life' which constitute, with prayer for unity, as the Second Vatican Council pointed out, 'the soul of the ecumenical movement' (Decree on Ecumenism, n. 8). All initiatives in view of unity would be vain if they were deprived of this foundation, if they were not based on the constant and sometimes painful pursuit of the full truth and of holiness. This pursuit, in fact, brings us closer to Christ and, through him, really brings us nearer to one another.

Pope John Paul referred to the 'various forms of collaboration in the service of the Gospel' already existing among the various Churches, and recalled his own often reaffirmed desire 'to see the Catholic Church fully enter the holy work which has its aim the restoration of unity'.

Certainly, the different countries and the different regions have each their religious history, that is why the methods of the ecumenical movement may differ, but its essential imperative always remains identical: the search for the truth in its very centre, Christ. It is he whom we seek above all, in order to find real unity in him.

Moving on from Zaire to Kenya, the Pope addressed Church leaders at Nairobi on 7 May, recalling that 'despite those factors that still divide us, we are nevertheless linked by a real fellowship that remains true even though it is still imperfect'.

Because of this one Baptism, in which we profess one basic faith that Jesus is Lord and that God raised him from the dead (cf. Rom 10:9), we stand together before the world of today with a common responsibility which stems from obedience to Christ. This common responsibility is so real and so important that it must impel us to do all we can, as a matter of urgency, to resolve the divisions that still exist between us, so that we may fulfil the will of Christ for the perfect unity of his followers.

Without full organic unity, Christians are unable to give a satisfactory witness to Christ, and their division remains a scandal to the world, and especially to the young Churches in mission lands. Your presence here testifies to a deep insight: that especially in the young Churches of Africa, in a continent that hungers and thirsts for God – a longing that can be fulfilled only in Christ – the common apostolic faith in Christ the Saviour must be held and manifested, for in Christ there can be no division. . . .

This task, I repeat, is an urgent one. Jesus calls us to bear witness to him and to his saving work. We can do this adequately

194

only when we are completely united in faith and when we speak his word with one voice, a voice which rings with that warm vitality which characterises the whole Christian community when it lives together in full communion. . . .

Although all Christians cannot yet share 'the fullness of Eucharistic worship',

wherever possible . . . let us find ways of engaging in acts of common witness, be it in joint Bible work, in promoting human rights and meeting human needs, in theological dialogue, in praying together when opportunity allows – as it does so beautifully today – or in speaking to others about Jesus Christ and his salvation.

The next country on the Pope's itinerary was Ghana, where he addressed representatives of the Christian Churches at Accra on 8 May.

All of us realise the great value that prayer has in accomplishing what is humanly difficult or even impossible. Jesus himself has told us: 'What is impossible with men is possible with God' (Lk 18:27). We know how important it is to turn humbly to God, day after day, asking him for the gift of constant conversion of life, which is so closely linked to the question of Christian unity. . . .
At the same time as we pursue our efforts towards the goal of perfect unity, we give thanks for the great bonds that already unite us in faith in the divinity of Christ.

Common faith in baptism and love of the Scriptures formed further links.

Because we believe in Christ and in 'the unsearchable riches of Christ' (Eph 3:8), we feel led by the Spirit to do everything possible to remove the divisions in faith that impair our perfect common witness to the Lord and his Kingdom, so that we may better serve our neighbour and more effectively bring the Good News of salvation to the world that continues to see in us a divided Christ.

By a coincidence, Dr Robert Runcie, who had been enthroned as Archbishop of Canterbury in March, was engaged on an African tour at the same time as the Pope. The Archbishop made a detour in order to meet Pope John Paul in Accra on 9 May. The following joint communiqué was issued after the meeting:

195

The first meeting of Pope John Paul II and the Archbishop of Canterbury, Robert Runcie, though a brief encounter in the midst of full programmes, has been a joyful and moving occasion. They were glad that it took place in Africa where the rapid expansion and the self-sacrificing zeal of the Church and the visible enthusiasm and love for Our Lord Jesus Christ has many lessons for Christians in Europe. They recognise the immense opportunities for the Christian Church in the countries of Africa to proclaim Christ in worship and in service and to make a contribution to the search for peace and justice. They believe that the time is too short and the need too pressing to waste Christian energy on old rivalries and that the talents and resources of all the Churches must be shared if Christ is to be seen and heard effectively.

Their much loved predecessors, Paul VI and Archbishop Donald Coggan, saw the urgent need for this common action and solemnly committed themselves to work for it in the common declaration of 1977. Pope John Paul II and Archbishop Robert Runcie endorse that commitment to 'collaborate more earnestly in a greater common witness to Christ,' and they share the recognition that common action depends on progress in the 'serious dialogue', now nearly fourteen years established, by which Roman Catholics and Anglicans have been seeking the way to that unity of faith and communion which Christ wills for his Church.

Today in Accra, the Pope and the Archbishop of Canterbury have established a personal friendship and trust upon which they intend to build in a fuller meeting in the future. They look forward to working together to achieve the unity for which Christ prayed to his Heavenly Father.

Back in Rome on 14 May, the Holy Father received a visit from the Syrian Orthodox Patriarch of Antioch, Mar Ignatius Jacob III, who had already visited Paul VI in 1971. It will be remembered that the Patriarch's Church did not accept the Chalcedonian definition of the two natures of Christ, though accepting his true humanity and divinity. The Pope's address to the Patriarch contained these words:

> Our love of that same Risen Lord, our devotion to that apostolic faith and the Christian witness received from our Fathers is what make our meeting today so full of meaning. Together we repeat the inspired words of Peter: 'You are the Christ, the Son of the living God' (Mt 16:16). Together we confess the mystery of the Word of God, made man for our salvation, who is the image of the invisible God, the firstborn of every creature (cf. Col 1:15), in whom it has pleased the Father to re-establish all things (cf. Eph 1:10). This is the Lord we proclaim: this is the Lord we seek to serve, in fidelity and truth; this is the Lord whose Spirit

196

impels us to search with ever greater zeal for the fullness of communion with each other. . . .

Nine years ago, Your Holiness and my revered predecessor Paul VI met in this very place to give clear testimony to a mutual dedication to this task of Christian reconciliation. At that time you recognised that, even if over the centuries difficulties have arisen because of the different theological expressions which have been used to express our faith in the Word of God made flesh and become really man, the faith we intend to proclaim is the same.

Pope John Paul spoke of the theological dialogue which had proceeded between the two Churches. Moreover, 'on the level of pastoral care for Christian emigrants there has been fruitful co-operation for disinterested service towards those who, in search of an improvement of the material conditions of their lives, feel the deep need of spiritual support in their new surroundings.' The Pope's recent journey to Africa had convinced him more than ever

> that the world in which we live hungers and thirsts for God, a longing that can be fulfilled only in Christ. As pastors of Churches sharing in apostolic traditions, we are called upon in a special way to carry on the apostolic mission of bringing Christ and his gifts of salvation and love to our generation.

In his reply the Patriarch stated:

> We together inherit very ancient rich traditions of the Apostolic times and the basic Christian creeds and dogmas embodied and proclaimed in the very famous Nicene Creed and the faith of the first three Ecumenical Synods. We are aware of the commonality of our faith. Now the theologians must find concrete ways to put aside the tragic heritage of our division and to solve the most painful and ordinary problems which beset the people of our Churches where they live side by side. For example, in India, which is predominantly a Hindu country, the Holy See of Antioch has allowed our people to celebrate the church festivals along with their Roman Catholic brethren. Today in India all Christians observe the Christmas and Easter festivals on the same day.

The Pope then took the Patriarch with him into the Audience Hall and introduced him to the people.

On May 15 1980 Pope John Paul wrote a letter to the German Episcopal Conference. In it he spoke of the 'certainty in faith' which is required for 'authentic dialogue' with the world.

Undoubtedly such faith in the power of Christ also calls for the ecumenical work of Christian unity undertaken by the Second Vatican Council. . . .

The Decree on Ecumenism (n. 4, 11) 'did not speak of compromise, but of meeting in an ever more mature fullness of Christian truth'.

> Thus, from the ecumenical point of view of the union of Christians, one cannot in any way pretend that the Church renounces certain truths professed by it. . . .
> Previously, I already pointed to the 'hierarchy' or order of truths of Catholic doctrine, of which theologians must be reminded, particularly 'when comparing doctrines'. The Council evokes such a hierarchy, given that 'they vary in their relation to the foundation of the Christian faith' (ibid., n. 11).

At the end of May, after years of patient preparation and diplomacy, the first meeting of the Catholic/Orthodox Joint Commission for Theological Dialogue took place at Patmos and Rhodes. This dialogue was one of the subjects of the Pope's Whit Sunday address on 25 May, when he asked for prayers that 'Almighty God, through Jesus Christ our Lord, the Head of the Church, will send his Spirit upon us to lead Catholics and Orthodox back into full unity'. The Holy Father used the expression 'symphonic' to refer to the need for different traditions to coexist in a united Church:

> The occurrence of this feast reminds us that the unity of the Church is 'symphonic', and that in full unity there is place for the expression of all the gifts of the Spirit.
> And it is in a spirit of inner conversion and of total trust in the work of God that the dialogue can help Catholics and Orthodox to rediscover the warmth and the power of full charity, in full truth, in full unity.

On 30 May Pope John Paul landed at Orly airport for a three-day visit to France. The following day he spoke to representatives of other Christian communities, reminding them 'of the requirements that the fact of being a Christian involves for us today'.

> First and foremost, and in the dynamics of the movement towards unity, our personal and community memory must be purified of the memory of all the conflicts, injustice and hatred of the past. This purification is carried out through mutual forgiveness, from the depths of our hearts, which is the condition of the blossoming

198

of real brotherly charity, a charity that is not resentful and that excuses everything (cf. 1 Cor 13:5 and 7). I say so here for I know the cruel events which, in the past, have marked the relations of Catholics with Protestants in this country. To be a Christian today requires us to forget this past in order to be wholly available for the task to which the Lord calls us now (cf. Phil 3:13). You are facing this task and I rejoice particularly at the quality of the collaboration that exists among you, especially as regards the service of man, a service understood in its whole dimension and which requires urgently and immediately the testimony of all Christians, the necessity of which I have already stressed in the encyclical *Redemptor Hominis*.

But, today more than ever perhaps, the first service to render to man is to bear witness to the truth, the whole truth . . . 'speaking the truth in love' (Eph 4:15). We must not cease until we are once more able to confess together . . . this whole truth in which the Spirit guides us (cf. Jn 16:13). I know how frank your collaboration also is in this field. . . . We must be able to confess the whole truth together in order to be able really to bear witness in common to Jesus Christ, the only one in whom and through whom man can be saved (cf. Acts 4:12).

Pope John Paul then added some impromptu remarks, in which he reaffirmed the need for different traditions in the Church, and acknowledged that dialogue required one to question one's own position:

We must consider well that we have now to restore again the work of centuries; and the work of centuries cannot be restored again in a few years, at least by human standards. But the work itself, the fact that we meet, the fact that we dialogue and put questions and seek to answer, the fact that we seek to examine our own truth, all this . . . is already a fruit, and we can do nothing other than continue, continue.

I should say that I am living in a very profound way the anniversary you are living this year, I mean the 450th anniversary of the Confession of Augsburg – yes, in a very profound way. I am living it in a way that I find almost beyond my comprehension, for there is someone who is living it in me. 'Someone will lead you!' I think that these words the Lord spoke to Peter are, perhaps, the most important of all the words he heard: 'Someone will lead you!' . . .

I think that here we are, you may say, on the right lines: we have recognised the signs of the times and we are seeking to respond to them, in ourselves, with our powers, our human powers, we are all seeking to respond to them. But there is, as you have stressed in your address, another element that is much more important than our efforts, and that is time. To say time is to say hope. We hope that the Lord will grant us the day when we shall find ourselves united and perhaps on that day we shall have – we can be sure we shall have – a different view of the difficulties which we see as such today. A vision of different approaches to the same source, the same truth, the same Jesus Christ, the same Gospel. I am convinced that the Lord is preparing us for this. . . .

And it is for this that we must always pray. I think, I am convinced, that the function, the fundamental task of Christian communities, of Churches, the fundamental task of all believers, is prayer.

That same day Pope John Paul addressed representatives of the Jewish community, recalling its 'long and glorious history', and paying homage to the victims of 'the dark years of the occupation and the war'. He was glad that dialogue and collaboration 'are very much alive and active here in France'.

Between Judaism and the Church, there is a relationship, as I said on another occasion to Jewish representatives, a relationship 'at the very level of their respective religious identities' (Address of 12 March 1979). This relationship must be further deepened and enriched by study, mutual knowledge, religious education on both sides, and the effort to overcome the difficulties that still exist. That will enable us to work together for a society free of discriminations and prejudices, in which love and not hatred, peace and not war, justice and not oppression, may reign.

On 1 June the Holy Father answered the questions of the young people of Paris:

What do you expect to do for the unity of Christians? How do you see this unity?
The work for the unity of Christians is, in my opinion, one of the greatest and finest tasks of the Church of our age.

You would like to know if I am expecting unity and how do I view it? I will give the same answer as I gave in connection with the implementation of the Council. There too, I see a special call of the Holy Spirit. As regards its implementation, and the different stages of this implementation, we find all the fundamental elements in the teaching of the Council. They must be put into practice, and their concrete applications must be sought; and above all it is always necessary to pray, with fervour, constancy and humility. The union of Christians cannot be realised otherwise than through deep maturation in the truth and a constant conversion of hearts. We must do all that in accordance with our human capacities, taking up again all the 'historical processes' that have lasted for centuries. But finally this union, for which we must spare no efforts or work, will be Christ's gift to his Church, just as it is already one of his gifts that we have already entered upon the way to unity.

On 6 June 1980 the Pope received a visit from the Catholicos Patriarch of all Georgia, His Holiness Ilia II. The Georgian Church was among the Orthodox Churches which took part in the Patmos dialogue with Catholic theologians. The Patriarch alluded to the 'complexities of history' which had sadly brought about the division of the Church, and stated:

> We have come to the city in which there is the Chair of St Peter, to re-establish those ancient and brotherly relations which traditionally existed between our two ancient Churches.

Despite divisions, 'there have always been good mutual relations between

> our two Churches, and these have found expression in political, spiritual and scientific collaboration.

Pope John Paul pointed out that this was the first occasion on which a Catholicos Patriarch of Georgia had visited Rome to exchange the kiss of peace with its Bishop. 'We meet as brothers.' Both Churches were concerned for the renewal of the Church.

> It is this concern for renewal that has made us so keenly aware of the need and obligation to restore full communion between our Churches. The long course of our history has led to sad, and sometimes bitter, divisions which have led us to lose sight of our brotherhood in Christ; and our concern for renewal is one of the factors that has led us to see more clearly the need there is for unity among all who believe in Christ. . . .
> Today this task of restoring full communion between divided Christians is a priority of all who believe in Christ. It is our duty to Christ, whose seamless robe is rent by division. It is our duty to our fellow men, for only with one voice can we effectively proclaim our faith in the Good News of salvation and thus obey our Lord's command to bring his Gospel to all mankind. And it is our duty to each other, for we are brothers and must express our brotherhood.

The Pope repeated the words he had spoken during his visit to the Ecumenical Patriarch of Constantinople the previous year:

> Union can be only the fruit of the knowledge of the truth in love. They must both operate together: one apart from the other is still not enough, because truth without love is not yet

the full truth, just as love does not exist without truth (General Audience, 5 December 1979).

The present visit showed that the theological dialogue which had begun must 'be rooted in a dialogue of brotherly love'.

In mid June a delegation from the Church of Ethiopia visited the Vatican. Like the Egyptian, Syrian and Armenian Churches, the Ethiopian is described as monophysite, because it does not accept the Council of Chalcedon's definition of the two natures of Christ. The Ethiopian Patriarch, Abba Tekle Haimanot, in a letter conveyed by his representatives affirmed:

> In our Churches there is one God, one Christ. We believe the Church is one in God and in Christ. Though there is division amongst us, as Christians the time is however ripe when this division of our Churches will have to be completely narrowed down.

After the visit the Pope sent a letter to the Patriarch thanking him for the meeting, seeing it as a sign of 'our common faith in Jesus Christ' (despite the different traditions of Christological language).

> This will help up to realise more fully the degree of communion we already enjoy and so to see more clearly the ways and means of overcoming the differences that still remain between us, in order that we may come to that full communion for which we long.

Pope John Paul spoke of 'our shared concern for increasingly close and wide-ranging collaboration', referring especially to 'ways of co-operating in the relief of the needs of your faithful, who are affected by drought'.

25 June 1980 was the 450th anniversary of the presentation of the Confession of Augsburg, the classical expression of Lutheran faith, which was, however, formulated in language calculated to avoid offending Catholics as much as possible. At a General Audience on that day, Pope John Paul spoke of this achievement of 'the forerunners of our brothers and sisters of the Evangelical Lutheran Confession'.

> To look back at the historical events of 450 years ago and, still more, at the developments that followed, fills us with sadness and sorrow. We must recognise that, despite the honest desire and the serious effort of all concerned, they did not then succeed in avoiding the tensions that threatened between the Roman Catholic Church and the evangelical reform. The last real attempt

202

to restore peace at the Diet of Augsburg foundered. Soon afterwards the point of clear division was reached.

We are all the more grateful that today we see with even greater clearness that at that time, even if there was no success in building a bridge, the storms of that age spared important piers of that bridge. The intense and long-standing dialogue with the Lutheran Church, called for and made possible by the Second Vatican Council, has enabled us to discover how great and solid are the common foundations of our Christian faith.

Today as we look at the history of the divisions of Christianity, we are more aware than ever what tragic and scandalous consequences human failure and human guilt have over a long period, and how they can obscure Christ's will and damage the dignity of faith in the Good News. The Second Vatican Council has reminded us that there is an intimate relationship between the constant renewal of the Church in the power of the Gospel and the safeguarding of its unity and also the restoration of its unity.

The Pope urged all the faithful, and particularly theologians, that

faithful to Christ and to the Gospel, faithful to the 'primitive Church', faithful to our common Fathers of the Church and to our common Ecumenical Councils, we may seek all there is in the apostolic heritage that unites us with our brothers and sisters, in order that we may discover anew the treasure of one common creed. The world of the late twentieth century in which we live is characterised by the mark of an indescribable hunger. The world is hungry and thirsty for the confession of Christ and for witness to Christ by word and by deed, Christ who alone can satisfy this hunger and thirst.

Pope John Paul sent a greeting to Christians gathering at Augsburg

to confirm, in the face of the fears and pessimism of a troubled humanity, that Jesus Christ is the salvation of the world, the Alpha and the Omega of everything that exists. I greet also all Christians who are gathering in many other places all over the world on the occasion of this 450th anniversary of the Confession of Augsburg, so that from the Gospel of creation by God, of Redemption in Jesus Christ, and of the call to one People of God, there may develop a new force for a confession of faith full of hope, today and tomorrow. The will of Christ and the signs of the times are leading us to a common witness in a growing fullness of truth and love.

The Holy Father devoted a large part of his address to the Roman Curia on 28 June 1980 to the subject of ecumenism.

The special task of the way that concerns the mission of the Church is ecumenism: the trend to the union of Christians. It is a question of a priority that is imposed on our action, in the first place because it corresponds to the very vocation of the Church. The ecumenical effort is not engaged in for reasons of opportuneness and it is not dictated by contingent situations or conditions, but is based on God's will.

After summing up the progress made in contacts and dialogue with the Orthodox, he turned his attention to the Churches of the West.

The effort to re-establish full communion with the Churches that are heirs to the various Eastern traditions, does not make us neglect, however, the concern to overcome the divisions that came into being in the sixteenth century in the West. In less than two years, and in a spirit of Christian friendship, I have had exchanges with two Archbishops of Canterbury: Dr Coggan, who kindly attended the solemn inauguration of my pontificate, and Dr Runcie, who met me in Africa. At these meetings I saw reflected the intentions of so many Anglicans for the restoration of unity.

This intention instils strength in so many dialogues and so much collaboration in progress in the English-speaking world. This is an experience that must lead us to follow in prayer the work carried out by the joint Commission between the Catholic Church and the Anglican Communion, the results of which, very important ones, will be presented at the end of next year.

The Methodists followed the Second Vatican Council closely, and they found in the renewal that it has produced many inspirations close to their ideals of holiness of life.

He then spoke of the Catholic Church's relations with the Lutheran World Federation, the World Alliance of Reformed Churches, the Pentecostal Churches and the World Council of Churches.

During each of my journeys I endeavoured to meet my brothers of other Churches and ecclesial communities. This happened particularly in Ireland, in the United States of America, in various African countries, and in Paris. These meetings made it possible, with the help of experience, to carry out brotherly exchanges progressively and they permitted mutual listening and mutual understanding. And I hope they will grow and develop in this direction during future journeys.

Pope John Paul then spoke of the importance of prayer in the ecumenical movement:

204

Once more and insistently, I urge the Catholic faithful, and especially those called to the contemplative life, to raise incessantly their supplication for the real and complete unity of all disciples of Christ. The Week of Prayer for the Unity of Christians must be, every year, the very special time, the heart, of his supplication.

He had, he said, reminded the German Episcopate recently that

the union of Christians cannot be sought in a 'compromise' between the various theological positions, but only in a common meeting in the most ample and mature fullness of Christian truth. This is our wish and theirs. It is a duty of mutual loyalty. The Second Vatican Council stated: 'Nothing is so foreign to the spirit of ecumenism as a false irenicism which harms the purity of Catholic doctrine and obscures its genuine and certain meaning' (Decree on Ecumenism, n. 11).

True ecumenical dialogue demands, therefore, on the part of theologians particular maturity and certainty in the truth professed by the Church; it demands particular faithfulness on their part to the teaching of the Magisterium.

At the end of June 1980 the customary delegation came to Rome from Constantinople to join in celebrating the feast of SS Peter and Paul. The Ecumenical Patriarch sent a letter saying that he would have liked to be able to reciprocate in person the Pope's visit to Constantinople, but was unable to do so, and had to be content with sending a delegation. The Patriarch thanked God 'who has permitted the two sister-Churches to honour, by celebrating them together, the memory of their Holy Apostles and Patron Saints', and to plan and inaugurate the theological dialogue.

In this important new phase of our reconciliation in Christ, when we are entering communion in theological thought, in order to serve, in faithfulness to truth, the holy cause of unity, we are called more and more to cultivate and deepen communion between us in charity, in order to serve the Lord's holy will more precisely and more fruitfully, and to hasten the coming of this holy and glorious day, desired by everyone, when we will concelebrate, in full communion, the mystery of the Church in the mystery of the divine Eucharist, to the glory of the mystery of the Holy Trinity.

As usual the Orthodox delegation was led by Metropolitan Meliton of Chalcedon. In his address to the Pope he said that the common celebration of the feast of SS Peter and Paul was not of the order of worldly conventions. It is a common ecclesial celebration, testified by the ecclesial presence of our humble persons, the representatives of the Patriarch of Constantinople.

The same was true of the celebration of the feast of St Andrew at Constantinople.

> In the mutual commemorations of the feasts of our common Apostles there is something more than mere custom. It is the fact that the Head of our faith and of the Church, he who completes everything, Jesus, has led us to this situation in which we exchange a mutual kiss, as was the case for Peter and Paul.
> In this event, our ecclesial meeting on this day of commemoration of the Apostles becomes a holy service and contributes to the reunification of the Church, that is, to the accomplishment of the will of the Lord who wishes us to be one. . . .

Pope John Paul in reply said that he experienced special joy at the meeting 'because this year the experience of the common bonds between our Churches has been more intense and because our common commitment to live together the communion of faith already existing between us, has been more explicit'.

> I would like these meetings, according to places and circumstances, but in the same spirit, to take place where Catholics and Orthodox live, in order to create gradually the necessary conditions for full unity.

The Pope spoke of the first steps in the theological dialogue.

> On our side, attentive to what the Spirit will wish to say, we will spare no effort, rest assured, for the pursuit of full unity. The ultimate perspective of the theological dialogue . . . remains that of the eucharistic celebration, after having overcome the difficulties owing to which the communion between our two Churches is not yet full and perfect today.

Afterwards the Pope wrote to the Ecumenical Patriarch expressing the joy the visit had given him, picking out

> the moment when your delegate joined with us in prayer and when we exchanged the kiss of peace, a pledge of the common celebration of the Eucharist in full unity, when God wills it, a celebration towards which we have committed ourselves to progress with all our determination. The warm and spontaneous applause with which the numerous faithful present in St Peter's emphasised this liturgical and brotherly gesture shows us how strongly the Christian people feel today the call to unity and to understanding and collaboration between our Churches.

This confirms our desire to do everything possible to hasten, with all due prudence but also with the courage God demands of us, the day of full unity.

Speaking of the new theological dialogue, he said:

I have asked all the Catholics in the world to take part in this dialogue by their prayers. It is a decisive moment in the relationships between our two Churches. It is a matter of eliminating the remains of age-old misunderstandings, of overcoming a lack of understanding inherited from the past, of definitely resolving the questions in controversy between our two Churches. All that is indispensable for the attainment of a stable unity in which, in full communion, we shall be united with one voice in praise of God and in the bearing of a common witness to him before the world.

On 30 June 1980 the Pope set out on a twelve-day visit to Brazil. On 2 July he touched on the subject of ecumenism in the course of an address to the Council of Latin American Bishops in Rio de Janeiro:

The pursuit of ecclesial unity takes us to the heart of ecumenism: 'And I have other sheep, that are not of this fold; I must bring them also, and they will heed my voice. So there shall be one flock, one shepherd' (Jn 10:16). The ecumenical dialogue, which takes on special characteristics in Latin America, must be set in this perspective. Prayer, trust, faithfulness must be the climate of real ecumenism. The dialogue between brothers of different confessions does not erase our own identity, but presupposes it. I know very well that you are endeavouring to create an atmosphere of greater rapprochement and respect, which is hindered by some people who have recourse to methods of proselytism that are not always correct.

On 3 July Pope John Paul met representatives of the Orthodox Church at São Paulo. After speaking of the good relations between the Catholic and Orthodox communities in Brazil, he turned his attention to his recent meeting with the Ecumenical Patriarch in Constantinople:

Returning from my brotherly visit to the Ecumenical Patriarchate, I had occasion to stress that what has very opportunely been called the dialogue of charity should become a necessary element of the pastoral programmes of each of our two Churches, Catholic and Orthodox. Deepening of this brotherly attitude, intensification of mutual relations and of collaboration between the Churches, create the vital environment, if I may express myself in this way, in which the theological dialogue can be born and should develop until it arrives at results that the Christian people will be prepared to accept. No one is dispensed from this effort. The Second Vatican Council declared this firmly as regards Catholics (cf. Decree on Ecumenism, n. 4). The same Council dedicated special attention to the collaboration of Catholics with their Orthodox brothers who, leaving the East, came to settle in countries far from their country of origin (cf. ibid, n. 18). This is precisely what happens here in Brazil, and, therefore, Catholics and Orthodox are called to contribute actively to the good outcome of this new phase of our progress towards full communion.

Also in the Brazilian situation, with an urgency and a scope that calls for the closest collaboration between the Churches, these must set to work together in the service of man. I am certain that this collaboration will not fail. May light and strength from above always assist us in this enterprise, and make us both became fervent in prayer, assiduous in knowledge of the other Church, zealous in keeping our own religious identity, and respectful of the identity of the other. Without this, either there is no dialogue, or the dialogue will turn out to be empty and insubstantial, if not falsified.

I renew here the expression of my admiration for the great and remarkable traditions of the Orthodox Church: the quality of its doctors, the majestic beauty of its worship, the value of its saints, the fervour of monastic life, as the Second Vatican Council already said so well (cf. ibid. 14–18).

While at São Paulo he also spoke to representatives of the Jewish community, and referred to the 'closer bonds that unite the Catholic Church and Judaism'.

The relationship between the Church and Judaism is not something external to the two religions: it is something based on the religious heritage characteristic of both, in the specific origin of Jesus and the Apostles, and in the environment in which the early Church grew and developed. If, in spite of all this, our respective religious identities divide us, and at times they have divided us painfully through the centuries, this must not prevent us now with respect to these same identities, from desiring to make the most of our common heritage and thus cooperate, in the light of the same heritage, in the solution of the problems that afflict modern society in need of faith in God, obedience to his holy law and active hope in the coming of his Kingdom.

The spirit of co-operation between the two communities in Brazil made possible

co-operation for the benefit of the individual man, for the advancement of his rights, frequently trampled on, and his just participation in the pursuit of the common good without exclusivism or discrimination.

On 4 July the Holy Father spoke to representatives of the Protestant communities, taking as his text the words of Psalm 133: 'behold how good and pleasant it is when brothers dwell in unity.' The occasion was a 'spiritual moment of prayer and meeting in the Lord'. They were all united by God's grace and received his strength to confess Jesus Christ as God and Lord and only Mediator. Remaining differences should lead them 'to seek full union more intensely and faithfully'. The plan for the establishment of a National Council of Churches, in which the Catholic Church was participating, could be 'the prelude to other initiatives'.

> In this way, all Christians together can bear a renewed witness to their faith in the Lord, and to their common hope, while trying, also together, according to the specific vocation of the disciples of Christ, to ensure that the requirements of this same faith, the source of charity and justice, will be expressed in the concrete private and public life of your nation.
> I cannot refrain from mentioning here, therefore, what has been done in the area of collaboration among Christians, on behalf of human rights and the complete respect for them. In saying this, I am referring not only to some important initiatives on the level of the explanation and research of the evangelical bases for these rights, but also to the daily work, in such diverse places and circumstances, for the defence and advancement of men and women, especially the poorest and most forgotten, whom present-day society often tends to abandon to themselves and to exclude, as if they did not exist, or as if their existence did not count. 'Man is in fact the way for the Church', as I wished to explain in my first encyclical *Redemptor Hominis* (n. 14).

These words were a gentle rejection of the view of some Protestants that the Church's mission is to preach faith in Christ, and not to act in protection of human rights.

Back at his summer residence at Castel Gandolfo, Pope John Paul received the members of the Anglican/Roman Catholic International Commission, whose final report was due to be completed in 1981. After welcoming them, he continued:

> I greet you with honour, veterans, seasoned workers in a great cause – that unity for which Christ prayed so solemnly on the eve of his sacrificial death.
> We know that this cause is the responsibility of all who are

committed to Christ (cf. Decree on Ecumenism, n. 5). It can be served in many ways; the way assigned to you by the Common Declaration of Paul VI and Archbishop Michael Ramsey was that of 'serious theological dialogue based on the Scriptures and on the ancient common Tradition'. You see that the very words of this programme are revealing. Unity is a gift of our Lord and Saviour, the founder of the Church. Although it was marred by the sin of men, it was never entirely lost. We have a common treasure, which we must recover and in the fullness of which we must share, not losing certain characteristic qualities and gifts which have been ours even in our divided state.

Your method has been to go behind the habit of thought and expression born and nourished in enmity and controversy, to scrutinise together the great common treasure, to clothe it in a language at once traditional and expressive of the insights of an age which no longer glories in strife but seeks to come together in listening to the quiet voice of the Spirit.

I do not need to tell you – you can tell me – that the task is not easy. It is not a task for man unaided. In seeking unity, man must first imitate Christ in praying for it. You have grasped and practised this, praying together; and you have reflected together, sharing in each other's liturgies and offices so far as is proper to our still divided state. This support was put behind your work of study, reflection and formulation from the beginning, fourteen years ago. You have prayed and countless others have prayed with you and for you.

Now your appointed task draws to an end. No doubt you look back in love and brotherhood on those years of labour. Some of its fruits are well known, have been studied by many others, have influenced many. Now the time is approaching when you will make a final report, which the respective ecclesiastical authorities must assess.

Here is a great responsibility. Your work will be taken seriously – weighed with all the care and sympathetic attention it demands. I thank God for what has been achieved, and I thank you, who have worked in his Name, with a desire to be submissive to his Spirit.

As the two men who commissioned you realised deeply, oneness in faith lies at the roots and fertilises Christian life. Given that, there can be rich variety in growth. In three great fields of doctrine you have sought agreement in those matters in which doctrine admits no diversity. This effort calls for warm appreciation.

But you yourselves realise that much remains to be done. To understand the mystery of Christ's Church, the Sacrament of Salvation, in its fullness is an abiding challenge. Many of the practical problems which still face us (questions of order, of mixed marriages, of shared sacramental life, of Christian morality) can only move towards solution as our understanding of that mystery deepens.

But here and now we must think with gratitude of what you have done. Your work and its fruits are already in themselves manifestations of, and a contribution to that 'greater common witness' of which Paul VI spoke in *Evangelii Nuntiandi* (n. 77) and it is an enabling instrument for all Christians who increasingly feel the call to common witness. It is a reminder that such witness is no matter of sentiment, but must be the fruit of prayer and hard work, of honesty and willingness to speak the truth in love.

With gladness I bless and thank you all. I pledge my concern for your work and my support for those who may continue it, and I join you in praying that the 'Father of lights, in whom there is no variation or shadow due to change' (James 1 : 17) may shed his light on us as we seek untiringly to reach full unity in his Son Jesus Christ.

The Pope's words about agreement in 'matters in which doctrine admits no diversity' echo a phrase from the Commission's Agreed Statement on Ministry and Ordination (n. 17). It implies that this essential faith which admits no diversity can sometimes be expressed in diverse ways according to the traditions of various Churches. It asserts, in other words, that uniformity and pluriformity each have a place in the Church's proclamation of faith.

11. ROYAL VISITS, GERMANY, THE FAR EAST, THE *FILIOQUE*

ON 17 October 1980, Queen Elizabeth II, who was paying a State Visit to Italy, went to the Vatican to pay a further State Visit to the Pope. Greeting her and Prince Philip, Pope John Paul recalled that John XXIII had welcomed the same royal visitors nineteen years earlier, and expressed his pleasure at being able to discuss a number of issues 'in the context of collaboration in our common ideal of service'. Contacts between 'the Apostolic See of Rome and Great Britain', he said, spanned a period of nearly fourteen hundred years, since Pope Gregory I sent Augustine to take the Gospel to Britain.

> In the person of Your Majesty I render homage to the Christian history of your people, as well as to their cultural achievements. The ideals of freedom and democracy, anchored in your past, remain challenges for every generation of upright citizens in your land. In this century your people have repeatedly endeavoured to defend these ideals against aggression. . . .
>
> Last year, before the United Nations Organisation I had the opportunity to speak of the relationship that exists between genuine development and peace and the cultivation of spiritual values. . . . In the presence of Your Majesty and Your Royal Highness I express the ardent hope that your noble nation will face this great spiritual challenge with renewed enthusiasm and fresh moral vigour.

The Pope then spoke explicitly of Christian unity.

> During the two decades intervening since the last visit of Your Majesty to the Holy See, one notes with a sense of deep satisfaction an ever more cordial relationship existing between various Christian bodies and between other religious men and women of good will. This is eminently true of the situation in your own land; under God's grace it is owing to the patience and sustained effort of so many honest people moved by the insights of charity and dedicated to a profound conviction that was once expressed by Jesus Christ. 'The truth will make you free' (Jn 8 : 32). Worthy of special mention in this regard is the zeal with which representatives of the Catholic Church and the Anglican Communion have pursued this noble goal of drawing closer together in Christian unity and in effective common service to humanity.

With great anticipation I look forward to having the opportunity of making a pastoral visit to the Catholics of Great Britain. On that occasion I hope to meet them both as sons and daughters of the Catholic Church and as loyal citizens of their nation; at the same time I hope to greet with fraternal respect and friendship other fellow Christians and people of good will. . . .

The Queen's reply included the following paragraphs:

. . . We in turn welcome the visit Your Holiness is planning to pay in 1982 to the Roman Catholic community in Great Britain, where some four million of my people are members of the Roman Catholic Church. We support the growing movement of unity between the Christian Churches throughout the world, and we pray that Your Holiness' visit to Britain may enable us all to see more clearly those truths which both unite and divide us in a new and constructive light. . . .

As Your Holiness knows well and has seen on your journey to Africa, many citizens of the Commonwealth of which I am head are members of the Roman Catholic Church. The interests of the Anglican and of the Roman Catholic Churches in these countries are often close and we welcome their growing dialogue on the many problems facing the international community.

We wish Your Holiness strength and inspiration in the great task to which you are committed.

Meanwhile the Synod of Bishops had been meeting in Rome, taking the family as the subject of their deliberations. The bishops gave considerable attention to the problems connected with mixed marriages, i.e. between Christians belonging to different Churches. The President of the Secretariat for Unity, Cardinal Willebrands, gave an important speech on this subject. In Catholic teaching, he said, every valid marriage between baptized persons was a true sacrament, and this was not only a juridical matter but 'a fundamental truth of Catholic doctrine concerning baptism'.

Therefore it can be said of the marriage of two Christians who have been baptised in different Churches, as it is of a marriage between two Catholics, that their union is a true sacrament and gives rise to a 'domestic church'; that the partners are called to a unity which reflects the union of Christ with the Church; that the family, as a family, is bound to bear witness before the world.

Consequently the Cardinal asked

whether the time has now come to study afresh the possibility of

213

admitting the non-Catholic partners in mixed marriages to Eucharistic Communion in the Catholic Church, obviously in individual cases and after due examination.

He recalled that, according to the Instruction of June 1972, one of the conditions for admitting non-Catholics to the Eucharist was 'a need for an increase in spiritual life and a need for a deeper involvement into the mystery of the Church and of its unity', a condition often fulfilled in a mixed marriage.

But there is a fourth condition: it is required that the non-Catholic Christian be unable for a prolonged period to have recourse to a minister of his own Church. To my mind this condition is less closely connected with eucharistic doctrine and faith.

Cardinal Willebrands recalled that the Council had spoken of the 'communion' existing, though in an imperfect form, between Catholics and other Christians. It should 'find expression in our pastoral practice regarding family life':

The Catholic Church cannot acknowledge mixed marriages to be the *ordinary* means for the restoration of unity among Christians, but it should show a real 'solicitude' for mixed families. For a mixed marriage that is inspired by a Christian spirit can do much to further the unity of Christians.

The Cardinal spoke of the need of

joint pastoral care of mixed marriages. This has been widely accepted in principle (a principle stated in norm 14 of *Matrimonia Mixta*), but much remains to be done to put this principle into practice, particularly as regards preparation for marriage and also the provision of proper help in the first years of family life. It is to be hoped that this Synod will urge priests to take this duty very seriously and to seek suitable collaboration with ministers of other Churches.

Cardinal Willebrands was speaking as an individual bishop; his words did not commit either the Secretariat for Unity or the Holy See. Nevertheless his position gave them great authority. The Pope himself referred to the ecumenical challenge of mixed marriages in his final address to the Synod:

All couples are called to holiness in marriage according to the divine plan; and the dignity of this vocation becomes effective when a person is able to respond to the command of God with a serene mind, trusting in divine grace and his own will. So it is

214

not enough for couples – if they are not both of the same religious persuasion – to accommodate themselves passively and easily to their circumstances, but they should strive with patience and good will to come to a common intention to be faithful to the duties of Christian marriage.

On 30 October 1980 the Pope received a visit from Prince Bertil and Princess Lilian of Sweden, the Primate of the Swedish Lutheran Church, and other visitors from the same country. The Pope spoke of 'the friendship of the Catholic Church towards the still separated brethren in those lands'.

I know that you join me in my prayer that God will, in ways known only to himself, hasten the day when full unity of faith and Christian life will be established between us.

On 3 November the Holy Father received a visit from participants in the working group of the 'Faith and Order' Commission of the World Council of Churches, which had been discussing 'Baptism, the Eucharist and the Ministry'. Pope John Paul expressed his interest in their work, which dealt with

realities that are at the heart of the mystery of the Church and her structure, but you are also tackling questions which were, if not the cause of our divisions, at least among the main subjects about which opposition arose. Now there cannot be a true and lasting re-establishment of unity without our succeeding in expressing our faith clearly together in these aspects of the mystery on which we opposed one another. The question of the ministry certainly remains a key question for the re-establishment of full communion.

It would be necessary for 'competent ecclesiastical authority' to examine the results of their deliberations.

In this work, you have to examine the Scriptures thoroughly; you have to consider how the Christians, from the beginning, with their pastors, received this teaching and interpreted it, not only on the intellectual plane, but on the existential plane, in their everyday life, in their profession of faith, in their institutions; how this teaching brought forth a more intense spiritual life. But above all, we must all put ourselves constantly at the disposal of God, in search of his will, in ardent prayer, which it is good to raise to God in common.

Pope John Paul paid a visit to Germany from 15 to 19 June 1980. Replying to the President of the Federal Republic, who greeted him at Bonn airport, the Holy Father said:

215

I am anxious to greet all our separated brothers in faith. I am looking forward to the personal meeting planned with the representatives responsible for their Churches and ecclesial communities. God grant that my pilgrimage may contribute, beyond confessional boundaries, to greater mutual understanding and to a rapprochement among all Christians, and promote the peaceful coexistence of all men in this country.

I have come here to the Federal Republic of Germany precisely in the year in which our evangelical brothers and sisters have commemorated the *Confessio Augustana*, proclaimed 450 years ago. Allow me to tell them that I particularly wanted to be among them at this very time. Here, where the Reformation began, may the effort also be redoubled to do, in fidelity to the one Lord of the Church and to his message, everything that is humanly possible, so that the desire of his Heart and his prayer: 'that they may all be one' (Jn 17:21) may be fulfilled.

In his homily during Mass at Osnabruck on 16 November, the Pope urged Catholics to deeper contact with the Lutherans.

But I would like above all to encourage you to seek and deepen, in sincere faith, contact with your evangelical brethren. The ecumenical movement in the last few decades has clearly shown you how much evangelical Christians are united with you in their concerns and joys, and how much you have in common with them when you live faith in our Lord Jesus Christ together, sincerely, and consistently. So let us thank God from the bottom of our hearts that the various ecclesial communities in your regions are no longer divided by misunderstanding or even barricaded against one another in fear. You rather have already had the happy experience that mutual understanding and acceptance were particularly easy when both sides knew their own faith well, professed it joyfully, and encouraged concrete communion with their own brothers in faith. I would like to encourage you to continue along this way.

Live your faith as Catholics with gratitude to God and to your ecclesial community; bear a credible witness, in all humility and without any complacency, to the deep values of your faith, and encourage, discreetly and amiably, also your evangelical brothers to strengthen and deepen in Christ their own convictions and forms of religious life. If all Churches and communities really grow in the fullness of the Lord, his Spirit will certainly indicate to us the way to reach full internal and external unity of the Church.

Early in the morning of 17 November, Pope John Paul met the Council of the German Evangelical (Lutheran) Church. Expressing his gratitude for this meeting 'in the country in which the Reformation began', the Pope attached a symbolic meaning to the early hour of his address:

216

Our common desire is that Christ may shine forth in our midst and in this land as the light of life and truth.

I recall at this moment that in 1510–1511 Martin Luther came to Rome as a pilgrim to the tombs of the princes of the Apostles, but also as one seeking and questioning. Today I come to you, to the spiritual heirs of Martin Luther; I come as a pilgrim. I come to set, with this pilgrimage in a changed world, a sign of union in the central mystery of our faith.

Pope John Paul linked the points he wished to make with texts taken from the Epistle to the Romans, on which Luther had written his great commentaries, and which he had regarded as 'the real masterpiece of the New Testament and the purest Gospel'. St Paul taught that all need conversion and repentance. Similarly the Second Vatican Council had affirmed that 'there can be no ecumenism worthy of the name without interior conversion' (Decree on Ecumenism, n. 7).

'Let us no more pass judgment on one another' (Rom 14:13). Let us rather recognise our guilt. 'All have sinned' (Rom 3:23) applies also with regard to the grace of unity. . . . 'Where sin increased, grace abounded all the more' (Rom 5:20). God does not cease to 'have mercy upon all' (Rom 11:32). He gives his Son, he gives himself, he gives forgiveness, justification, grace, eternal life. We can recognise all this together.

You know that decades of my life have been marked by the experience of the challenging of Christianity by atheism and non-belief. It appears to me all the more clearly how important is our common profession of Jesus Christ, of his word and work in this world, and how we are driven by the urgency of the hour to overcome the differences that divide us, and bear witness to our growing union.

Jesus Christ is the salvation of us all. He is the only mediator, 'whom God put forward as an expiation by his blood, to be received by faith' (Rom 3:25). 'We have peace with God through our Lord Jesus Christ' (Rom 5:1) and among ourselves. By virtue of the Holy Spirit we are his brothers, really and essentially sons of God. 'If children, then heirs, heirs of God and fellow heirs with Christ' (Rom 8:17).

Reflecting on Confessio Augustana, and through numerous contacts, we have realised anew that we believe and profess all that together. This was testified by the German Bishops in their pastoral letter 'Thy Kingdom come' (20 January 1980). They said to the Catholic faithful: 'Let us rejoice to discover not only partial consent on some truths, but also agreement on the fundamental and central truths. That lets us hope for unity also in the areas of our faith and our life in which we are still divided up to now.'

But we must not be blind to what still divides us.

We must examine it together as far as possible, not to widen the gaps, but to bridge them. We cannot stop at the acknowledgement: 'We are and remain divided for ever and against each other'. We are called to strive together, in the dialogue of truth and love, to full unity in faith. Only full unity gives us the possibility of gathering with the same sentiments and the same faith at the Lord's one table. We can let the lectures given by Luther on the Letter to the Romans in the years 1516–1517 tell us what this effort above all consists of. He teaches that 'faith in Christ through which we are justified, is not just belief in Christ, or more exactly in the person of Christ, but belief in what is Christ's'. 'We must believe in him and in what is his'. To the question: 'What is his, then?' Luther refers to the Church and to her authentic teaching. If the difficulties that exist between us were only a question of 'ecclesiastical structures set up by men' (cf. *Confessio Augustana*, VIII), we could and should eliminate them immediately. According to the conviction of Catholics, disagreement revolves around 'what is Christ's', around 'what is his': his Church and her mission, her message, her sacraments, and the ministries placed in the service of the Word and the Sacrament. The dialogue established since the Council has brought us a good way further in this respect. Precisely in Germany many important steps have been taken. That can inspire us with confidence with regard to problems not yet solved.

Another meeting followed with the leaders of other Christian denominations, at which the Pope took as his text: 'How good and pleasant it is when brothers dwell in unity (Ps 133: 1).

We have found ourselves together as *brothers in the Lord*. Brotherhood is not an empty word or a fleeting dream for us; it is a happy reality, today and here and wherever Christians obey their Lord and follow him. . . .

All the joy for our meeting, for our vocation and mission, must not make us forget how little we have responded and respond to the grace of God. In spite of our deep union, we are, in fact, divided in many things.

Our being together in your German homeland confronts us with the event of the Reformation. We must think of what preceded it and of what has happened since. If we do not evade the facts, we realise that the faults of men led to the unhappy division of Christians, and that our faults again hinder the possible and necessary steps towards unity. I emphatically make my own what my predecessor Hadrian VI said in 1523 at the Diet of Nuremberg: 'Certainly the Lord's hand has not been shortened so much that he cannot save us, but sin separates us from him . . . All of us, prelates and priests, have strayed from the right path and there is not anyone who does good (cf. Ps 14:3), Therefore we must all render honour to God and humble ourselves before him. Each of us must consider why he has fallen and judge himself rather than be judged by God on the day of wrath'. With the last German or Dutch Pope, I say: 'The disease is deep-rooted and developed; we must therefore proceed step by step, and first of all treat the most serious and dangerous ills with suitable medicines, so as not to make things even more confused with a hasty reform'. Today, as then, the first and most important step towards unity is the renewal of Christian life. 'There can be no ecumenism worthy of the name without interior conversion' (Vatican II, Decree of Ecumenism, n. 7).

Pope John Paul recalled what had already been achieved in Germany, remembering apparently how Christians of all denominations were united in suffering and in witness at the time of the Nazis.

Among those things are the coming together of separated brothers in the years of calamities and tribulations suffered in common, the martyrdom of those who sacrificed their lives for unity in Christ, the common scientific efforts made together for decades for the unity of Christians, the ecumenical translation of Holy Scripture made together, reciprocal and regular official contacts, the efforts made again and again to meet together the challenges of our time, reflection, animated by an ecumenical spirit, on the intention and testimony of the *Confessio Augustana* and the celebration of its 450th anniversary, union in the National Council of Christian Churches 'for common witness and service' . . .

Certainly everything depends decisively on our uniting more and more 'for common witness and service'. The unity of the Church undeniably belongs to her essence. She is not an end in herself. The Lord gives her 'that the world may believe' (Jn 17:21). Let us do everything in our power to bear witness together to what is given to us in Jesus Christ.

He is the 'one mediator between God and men' (1 Tim 2:5). 'There is salvation in no one else' (Acts 4:12). All steps towards the centre oblige us and encourage us at the same time to venture to take the necessary steps towards all our sisters and brothers.

The Pope's third meeting at Mainz that morning was with representatives of the Jewish community.

If Christians must consider themselves brothers of all men and behave accordingly, this holy obligation is all the more binding where they find themselves before members of the Jewish people! In the 'Declaration on the relationship of the Church with Judaism' in April of this year, the Bishops of the Federal Republic of Germany put this sentence at the beginning: 'Whoever

219

meets Jesus Christ, meets Judaism'. I would like to make these words mine too. The faith of the Church in Jesus Christ, the son of David and the son of Abraham (cf. Mt 1 : 1) actually contains what the Bishops call in that declaration 'the spiritual heritage of Israel for the Church' (n. 11), a living heritage, which must be understood and preserved in its depth and richness by us Catholic Christians.

Pope John Paul set the 'concrete brotherly relations between Jews and Catholics in Germany' against 'the grim background of the persecution and the attempted extermination of Judaism in this country'.

Before God all men are of the same value and importance.

In this spirit, during the persecution, Christians likewise committed themselves, often at the risk of their lives, to prevent or relieve the sufferings of their Jewish brothers and sisters. I would like to express recognition and gratitude to them at this moment. And also to those people who, as Christians, affirming they belonged to the Jewish people, travelled along the *via crucis* of their brothers and sisters to the end – like the great Edith Stein, called in her religious institute Teresa Benedikta of the Cross, whose memory is rightly held in great honour.

The Pope then spoke of the need for collaboration and dialogue.

It is not just a question of correcting a false religious view of the Jewish people, which in the course of history was one of the causes that contributed to misunderstanding and persecution, but above all of the dialogue between the two religions which – with Islam – gave the world faith in the one, ineffable God who speaks to us, and which desire to serve him on behalf of the whole world.

The first dimension of this dialogue, that is, the meeting between the people of God of the Old Covenant, never revoked by God (cf. Rom 11 : 29), and that of the New Covenant, is at the same time a dialogue within our Church, that is to say, between the first and the second part of her Bible.

The second dimension of the dialogue was the meeting between Christians and 'the present-day people of the covenant concluded with Moses'. The third dimension was the common task.

Jews and Christians, as children of Abraham, are called to be a blessing for the world (cf. Gen 12 : 2ff), by committing themselves together for peace and justice among all men and peoples. . . .

220

In the light of this promise and call of Abraham's, I look with you to the destiny and role of your people among the peoples. I willingly pray with you for the fullness of Shalom for all your brothers, in nationality and in faith, and also for the land to which Jews look with particular veneration.

Later on 17 November, the Holy Father addressed the German Episcopal Conference at Fulda. Speaking of the Reformation schism, which had now lasted for more than four and a half centuries, he told them not to resign themselves to the fact that 'disciples of Christ do not give the testimony of unity before the world'.

We often hear it said today that the ecumenical movement of the Churches is at a standstill, that after the spring of the changes brought by the Council, there has followed a period of coolness. In spite of many regrettable difficulties, I cannot agree with this judgment.

Unity, which comes from God, is given to us at the cross. We must not want to avoid the cross, passing to rapid attempts at harmonising differences, excluding the question of truth. But neither must we abandon one another, and go on our separate ways, because drawing closer calls for the patient and suffering love of Christ crucified. Let us not be diverted from the laborious way in order to remain where we are, or to choose ways that are apparently shorter and lead astray.

In the evening of that very crowded 17 November, Pope John Paul celebrated a Mass for young people at Munich. He concluded his homily with a reference to the Lutherans.

I would like to close with a special blessing for our Evangelical Lutheran brothers and sisters, who today in this country are celebrating their *Day of Repentance and Prayer*. This day is dominated for them by a knowledge of the necessity for constant renewal and by the calling of the Church to commemorate our communion as a people and as a State before God in prayer. The Roman Catholic Church is united with you in this matter. Please include your Catholic fellow-citizens, as well as your brother John Paul and his ministry, in your prayers this day. Amen.

On 19 November the Pope flew back to Rome from Munich. In his parting address at the airport he spoke of the motives for his visit.

I not only perceived a special *call* of the remote and recent past, but also *the challenge for the future* –

221

the challenge made by Jesus' prayer 'that all may be one'.

This prayer of the Lord becomes for us all the source of a new life and a new longing. As Bishop of Rome and Successor of St Peter *I put myself fully and completely in the stream of this longing*: in it I recognise the language of the Holy Spirit and the will of Christ whom I wish to obey and to be faithful to in everything.

I want to serve unity; I want to walk all the ways in which, after the experiences of the centuries and millennia, Christ is leading us towards the unity of that flock where he alone is the *only and reliable Good Shepherd*.

The jubilee of the Confession of Augsburg had therefore provided an appropriate occasion for his visit.

I hold the firm hope that the *unity of Christians is already on its way* in the power of the Spirit of truth and love. We know how long the times of separation and division have been. But we do not know how long the way to unity will be. But one thing we know with all the greater certainty: *We have to keep on walking this way with perseverance* – keep on going and do not stand still! There are many things we have to do for it; above all, we have to *persevere in prayer, in an ever more powerful and intimate prayer.* Unity can be given only as a gift of the Lord, as the fruit of his passion and resurrection in the 'fullness of time' appointed to it.

Back in Rome, the Holy Father spoke of his experiences in Germany at the General Audience of 26 November. Speaking again of the Confession of Augsburg, which had been conceived as a basis of reconciliation, he recalled that 'the efforts made then to maintain the unity of the Church did not yield the expected results'. Ecumenism was a way

on which we can no longer turn our backs; but we must always go forward, not desisting from prayer and interior conversion, and adapting our conduct in the light of the Holy Spirit, who alone can bring it about that the whole work will be accomplished together in love and truth.

The Feast of St Andrew 1980 was marked by the usual exchange of delegates and letters between Constantinople and Rome. Many references were made to the theological dialogue which had just commenced between the Catholics and Orthodox. The Pope, in a letter to the Ecumenical Patriarch dated 24 November 1980, spoke of the 'warm fraternal charity' which characterised the dialogue.

The old differences that had led the Eastern and Western Churches to cease celebrating the Eucharist together are going to be tackled in a new and constructive way. Both the subject chosen for the first phase of the dialogue and its general perspectives bear witness to this.

Our prayer will accompany the theological dialogue that it may be more and more deeply rooted in the truth, carried out in sincerity and in mutual faithfulness without shadows, animated by the Spirit of God and therefore fruitful for the life of the Church. For this purpose I have requested the prayer of all the Catholic faithful and, that we might grow together in Christ, I expressed the wish that where they live side by side, Catholics and Orthodox should entertain fraternal relations and a disinterested collaboration, which will progressively prepare for realising our unity.

The Pope's second encyclical, *Dives in Misericordia*, was published on 30 November 1980. At one point Pope John Paul explores the ecumenical implications of the letter's theme of mercy.

The contemporary Church is profoundly conscious that only on the basis of the mercy of God will she be able to carry out the tasks that derive from the teaching of the Second Vatican Council, and, in the first place, the ecumenical task which aims at uniting all those who confess Christ. As she makes many efforts in this direction, the Church confesses with humility that only that *love* which is more powerful than the weakness of human divisions *can definitely bring about that unity* which Christ implored from the Father and which the Spirit never ceases to beseech for us 'with sighs too deep for words' (Rom 8:26).

On 5 December Pope John Paul received the members of the Catholic/Methodist International Commission. He referred to the fourteen years of dialogue between the two Churches, and recalled that several of the Methodist members of the Commission had been observers at the Council.

You have often remarked in your reports how these attentive observers were struck by the deep affinities between Catholic and Methodist traditions and ideals: between the fervent preaching of personal holiness by the Wesleys and later Methodist leaders, and the work of the spiritual giants of Catholic history. In choosing this affinity as an anchor for your dialogue, you chose wisely; yours has been a truly 'holy converse', centred on a shared love of Christ, so that in it the thorny questions which are the legacy of the sad history of modern Christian division (questions which you have not shirked) have been faced with serenity, good will and charity. No one has more need than the

223

ecumenist to remember the words of Saint Paul: 'If I speak in the tongues of men and of angels, but have not love, I am a noisy gong or a clanging cymbal' (1 Cor 13:1).

Besides discussions of doctrinal differences, the dialogue had had a 'strong emphasis on the positive challenges which all Christ's witnesses face today' – in the social field, and also 'in the delicate inner realm of the Christian conscience, where no man or woman escapes the hard choices, the sacrifices inseparable from holding to Christ'.

Do not be upset by the cries of the impatient and the sceptical, but do all in your power to ensure that your search for reconciliation is echoed and reflected wherever Methodists and Catholics meet.

On December 8 a prayer which the Pope had composed was read at the shrine of Our Lady of Altötting. The prayer expressed his reflections on his German visit; part of it was concerned with the unity of Christians.

Mother of Christ, who before his Passion prayed: 'Father . . . that they may all be one' (Jn 17:11–21), how closely connected is my way through German land, precisely this year, with the deep and humble longing for unity among Christians, who have been divided since the sixteenth century! Can anyone desire more deeply than you that Christ's prayer in the Upper Room should come true? And if we ourselves must recognise that we shared responsibility for the division, and today pray for a new unity in love and in truth, could we not hope that you, Mother of Christ, will pray together with us? Could we not hope that the fruit of this prayer will in due time be the gift of that 'fellowship of the Holy Spirit' (2 Cor 13:14), which is essential 'so that the world may believe' (Jn 17:21)?

At the end of 1980 more than 30,000 young people came to Rome as part of a mass ecumenical youth gathering organised by the Community of Taizé. Each participant was the host of one of the 300 parishes of the Roman diocese. On 30 December Pope John Paul took part with them in a vigil of prayer, during which he delivered a long address, each section of which was in a different one of eight languages. In their assembly, he said, the participants had 'shared, in prayer and exchanges, the same aspiration to reconciliation, peace, and, I would say, your impatience for unity'. It was 'a way of preparing, at your level, the ways of unity, of living its mystery a little'.

For ecclesial unity, dear friends, is a deep mystery which transcends our conceptions, our efforts, our desires. The Fathers of the Second Vatican Council meditated at length on this mystery of the Church, of the People of God, as the Constitution *Lumen Gentium* and other texts bear witness. 'Christ bestowed the unity of the one and only Church on his Church from the beginning' (Decree on Ecumenism, n. 4). And at the same time, it must constantly be sought, reconstructed, for Christians as a whole.

In a certain sense, Christians do not exist before the Church, and they do not continue to exist, as such, independently of the Church. Let us say rather: men join the Church to become Christians, her who was born as one people from the plan of God the Father, the sacrifice of Christ, and the gift of the Holy Spirit . . . Unity does not come merely from listening to the same evangelical message, which, moreover, is transmitted to us by the Church; it takes on a mystical depth: we are joined to the very Body of Christ through faith and baptism in the name of the Father, the Son and the Holy Spirit; it is the Spirit himself who justifies us and animates our Christian life. . . .

The structure of the Church, with its hierarchy and sacraments 'merely expresses and realises this essential unity received from Christ the Head'. But not all Christians live according to the 'grace' and 'vocation' of unity. Unity is 'a fundamental characteristic of the Church', but its realisation is difficult. 'Faithfulness to Christ makes it an urgent duty for us to reconstruct full unity.' Although Christians have a 'common heritage', and progress in 'understanding, charity and common prayer',

> out of honesty and loyalty to ourselves and to our brothers and sisters, we cannot celebrate the Lord's Eucharist together, for it is the Sacrament of Unity. It is impossible, in fact, to separate eucharistic communion and ecclesial communion in one and the same faith.

The unity they were to seek

> is not a question of any kind of unity whatsoever, but of the one that corresponds to the ways laid down by the Lord in the foundation of his Church and followed by the most venerable tradition of the Church.

Their experience in Rome might help them better to understand this unity according to the mind of Christ. First, this unity, 'marred by Christians and therefore ceaselessly to be rebuilt', was entrusted to Peter.

It was not to John, the great contemplative, nor to Paul, the

225

incomparable theologian, and preacher, that Christ gave the task of strengthening the other Apostles, his brethren (cf. Lk 22:31–32), of feeding the lambs and the sheep (cf. Jn 21:15–17) but to Peter alone. It is always enlightening and moving to meditate on the Gospel texts expressing the unique and irreducible role of Peter in the College of Apostles and in the Church at her beginning. It is even overwhelming, for each of us, to see how much Christ continues to put all his trust in Peter, in spite of his momentary weakness. And Peter took this role seriously, even to the supreme witness of shedding his blood. His First Letter certainly seems to prove that he meditated deeply upon the astonishing words that Jesus had said to him. It reveals the personal spirituality of the one who had received the charge of gathering together the flock of the one Shepherd: 'Tend the flock of God that is your charge . . . not for shameful gain but eagerly. . . . And when the chief Shepherd is manifested you will obtain the unfading crown of glory' (1 Pet 5:2–4; cf. ibid, 2:25). Peter remembers that he is the rock but also the shepherd. And when he exhorts the Elders to carry out their pastoral task eagerly, it is because he remembers having received his own pastoral task in response to a threefold protestation of love.

The charism of St Peter passed to his successors.

The Pope gave examples of Rome's leadership in the early Church, and then turned to the second way in which Rome could help his hearers to understand Christ's will for unity: Rome was a Church of martyrs.

This glance at the Church in Rome makes me wish you an increasing interest in history. The knowledge of two thousand years of Christianity can instil two important things in Christians: the sense of continuity and the sense of the relative. The sense of continuity can preserve us from the naïve and presumptuous illusion that the generation to which we belong is the first to discover certain truths and to live certain experiences. The sense of the relative, which has nothing to do with scepticism, teaches us to discern what is essential. A certain number of difficulties in faith, of individual or collective religious crises, are due to relativising the absolute and absolutising the relative. We may wonder, so essential is this discernment, if it is possible today, in a civilised world, to be fully Christian while knowing nothing or hardly anything of the Church's past.

The third light that Rome could throw on the demands of ecumenism was their experience of brotherhood and prayer in the parishes of Rome. This led the Pope to speak of the need for the unity of the Church to have an 'institutional aspect', and to urge his young hearers to preserve their contacts with their parishes.

Communion in the Church necessarily has a visible countenance, an institutional aspect, thanks in particular to the service of unity which the papal, episcopal and priestly ministry is. This ministry, which you have directly witnessed all these days, brings about, in the strong sense of the word, communion among Christians because it is in the first place an apostolic ministry, a real link with the origins, with what founded the Church: bishops and priests preside, in fact, over the sacraments and the proclamation of the Word, which make the Lord Jesus our contemporary. . . Furthermore, you may perhaps grasp even better, through your temporary integration in the parishes of Rome, the importance of places of communion. While there may be various places, the parish is chief among them, with the advantage of having a geographical base and so being open to all environments. This material, visible, and institutional possibility seems necessary to embody the essential idea of communion in the Church; God accepts us such as we are, without discrimination. It is his gratuitous love that gathers us, beyond our particularisms, our merits, or our sins. I know, dear young people, that many of you have made well-known efforts in recent times concretely to rejoin your parishes, which you had tended to abandon for various reasons. Keep on doing it. You will certainly find, beyond possible disappointments, the roots of your Christian identity; you will hear there the Church's calls to evangelisation and you will bring to these communities the evangelical inspiration they are entitled to expect from you.

Fourthly, history showed Rome to have been a missionary Church.

Very early, the communities founded by the Apostles, the Eastern one – whose heritage was received by Constantinople – and that of Rome for the West, became apostolic centres of far-reaching influence, in the one Church of Jesus Christ. Thus Rome, for its part, showed concern to promote and harmonise the evangelisation of the new nations of the European continent. Particular ties were then woven between these new local Churches and the one that had helped to found them; a common spiritual culture, a common soul was established throughout this Europe, in your countries; it has remained through many vicissitudes and it may greatly contribute to inspiring and nourishing the unity that this continent is presently seeking. I can bear witness, for example, that Christianity in my country developed in close liaison with the Church of Rome.

In this way the Gospel, the history of the Church, and the experience you are having in Rome, enable you to approach the mystery of the Church in a better way, to grasp the requirements and the ways to the full unity of Christians, and to take your place better yourselves in the line of descendants of Christ's real disciples in search of full reconciliation. In this way you put yourselves in the true climate of faith, hope, and charity.

On the last day of 1980, in an Apostolic Letter entitled *Egregiae Virtutis*, the Pope declared SS Cyril and Methodius to be Patrons of Europe. These two brothers, Greeks from Thessalonica, were the founders of the Slavonic Church in the ninth century. Receiving their mission first from the Emperor of Constantinople and later from the Pope (in Methodius' case; Cyril died as a monk in Rome), they are fitting patrons of Church unity as well as political harmony.

Europe, in fact, as a geographical whole, is, so to speak, the fruit of the action of two currents of Christian traditions, to which are added also two different, but at the same time deeply complementary, forms of culture. St Benedict, who with his influence embraced not only Europe, first of all Western and central, but through the Benedictine centres also arrived in the other continents, is as the very centre of that current that starts from Rome, from the See of St Peter's successors. The Holy Brothers of Thessalonica highlighted first the contribution of ancient Greek culture and, subsequently, the significance of the influence of the Church of Constantinople and of Eastern tradition, which has so deeply marked the spirituality and culture of so many peoples and nations in the Eastern part of the European Continent.

Since today, after centuries of division of the Church between East and West, between Rome and Constantinople, from the Second Vatican Council decisive steps have been taken in the direction of full communion, the proclamation of SS Cyril and Methodius as Co-Patrons of Europe alongside St Benedict, seems to correspond fully to the signs of our time. Especially if that happens in the year in which the two Churches, Catholic and Orthodox, have entered the stage of a decisive dialogue, which started on the Island of Patmos, linked with the tradition of St John the Apostle and Evangelist. Therefore this act is also intended to make this date memorable.

During the 1981 Week of Prayer for Christian Unity, the Holy Father devoted several speeches to this subject. In his Sunday Angelus message of 18 January, he reminded his hearers that 'unity is a characteristic and a requirement of the Catholic Church', and that

the travail of history and the spirit of evil have led Christians to painful divisions. The Spirit of the Lord, however, has brought forth the ecumenical movement, which, in the last few decades, has started Christianity decidedly on the way of full unity.

He continued:

It is a good thing to recall today Fr Couturier, a convinced apostle of the importance of prayer for unity. This year the centenary of his birth (1881–1981) will be celebrated in France, precisely during this week. Together with him it is right to recall with gratitude all those, both Catholics and members of other Churches, who promoted and encouraged this practice, sometimes amid misunderstanding. First of all mention should be made of my great predecessor Leo XIII, who, as early as 1895, recommended to Catholics a novena of prayers for unity, in the period of Pentecost (Letter *Provida Matris*).

Recalling the theme of the 1981 Week, the Pope affirmed that

The subject of the week of prayer this year is rich in content and very inspiring: 'One Spirit, various gifts, one body' (cf. 1 Cor 12:3–13). The variety of gifts, ministries and tasks within the people of God comes from one and the same Spirit and is geared to common advantage and to the harmonious functioning of one body, that is, the Mystical Body of Christ.

Each one, therefore, is called to make his own contribution of life, action, study, and prayer. I emphatically and confidently call you to do so.

At a General Audience on 21 January, the Holy Father returned to the subject of Christian unity, and explained why he attached great importance to the Week of Prayer.

This week of prayer returns at a set time to urge the conscience of Christians to an examination before God on the subject of the restoration of full unity. It returns also to remind us that unity is a gift from God and that therefore it is necessary to ask the Lord for it intensely. The fact, moreover, that Christians of different denominations unite in common prayer – particularly at this time or in the week of Pentecost, but I should like to hope that this will happen more and more often on other occasions as well – takes on quite a special significance. Christians are rediscovering with growing clarity the partial, but real communion that exists, and they are moving together, before God and with his help, towards full unity.

They are moving towards this goal by beginning precisely with prayer to the Lord, to him who purifies and liberates, who redeems and unites.

Prayer for unity was becoming more and more common.

It is losing its character of an extraordinary event and is becoming part of the normal life of the Churches . . . This is a positive sign. But it is necessary to be very careful to prevent prayer from losing that stirring charge which must shake the conscience of everyone in the face of the division of Christians, which 'openly contradicts the will of Christ, scandalises the world, and damages that most holy cause, the preaching of the Gospel to every creature' (Vatican II, Decree on Ecumenism, n. 1).

The joint preparation of texts for the Week of Prayer together with the World Council of Churches 'expresses the common determination to listen attentively to the Word of God in order to carry out his will'. However,

> this week of prayers also creates a certain anxiety every year. It shows us, in fact, that, if we still must plead for unity, if we must seek it, the full unity of Christians is not yet reached and we are at fault before the Lord. Even this anxiety, which is sometimes veiled with bitterness, seems to me a positive sign. It should incite us to a greater commitment of faith and love, and in the pursuit of full unity.

Pope John Paul recalled his recent meetings with Church leaders of East and West, and other signs of ecumenical progress, especially the recently initiated dialogue with the Orthodox. But it must not be forgotten that, if

> Eastern and Western Churches have no longer concelebrated the Eucharist for almost a millennium, that means that they have considered the controversial problems serious ones. Not everything can be reduced to historical and cultural factors, even if the latter had a heavy and harmful influence in the progressive estrangement between East and West.

Dialogue is required both to 'solve all the major problems . . . that are connected with faith', and to constitute

> a valuable instrument for clarifying mutual misunderstandings and prejudices and also for reaching agreement on those legitimate varieties and differences compatible with the unity of faith.

It was for this reason that the Pope wished

> to declare the Eastern Saints Cyril and Methodius Co-patron Saints of Europe, together with St Benedict. For full unity we must all accustom ourselves to having a mentality mutually open both to the Eastern tradition and to the Western one.

The theme of the Week of Prayer – 'One Spirit, various gifts, one body' – provided the Pope with a cue for discussing the contribution which the charismatic renewal could and should make to Church unity.

St Paul, writing to the Christians of Corinth, whose exuberant vitality gave rise to expressions similar to the ecstatic phenomena of pagan religious assemblies, gives explanations on how to discern true from false charisms. Upright faith, adherence to Jesus Christ, is the first norm of their authenticity.

Another criterion is provided by St Paul's words: 'By one Spirit we were all baptized into one Body' (1 Cor 12: 13).

In the Christian community the variety of gifts received must be put into the service of the building up of the one Body of Christ and of the harmonious development of its vitality.

In this way not only must charisms not generate rifts or oppositions, but they must be in the service of unity. And when this unity is harmed, every gift must be used for its re-establishment. Unity and harmonious functioning are part of the health of the body itself and of its normal activity.

And so it is necessary that all charisms, present today in various forms, must also be put at the service of unity to give the Christian community the essential conditions to proclaim and bear witness that Jesus Christ is the Lord.

On Friday, 23 January, the Pope presided at an Hour of Prayer for Christian unity in the Sistine Chapel, attended by members of the Curia, and preached a homily based on the text: 'That they all may be one'.

Unity, the resplendent mark of the true Church, is the climax of Christ's priestly prayer at the Last Supper; it is his last Testament of love, the order that he left us before his passion: *antequam pateretur*. It is a distinctive mark of the Church that Jesus was at that moment preparing to found and to redeem by instituting the Eucharist, by shedding blood and water from his Heart on the Cross (cf. Jn 19: 34). And in the communion of affection and prayer of this particular hour, we have felt the Saviour's supreme aspiration re-echoing in us: *Ut omnes unum sint*.

It is not possible to evade the examination of conscience which these words impose on us. They are the touchstone for the credibility of discipleship of Christ in the world: *ut credat mundus quia tu me misisti* (Jn 17: 21). If we are not one, as the Father is one in Christ, and Christ is one in the Father, the world

231

will not believe: it lacks the concrete proof of the mystery of redemption, by which the Lord made of dispersed mankind one family, one organism, one body, one heart. . . .

For this reason we are here today to pray, all of us of the Roman Curia, to feel within us the whole power of prayer and supplication to the Father in those words which rose from Jesus' lips and heart in the night of the Eucharist and the agony. The night of Holy Thursday. The night of the betrayal, the scandal, the division: 'and the sheep of the flock will be scattered' (Mt 26: 31). But Christ's voice is louder: 'That they all may be one'.

The Pope reminded the members of the Curia that they were 'in the direct service of the Pope', and therefore 'in the service of unity'. They must be one with the Church all over the world – 'all the faithful in the world, all dioceses, all parishes, all convents and monasteries, all ecclesial communities, even the most remote missionary stations' – praying "that all may be one".

The beauty of the Church lies in unity, though in the diversity of ministries and operations: 'Where there is division, there is deformity, there is not beauty', St Augustine says (Sermon 46.37). And this beauty is the gift of the Holy Spirit, as the great Bishop of Hippo says further: 'By the Holy Spirit we are gathered in unity, not separated from it' (Sermon 8.17).

While we pray for unity, that the Holy Spirit, who moves everything that lives in the Church, may preserve it and restore it where it is broken, we must always feel in close dependence on the same Spirit: we, too, form one body in him; and, in the exercise of the various ministries entrusted to us, all of us, from the first to the last, know we are an integral part of a great plan of unity: we must exert ourselves, in silence, in obedience, in sacrifice, even in the humblest duties, because we are certain that our work, like a seed placed in fertile ground, will yield its fruit in due time.

The 'orderly team of the whole Roman Curia' co-operated in 'a service for the complete unity of all believers in Christ; a *diaconia* for *koinonia*' (a service for communion). But this service will not be accomplished if we have not reached this close intimacy with the Lord Jesus: if we are not truly consecrated in Truth with him and like him (cf. Jn. 17: 17-19).

The external unity for which we pray will be the germinating, the flourishing, of this close union with Christ which all the faithful alike – bishops, priests, consecrated souls, laity – must have. . . .

If we lack genuine union with God in Christ, in the life of

grace, our ecumenism remains a mere *flatus vocis*. 'For although the Catholic Church has been endowed with all divinely revealed truth and with all means of grace, yet its members fail to live by them with all the fervour that they should. As a result the radiance of the Church's face shines less brightly in the eyes of our separated brethren and of the world at large, and the growth of God's kingdom is retarded. Every Catholic must therefore aim at Christian perfection' (Decree on Ecumenism, n. 4).

Giving his Sunday Angelus message on 25 January, the last day of the Week for Prayer, the Holy Father reiterated his belief that unity was the gift of the Holy Spirit. 1981 marked the sixteenth centenary of the First Council of Chalcedon, which had added to the Nicene Creed the clauses professing the divinity of the Holy Spirit.

We shall invoke him in order that he may carry out and lead to its definitive accomplishment the work of unity, which can be accomplished only by him. Only by him, through him, in fact, can those obstacles which make the way of union difficult be overcome in us and among us; only by him, through him, can all our efforts aiming at the unity of the Church be crowned with success. Such unity cannot but be, in a word, a gift. We often repeat: the fellowship of the Holy Spirit . . . ! And precisely today, at the end of the octave, I wish to address once more to all those throughout the world who are taking part in it, the words 'The fellowship of the Holy Spirit be with you all' (cf. 2 Cor 13 : 14).

On 16 February 1981, Pope John Paul set out on a visit to the Far East. While his plane was refuelling at Karachi, the Pope celebrated Mass in a stadium. A few minutes before the Holy Father's arrival, a man was killed by a bomb he was carrying. In his homily the Pope spoke of the close connection between the Eucharist and Christian unity.

Because the mystery of the Eucharist is so closely linked to the mystery of the Church, we cannot but feel a sadness at the divisions which still affect the one Body of Christ – divisions between fellow Christians. We are saddened because we cannot yet share together in the one bread and the one cup. May this sadness prompt us to action. When we who are Catholics partake of this Sacrament of unity may we have a deep longing for the reunion of all the Churches; may we feel the urgency of the prayer of Jesus: *'Ut unum sint* – May they all be one' (Jn 17: 21); and may we be more deeply convinced of the need to pray and work for the unity of all who have been baptized in Christ.

233

Our participation in the Eucharistic Sacrifice should also deepen our desire for the whole human family to come to the light of faith. It should inspire us to bring the Gospel of Jesus Christ to all those who do not yet know him. For the Eucharist is 'Bread for the life of the world', bread for every man and woman on earth.

On 21 February, Pope John Paul spoke to the leaders of other Churches in Manila. He commented on the 'warm community feeling' which was characteristic of the Filipinos.

In view of this spirit, divisions among Christians look even more strange and unnatural. This is surely an important basis for your ecumenical sensitivity, but of course our concern for the unity of Christians has a more profound reason. All that is noble and good in human community has been realised and perfected in that deeper world-wide fellowship of which Saint Paul says: 'For as many of you as were baptized into Christ have put on Christ' (Gal 3: 27).

The Church's unity is God's gift, which Christians obscure by their divisions, and so obscure their witness to Christ. 'It is a great grace, and a power for renewal, that in our days God has awakened in the hearts of Christians a deep longing' for one visible Church. Christians are already linked in a 'real, although still imperfect, communion'.

It is our responsibility as far as possible to express and make visible this communion which links us in Christ, 'maintaining the unity of the Spirit in the bond of peace' (Eph 4: 3).

Christian co-operation must express the bond that already unites them.

You have an opportunity to combine or co-ordinate your efforts to promote the human condition, by alleviating need, by helping to create in society those conditions which make life more worthy of the dignity of every man and woman.

These efforts can give a common witness to the one Gospel of Jesus Christ. It is the Gospel which is our common treasure, and the missionary task which is yours as Christians must lead you also to look for ways to proclaim together, as far as possible, the basic truths about Jesus Christ which it contains, finding what already unites you even before your full communion is achieved (cf. *Redemptor Hominis*, n. 12). Here you at once come face to face with the things which still divide you and which limit the witness that can be given together. That is the tragedy of our divisions.

Far from rendering fruitful and effective our witnessing to Christ, the scandal of our divisions has diminished our credibility. This is true not only among non-Christians but even among Christians of simple faith. In all honesty we must bear responsibility for this. That is why it is so urgent that at every level Christians should be prepared to work actively and to pray for the restoration of full communion. The effort of theological dialogue is an integral part of this, but its very soul is personal conversion, holiness of life and prayer for Christian unity (Decree on Ecumenism, n. 8).

As the majority of Christians in the Philippines were Catholics, they bore a special responsibility for unity.

I want to end with a word of encouragement to all Christians in the Philippines. Your task is a real one, for the divisions are in many cases of recent origin; there has been a proliferation of many different groups; for some, the divisions still find expression in open ill-will and in proselytism. But remember, the unity Christ wills for his Church is his gift. Your patient, well-informed efforts to overcome separation and to restore communion, the common witness which even now you are able to give, are a loving obedience to the will of our Lord.

On 24 February the Holy Father made a similar speech to the leaders of other Churches in Tokyo. He reminded them of their need to 'recognise each other in Christ, ... to discover and to appreciate the values in each other's Christian lives, "whether as individuals or as communities and Churches" (Decree on Ecumenism, n. 3)'. Above all they were to pray for each other and for unity, because 'there are still serious matters of faith on which we have not yet reached agreement', so that there must be 'intense prayer for reconciliation and for the complete unity that our Lord wills for his people'.

Such prayer would help Christians to use 'the opportunities that are ours to bear a common witness to Jesus Christ and to his Gospel'. (Here the cases of Japan and the Philippines are very different.)

All the Christians of Japan taken together are such a small number. Yet what a splendid mission is yours – to try to be a leaven of love amid competition in society, to exemplify and proclaim unselfishness and all the other Gospel values in the face of the materialistic values of consumerism, to emphasize human dignity and the value of human persons against everything in modern society that might detract from them. With a sense of the worldwide fellowship of Christians, surely you

235

have a special ability to promote in your own land an awareness of Japan's responsibility to the many countries and peoples of Asia which are in a less advantaged position. Especially in the dialogue with peoples of other faiths, may Christians join together to promote religious and human values. In all of these ways, amidst the existing divisions, you may be a leaven, a seed of salvation.

On the Feast of the Annunciation 1981, Pope John Paul wrote to all bishops announcing his intention of celebrating on the Feast of Pentecost the 1600th anniversary of the First Council of Constantinople (381) and the 1550th of the Council of Ephesus (431). The first of these councils asserted the divinity of the Holy Spirit, the second asserted the unity of Christ's divine and human natures by declaring Mary to be *Theotokos* (God-bearer; Mother of God).

The Council of Constantinople enlarged the Nicene Creed and so provided '*the expression of the one common faith* of the Church of the whole of Christianity.' (No mention here of the word which the West added to the text to the enduring anger of the East: 7 June would see the Pope grasping that nettle). When reciting this creed and commemorating the centenary, 'we wish to emphasize the things which unite us with all our Brothers, notwithstanding the divisions that have occurred in the course of the centuries.'

I also venture to hope that the commemoration of the Councils of Constantinople and Ephesus, which were expressions of the faith taught and professed by the undivided Church, will make us grow in mutual understanding with our beloved Brothers in the East and in the West, with whom we are still not united by full ecclesial communion but together with whom we seek in prayer, with humility and with trust, the paths to unity in truth. What indeed can more effectively hasten the journey towards that unity than the memory and, at the same time, the re-living of that which for so many centuries has been the content of the faith professed in common, indeed which has not ceased to be so, even after the sad divisions which have occurred in the course of the centuries?

1981 marked the centenary of the birth of Angelo Roncalli, later Pope John XXIII. Pope John Paul visited his predecessor's birthplace, Sotto il Monte, on 26 April. In his *Regina Caeli* message he spoke of Pope John as 'the Pope of goodness and peace, the Pope of the Council, the Pope who reopened the way to the unity of Christians, the follower of the Good Shepherd'. That evening he celebrated Mass at Bergamo, where he described the

Church as it emerged from Pope John's Council as 'the Upper Room of all people and continents, open to the future'.

It is difficult to make a deep analysis here of the perspective of this opening. But it is also difficult not to mention at least what, in a particular way, came out of Pope John's heart. It is the new impetus towards the unity of Christians and a special understanding for the mission of the Church with regard to the modern world. These themes underwent an essential probing on the bench of the Council. Even though, in this spacious Upper Room of the Church of our times, spread all over the earth, there is no lack of difficulties, tensions and crises which create justified fears, it would be difficult not to recognise that, thanks to the Pope who came from your Bergamo region, from Sotto il Monte, a providential work was started. We must just remain faithful to the Spirit of Truth, who guided this work; we must be honest in understanding and implementing the Council, and it will prove to be precisely that way along which the Church of our time and future times must walk towards the accomplishment of her destiny.

On 6 May 1981, at the end of a General Audience the Pope greeted a group of Orthodox visitors who had come to Italy to 'meet the Focolarini and meditatetogether on their common effort to be witnesses to the Gospel in their own surroundings'.

May such meetings help to overcome what separates us! I hope that they will increase and that they will contribute to weaving closer and closer bonds of love, reciprocal respect, mutual esteem and understanding among Christians, who have been baptized in the death and resurrection of Christ and who live by the same Spirit.

The next day the Holy Father addressed about six hundred people taking part in the Fourth International Leaders' Conference of the Charismatic Renewal, and spoke of their 'desire for the unity to which the Spirit guides us' and of their 'commitment to *the serious task of ecumenism*'. The Council had said that the Catholic ecumenist's 'primary duty' was to renew the Catholic Church itself.

Genuine ecumenical effort does not seek to evade the difficult tasks, such as doctrinal convergence, by rushing to create a kind of autonomous 'church of the Spirit' apart from the visible Church of Christ. True ecumenism rather serves to increase our longing for the ecclesial unity of all Christians in one faith, so that 'the world may be converted to the Gospel and so be saved, to the glory of God' (Decree on Ecumenism, n. 1). Let us be confident that if we surrender ourselves to the work of genuine renewal in the Spirit, this same Holy Spirit will bring to light the strategy for ecumenism which will bring to reality our hope for 'one Lord, one faith, one baptism, one God and Father of all, who is over all, and works through all, and is in all' (Eph 4: 6).

On the evening of 13 May Pope John Paul was shot in St Peter's Square. Messages of sympathy, appreciation and good wishes flooded in; Cardinal Willebrands received one from a Church of Scotland minister which began: 'At a time like this no brethren can feel separated.'

The Pope had marked Pentecost Sunday, 7 June, as the day for celebrating the anniversaries of the Councils of Constantinople and Ephesus. Though unable to be present in person, he participated as best he could from his sick-bed.

The occasion was one that called for great delicacy, as the deepest theological dispute between Constantinople and Rome centred on the very Constantinopolitan Creed whose composition the two Churches were celebrating. The Creed of Nicaea (325) had no more than this to affirm of the Third Person: 'And [we believe] in the Holy Spirit.' The Council of Constantinople fifty-six years later considerably enlarged this clause:

> And [we believe] in the Holy Spirit, the Lord, the giver of life,
> who proceeds from the Father.
> With the Father and the Son he is worshipped and glorified.
> He has spoken through the Prophets.
> We believe in one holy catholic and apostolic Church,
> We acknowledge one baptism for the forgiveness of sins.
> We look for the resurrection of the dead,
>   and the life of the world to come. Amen.

By the end of the sixth century a further development of the creed had taken place in Spain: the words 'and the Son' (*Filioque*) were added after the clause 'who proceeds from the Father'. The purpose of this addition was apparently to reinforce the Church's anti-Arian profession of faith in the Son's equality with the Father by affirming that the Spirit proceeded from the Son as well as from the Father. From the ninth century the creed began to be sung during Mass throughout the Frankish Empire, and in this expanded form. Rome at first refused to accept the change, but by the eleventh century this form was adopted in the liturgy throughout the West. The Greeks strongly denounced the innovation, both as a modification of a canonical formula which could not be changed by part of the Church alone, and also as a heretical expression of trinitarian faith.

238

On 4 June Pope John Paul wrote to the Ecumenical Patriarch about the centenary. He began by reflecting how the Holy Spirit had led the Church between 325 and 381 to formulate its faith in the Spirit's divinity more explicitly. With great tact the Pope then quoted the relevant clause from the Constantinopolitan Creed without the addition of the *Filioque*, and repeated the words from his letter of 25 March in which he stated that 'the teaching of the First Council of Constantinople is still and always the expression of the one common faith of the Church of the whole of Christianity'. He then referred to the historic dispute over the *Filioque*, without suggesting how it could be resolved. (Silence was wise, because the issue was to be considered by the Catholic/Orthodox Dialogue.)

I am aware, it is true, that in the course of history controversies have taken place between our Churches with regard to the doctrine on the Holy Spirit, particularly on the eternal relationship of the Son and the Spirit.

This question, like all those which are not yet entirely cleared up between our Churches, will have to be the object of the dialogue so happily begun, which, we all expect, will contribute to hasten the longed-for day when, in light and without mental reservations, we will be able to proclaim our faith together by concelebrating the Holy Eucharist.

I will not say more. You are aware, Venerated Brother, of the situation in which I find myself as the result of recent events. The designs of Divine Providence surpass all understanding but we know that they are always inspired by his mercy. Personally, I am happy to offer my sufferings for the Body of Christ, that is, the Church, (cf. Col 1: 24) in order that the moment may be hastened when the Lord's prayer *ut omnes unum sint* (Jn 17: 21) may be fulfilled.

Pope John Paul, wishing to make the celebration an ecumenical occasion, had invited representatives of other Churches to Rome and sent a Catholic delegation to Constantinople. On the Eve of Pentecost, at First Vespers presided over by Cardinal Hume in the name of the Pope, the homily was preached by the Metropolitan Damaskinos, representing the Ecumenical Patriarch. The Metropolitan's words were a meditation on 'the Holy Spirit who gives the Church her existence and keeps her in brotherly communion'.

As ecclesial communion in the Holy Spirit is not juridical, it is characterised by the grace of our Lord Jesus Christ, the love of God the Father and the Spirit of truth. . . .

239

Today the Holy Spirit imposes on us a great task: to re-establish the unity of divided Christendom.

Living today the tragedy of separation and the necessity of putting it right, we are particularly called – in this year of the celebration of the 1600th anniversary of the meeting of the Second Ecumenical Council at Constantinople – to study the creed of faith of this Council, which constitutes the basis of the ecumenical dialogue for the reestablishment of unity.

This year should be for all the Churches and Confessions the year of an urgent invitation to examine in common – through bilateral and multilateral dialogues – to what extent they are obliged, in fidelity to their origins and to their faith, to re-establish unity or not.

This appeal and this invitation apply particularly to those among the Churches which claim to continue exclusively the one, holy, catholic and apostolic Church. They must seek and recognise as the Church, in the full sense of the term 'Church', outside their own canonical frontiers, with which they identify the one, holy, catholic and apostolic Church (naturally, if and to the extent to which that is possible) the Churches with which they will be called to eucharistic communion.

At the Solemn Mass of Pentecost on 7 June the Pope's pre-recorded homily was broadcast in the basilica of St Peter's. He expressed his wish

to confess with a loud cry of our voices and our hearts the truth that sixteen centuries ago the First Council of Constantinople formulated and expressed in the words we know so well.

He then recited the words of the Constantinopolitan Creed concerning the Holy Spirit 'as it was then expressed', i.e. without the *Filioque*. The Creed of Constantinople, 'has throughout so many generations maintained in the unity of the faith then professed the great family of those who confess Christ'.

Although at different times and places that unity of the Church has undergone divisions, the faith professed by our holy pre-decessors in the Creed of Nicaea and Constantinople testifies to the original unity and calls us again to rebuild full unity.

The Pope greeted the legates from Constantinople and the representatives of other Churches, and expressed his joy that the Roman delegation

can participate in the splendid Liturgy commemorating the historic event, a Liturgy through which the two Sister Churches of Rome and Constantinople wish to venerate the Divine

Majesty for the work done by the Council of sixteen hundred years ago. . . .

(During the Mass itself the Creed was recited *with* the *Filioque*.)
In a second recorded address, broadcast as a message preceding the recital of the *Regina Caeli* in St Peter's Square, the Pope explained once more the significance of the celebrations. A third recorded address was broadcast as the homily at Second Vespers of Pentecost in St Mary Major. After Vespers, as an ecumenical gesture, the Orthodox Acathistos Hymn in honour of the Blessed Virgin was sung. The homily treated of the role of Mary in the Church, and ended with a prayer to her, which included a prayer for the unity of Christians:

> You, who are the first Handmaid of the unity of Christ's Body, help us, help all the faithful who feel so keenly the tragedy of the historical divisions of Christianity, to seek persistently the path to the perfect unity of the Body of Christ through unreserved fidelity to the Spirit of Truth and Love, granted to them at the price of the Cross and Death of your Son.

At the parallel celebration at Constantinople, the Ecumenical Patriarch Dimitrios preached at the Divine Liturgy at the Phanar. The Patriarch spoke of the way the Eucharist, celebrated in a local Church, is at the heart of the unity of the Church.

> In this ecumenical celebration and offering of the Divine Eucharist by the local bishop for the good of the Holy Catholic and Apostolic Church, you are all included, you Christians, dear and honoured brothers, who have gathered from West and East, from North and South, for this liturgical blessing: 'May the grace of Our Lord Jesus Christ, and the love of God, and the fellowship of the Holy Spirit be with you all.'
> We would depart from the spirit and the teaching of the Great and Holy Second Ecumenical Council were we to seek its heart anywhere else than at the altar of the Divine Eucharist celebrated by a canonical bishop of that place on behalf of the whole.
> The Council gathered in one place on behalf of the whole. . . .
> Today, sixteen hundred years later, we Christians are again gathered on the soil of the undivided Church in the fellowship of the Holy Spirit; but also – through sins known only to God, but largely because of reasons that derive from non-theological, linguistic and general cultural factors – we return here in division, as pilgrims homesick for the ecumenical Christian unity, for the undivided Church, for the One, Holy, Catholic and Apostolic Church of our common Symbol of Faith.

241

This seems to be an appropriate place at which to conclude this account of the papal statements on ecumenism. We thus end at a point where the Churches are studying their common past in order to rediscover a unity which will help them view historic differences in a new light. In the words of the Ecumenical Patriarch, the common statements of faith of the early councils 'were not meant solely for the past; they looked towards today; they envisaged the future.'

12. PAPAL PRINCIPLES OF ECUMENISM

IN the first eleven chapters of this book I have presented the three Popes' statements on ecumenism in chronological order. This method has the advantage of exhibiting a continuous history of a growing relationship between Rome and her partners in dialogue. At times the reader may feel himself buried under an avalanche of words; but even when ideas recur frequently, one may admire the way in which they are expressed in different forms for different circumstances. At least they may have a cumulative effect so as to make it impossible to doubt that 'they are in earnest'.

In this last chapter however it seems desirable to set out systematically the ecumenical principles which are to be found scattered through the preceding pages. The reader will therefore find it easy, if he wishes, to compare the ecumenical emphases of the three popes.

Unity is an essential quality of the Church,[1] which is a gift of the Holy Spirit.[2] At the same time, this unity is not fully realised, and needs to be sought.[3] The incompleteness of the Church's unity is due to human failure, sin, guilt and evil,[4] for which we need to ask pardon of one another, do penance and make atonement.[5] Nevertheless the bonds and the reality of unity remain,[6] though they need to be rediscovered.[7] Divided Christians are in real but imperfect communion, and in fundamental unity,[8] they are brothers,[9] they share an affinity.[10] This is based above all on baptism,[11] and a common faith,[12] scriptures,[13] and creeds.[14] They are linked in love of the Lord and in the mystery of Christ.[15] They are not strangers to each other.[16] They share apostolic and patristic traditions.[17] The prayers which they share, especially the invocation of the Trinity, express a common belief.[18] For this unity we should thank God.[19]

The search for complete unity is one of the foremost tasks of the Church and a duty incumbent on all Christians.[20] It is the foremost demand of the Spirit.[21] This duty is based on several facts: unity is God's will;[22] Christ prayed for it (Jn 17),[23] and told his followers to love one another (Jn 13: 34);[24] it is required by obedience to the Church and the Council,[25] by faithfulness to God's word,[26] and by Christians' baptismal calling.[27] Christians have no right not to seek unity.[28] They are obliged to repair

243

Christ's seamless robe.[29] Unity was laid down by Christ as a foundation of the Church.[30] The need for unity follows from the Church's vocation,[31] its need of renewal,[32] and its ministry of reconciliation.[33] It accords with the signs of the times.[34] The model and the source of this unity is the Trinity.[35]

The Church's unity is needed 'that the world may believe' (Jn 17:21).[36] It is the sign that is to call forth faith,[37] it is the Good News made visible,[38] and reveals the features of Christ.[39] The credibility of Christian witness depends upon it.[40] Disunity is a countertestimony,[41] which is a scandal and a source of confusion to the world.[42] It is needed for the greater good of souls,[43] and for the coming of the Kingdom.[44] All Christians must be united before grace can be restored to all men.[45] While still divided, Christians can unite in giving witness to Christ.[46]

The Church cannot serve the world as it ought while it is disunited.[47] Disunited it cannot bring peace, unity and reconciliation to the world;[48] its announcement of the hope of liberation is hindered.[49] The unity of Christians is urgently required for the spiritual destiny of all men.[50] Ecumenism is part of the Church's pastoral programme.[51] Love of mankind and respect for human liberty and dignity provide motives for ecumenism.[52]

Ecumenism should be motivated and characterised by charity,[53] by love of Christ and his Church.[54] One stage in the recovery of Christian unity is the dialogue of charity.[55] Progress depends on Christians' loving one another more.[56] Charity is linked with truth: [57] it enables us to discern the truth in others;[58] to speak the truth to them, and to seek it with them.[59] We need to acknowledge the good faith of other Christians.[60] Charity will be inventive of ways of bringing Christians together.[61] Charity requires communion of faith, which is a condition for eucharistic sharing, the expression of charity.[62]

The unity of Christians requires a common understanding and expression of the faith,[63] perfect unity in faith,[64] identity of faith.[65] There are some matters concerning which doctrine admits no diversity.[66] Nevertheless a common faith in Christ, in the central mystery, is already possible.[67]

The Church is a communion,[68] a spiritual relationship on the level of mystery.[69] But God's will for his Church is real, full communion,[70] complete, perfect unity,[71] in faith and sacramental life.[72] This unity must be visible,[73] stable,[74] organic,[75] institutional,[76] hierarchical,[77] canonical,[78] ecclesial;[79] it needs a community perspective.[80] It should be a communion of priesthood and rule,[81] of faith and discipline,[82] of ministry.[83] The structure of hierarchy and sacraments expresses the ecclesial unity received from Christ its head.[84] The Church is therefore not an autonomous Church of the Spirit.[85]

The Eucharist is the consummation of perfect communion,[86] the full manifestation of charity,[87] the seal on full reconciliation,[88] the sacrament of unity,[89] the communion of sacramental life.[90] Sharing the chalice symbolises perfect unity.[91] The Eucharist is the decisive and final meeting.[92] Eucharistic sharing is a spiritual reality,[93] which is not possible among divided Christians.[94] It requires communion of faith,[95] in a single ecclesial communion.[96] The inability of partners of mixed marriages to share the Eucharist together shows the tragedy of Christian division.[97] Shared prayer can prepare the way for eucharistic sharing.[98] Separated Christians can pray together at the Eucharist, even if they cannot receive.[99]

By the grace of God, Christians today desire reunion;[100] they have an increased awareness of the need for unity;[101] disunity causes them suffering,[102] impatience,[103] anxiety and bitterness.[104] There is a unanimous sentiment of charity.[105] The desire for reunion is a sign of the times,[106] a trend.[107] This desire, and ecumenical progress, are the gift of God, of his Spirit.[108] Full restoration of unity will also be God's gift,[109] though it will have to be merited,[110] and requires growth in the fullness of the Lord.[111] God has set an hour for the restoration of unity.[112] The popes share this desire for unity,[113] and seek it passionately.[114] Christians must not acquiesce in division or be satisfied with the results already achieved by the ecumenical movement.[115]

The recovery of full unity is something for which all Christians should pray;[116] such prayer is a fundamental task,[117] and the soul of the ecumenical movement;[118] it is a stirring charge which must shake the conscience.[119] The Week of Prayer for Church Unity has a special value.[120] It is important that Christians not only pray *for* unity by pray also *with* Christians of other Churches;[121] such prayer can lead to full communion in the Eucharist.[122]

The search for unity requires conversion of heart,[123] the cleansing and purifying of heart and soul,[124] renewal of the spirit and the Church,[125] a change of heart,[126] liberation,[127] the search for holiness and authentic Christian living,[128] maturation in truth,[129] the growing closer to Christ and therefore to one another.[130] This process can be called spiritual ecumenism.[131]

An essential means for the recovery of unity is dialogue. This involves listening to the other side,[132] and looking for the truth in the other side's beliefs,[133] so as to recognise one another in Christ,[134] and respect one another.[135] Catholics must explain their position to non-Catholics,[136] presenting their beliefs in terms that will be best understood,[137] and avoid where possible the use of expressions that may offend the sensibilities of others.[138] In this way Christians will challenge one another to greater faithfulness,[139] and encourage them to deepen their own convictions.[140] Such dialogue may lead Catholics to re-examine and modify their point of view,[141] e.g. in matters of canon law.[142] For Christianity is not static,[143] but is adaptable[144] and evolves,[145] and brings liberation.[146] One must go beyond the limits of one's history;[147] tradition is living.[148] Dialogue requires fidelity to one's own tradition,[149] which is a principle of unity not of separation,[150] but excludes false irenicism, compromise, syncretism, false pluralism and harmonisation which exclude consideration of truth.[151] Authority should not have to intervene but may have to.[152] Ecumenism can involve sacrifices, in the spirit of the cross;[153] one should impose no burden beyond what is necessary (Acts 15: 28);[154] one should be more solicitous for the convenience of the other side than one's own.[155] Proselytising and polemics should be eschewed, but are still in evidence.[156] Dialogue requires maturity,[157] a solid grounding in one's own position,[158] and faithfulness to the Magisterium.[159] Mutual acceptance is easy when both sides know their faith well and profess it joyfully.[160] Dialogue should begin with what is held in common before discussing what divides.[161]

Ecumenism involves a search, a rediscovery,[162] which is made together with Christians of other Churches,[163] searching for truth in its centre, Christ.[164] Christians must together discern the causes of divisions,[165] and not be content with applying painkillers.[166] The process calls for patience;[167] the work of centuries has to be repaired;[168] but the patient waiting for God's will is no substitute for action.[169] Perseverance is also required.[170] One must exchange forgiveness,[171] and forget the bitterness[172] and the rivalries of the past;[173] there must be a purification of the collective memory,[174] for many of the obstacles to reunion are non-theological.[175] All, especially pastors, must contribute to the ecumenical process; no one is exempt.[176] Unity is possible only if *all* play their part;[177] a change in canonical rules can help the faithful to recognise that progress is being made.[178] Internal ecumenism among members of the Catholic Church is a means towards reunion with other Christians.[179]

Even before full communion is re-established, separated Christians can collaborate, and should do so without delay.[180] This is possible in matters of pastoral concern,[181] especially in defence of moral values;[182] Christians should be a leaven of love.[183] Collaboration is also called for over social and political issues;[184]

these include matters of peace and justice,[185] poverty,[186] human dignity,[187] and the generation gap;[188] Christians should act together in the service of humanity,[189] so as to provide a civilisation of love.[190] There is also scope for co-operation in the intellectual sphere,[191] especially in the study and translation of the Bible.[192] Christians should also join in witness and evangelisation,[193] in catechesis,[194] and in other spiritual matters.[195] In collaborating Christians will experience the limits imposed by their divisions and so be moved to work harder for unity.[196] They need to be united in Christian living.[197]

The relationship between non-Catholics and Christ's Church is viewed in two main ways. On the one hand, non-Catholics are summoned to the one Church;[198] they are not in the house of God;[199] the Catholic Church aspires to be unique and universal,[200] and only Catholics have communion with the universal Church;[201] the Catholic Church is the organism of the Church of Christ.[202] These are all expressions of Paul VI, but they are not typical of his understanding of Christian division, which he shares with John Paul II. In this view, non-Catholic Christians are in the full flock of Christ,[203] the whole Church of Christ,[204] are already united in the mystery of the Church,[205] and are joined to Christ's Body through faith and baptism.[206] Divisions seem to be seen as divisions *within* Christ's Church rather than separation from it: a wound is inflicted on it;[207] its ecumenicity is incomplete;[208] the fullness, truth and charity of the Church are not fully manifested;[209] the whole organic structure of the Mystical Body is lacerated.[210] The unity of Christians is something which needs to be recomposed.[211] Nevertheless the Catholic Church has prerogatives which other Churches lack:[212] namely, the fullness of revelation,[213] the perfect unity of Christ,[214] Catholic fullness, the fullness of truth and charity.[215] Other Christians are missing;[216] they need to be recomposed with honour in the one fold of Christ,[217] to draw closer and be merged in communion with the Catholic communion.[218] Unity and catholicity do not coincide.[219] The Catholic Church is the Mother Church; other Churches belong to the family.[220] Rome's distinctive prerogatives are for the benefit of all.[221] The expression 'sister-Churches', frequently applied to the relations between the Catholic and Orthodox Churches,[222] is once applied to the Anglican Church.[223]

The function of the papacy is to be the source, the heart, the hinge and the guarantee of unity,[224] to recapitulate the universal Church,[225] to exercise a ministry of communion.[226] The papacy is founded on Peter's faith,[227] and so serves the communion of faith and spiritual life,[228] guarding the gifts of truth and grace.[229]

247

The Pope presides over charity,[230] and protects the rights of all.[231] It is because of his office that greater variety in the Church is possible.[232] Other Christians sometimes regard the papacy as an obstacle to unity;[233] but it should be seen as involving not servitude but brotherhood,[234] not domination but service.[235] It does not challenge legitimate positions within the Church;[236] it does not imply the old trappings of temporal sovereignty,[237] or vain prestige.[238] A measure of decentralisation of curial functions is desirable.[239] The Pope is not apart from the college of bishops but belongs to it as its head and their brother.[240] The Popes on occasion offer leadership to Christians of other Churches.[241]

Pluriformity is not only legitimate in the Church, but is advantageous, necessary, a source of beauty and a gift of the Spirit.[242] This principle applies to traditions, canon law and usages;[243] Churches reconciled to Rome will be united not absorbed;[244] there can be a pastoral pluralism.[245] The principle applies also to expressions of faith, theologies, vocabulary.[246] Theologians should not just repeat dogmatic formulations;[247] there is room for different approaches to the same source.[248] Unity is symphonic.[249] *In dubiis libertas.*[250] However there needs to be substantial agreement in reality;[251] the purity of the deposit must be preserved; there must be convergences.[252] Difficulties arise from relativising the absolute or absolutising the relative.[253] An example of convergent diversity is provided by the legitimacy of speaking of either one nature or two natures in Christ.[254] The Church is also enriched by diversity in spirituality;[255] the *lex orandi* is linked with the *lex credendi.*[256]

The Popes commend different Churches in different terms. The Orthodox enjoy nearly perfect communion with Rome because of faith, sacraments and apostolic succession.[257] With the Anglicans also there is a dawning communion;[258] they are not strangers;[259] they enjoy a special place in Rome's relations;[260] Rome and Canterbury are sister-Churches;[261] the prestige, piety and usage of Anglicanism would not be impaired in a united Church.[262] The Popes also make special mention of Methodists[263] and Lutherans.[264] John Paul II also speaks of points which Catholics have in common with Jews[265] and Moslems.[266]

Among special ecumenical problems which the Popes discuss are those connected with mixed marriages.[267]

The Popes' attitude to other Churches is revealed not only by their words but also by their gestures.[268]

Ecumenism is carried on in hope, based on the power of the Resurrection and the Holy Spirit.[269] 'Hope does not disappoint us' (Rom 5: 5).[270]

NOTES AND INDEX
OF PROPER NAMES

NOTES

1. 219, 225, 228, 231.
2. 110, 155, 157, 192, 210, 222, 223, 229, 233, 234, 235.
3. 225.
4. 7, 94, 103, 110, 185-6, 189, 203, 210, 217, 218, 224, 225, 226, 235.
5. 52, 54-5, 79, 111, 117, 124.
6. 83, 86, 110, 114, 131, 132, 184, 195.
7. 114, 130, 229.
8. 64, 85, 92, 158, 202, 234.
9. 131, 140, 151, 153, 155, 201, 218, 226.
10. 4.
11. 9, 92, 94, 128, 129, 132, 161, 189, 225, 237.
12. 9, 86, 103, 128, 131, 161, 167, 170, 171, 174, 189, 196, 209, 210, 225, 236, 239, 240.
13. 9, 169, 172, 234.
14. 102, 179, 203, 236, 239, 240.
15. 86, 114, 154, 158, 193, 218.
16. 4, 59, 140.
17. 8, 15, 20, 60, 77, 103, 115, 134, 161, 179, 186-7, 196, 197, 203, 210, 225.
18. 64, 127.
19. 195.
20. 139, 176, 200, 201, 204.
21. 76.
22. 87, 106, 178, 203, 215.
23. 15, 54, 60, 85, 86, 87, 91, 109, 121, 135, 136, 139, 145, 152, 153, 155, 156, 159, 164, 168, 171, 172, 173, 183, 185, 194, 196, 203, 209, 216, 222, 223, 230, 231, 235.
24. 60, 167.
25. 64, 176, 191, 204, 225.
26. 130, 165, 230.
27. 175.
28. 160, 183.
29. 201.
30. 225.
31. 204.
32. 96.
33. 118.
34. 203.
35. 130, 140, 231.
36. 14, 88, 124, 125, 128, 130, 131, 136, 153, 156, 158, 159, 166, 170, 181, 182-3, 189, 192, 194, 195, 199, 201, 207, 217, 230, 231, 234.
37. 76, 109, 189.
38. 83.
39. 86.
40. 139, 168, 172, 176, 231, 235.
41. 162.
42. 136, 146, 152, 153, 154, 163, 176, 194, 203, 230, 235.
43. 55.
44. 55, 190.
45. 117.
46. 128, 133, 135, 160.
47. 164, 195.
48. 12, 121, 165-6, 176, 179, 189, 216.
49. 153.
50. 64.
51. 189.
52. 151, 160.
53. 9, 19, 20, 54, 55, 59, 64, 65, 69, 76, 77, 84, 106, 117, 119, 124, 125, 131, 140 141, 145, 151, 152, 157, 164, 170, 171-2, 181, 193-4, 210, 212, 222, 223, 225, 226, 230.
54. 15.
55. 179, 187, 202, 207, 218.
56. 53, 60, 61, 64, 78, 80, 118, 138, 140, 141, 147, 162, 165, 198-9, 201, 237.
57. 162, 173, 201-2, 203, 218, 222, 224.
58. 69, 183.
59. 155, 211.
60. 9.
61. 162.
62. 70, 172.
63. 55.
64. 59, 60, 77, 135, 136, 147, 155, 161, 171, 172, 199, 210, 215.

225. 28, 46, 178.
226. 85.
227. 156.
228. 164.
229. 24, 66, 182.
230. 19, 111, cf. 66.
231. 66.
232. 128.
233. 26, 66.
234. 21, 66.
235. 26, 66.
236. 66, 95.
237. 18.
238. 52, 65.
239. 4.
240. 27, 28-9, 39-40, 41, 48, 85, 105, 146, 153, 157, 170.
241. 4, 5, 19, 44, 48, 49, 56, 117.
242. 6, 26, 30, 31, 43, 48, 70, 74, 95, 104, 105, 118, 120, 124, 127, 130, 161, 164, 182, 186, 192, 208, 210, 228, 229, 230, 232.
243. 26, 70, 120, 130.
244. 4, 133.
245. 158.
246. 6, 25, 69, 93, 95, 102, 103, 105, 113, 114, 120, 124, 128, 164, 183, 191, 197.
247. 174.
248. 200.
249. 198.
250. 152, 158.

251. 114.
252. 174.
253. 226.
254. 102, 103, 197, 202.
255. 26, 114, 183, 187, 215.
256. 127.
257. 3, 11, 64, 69, 72, 73, 74, 92, 93, 99, 105, 107, 119, 124, 139, 141, 157, 162, 177, 180, 181. 181-2, 183, 187, 191, 207-8, 228, 230, 236, 239.
258. 64-5.
259. 59.
260. 81, 118, 133, cf. 48, 204, 212-3.
261. 95.
262. 95.
263. 223.
264. 79, 191, 199, 203, 216, 217, 218, 219, 221, 222.
265. 82, 121, 158, 171, 177, 193, 200, 208, 219-20.
266. 74, 177-8, 220.
267. 65, 77-8, 91-2, 134-5, 210, cf. 214.
268. 14, 21, 22, 46, 53-4, 55, 67, 126, 139, 145, 180, 187, 188, 206.
269. 9, 47, 52, 87, 118, 120, 128, 132, 135, 140, 141, 145, 152, 160, 169, 172, 179, 189, 193, 198, 199, 224, 232.
270. 121, 122, 135.

INDEX OF PROPER NAMES

256